## Early Praise for *Programming Elm*

*Programming Elm* is wonderfully accessible for folks coming to Elm from JavaScript. Jeremy Fairbank takes the time to introduce each concept thoroughly and thoughtfully, so the learning path is quite smooth.

➤ **Brian Hicks**
 Organizer, elm-conf

*Programming Elm* is a joyful and empathetic primer on building software with Elm, and I recommend it to anyone interested in adding Elm to their front-end development toolkit.

➤ **Luke Westby**
 Engineer, Creator of Ellie, NoRedInk

I love the approach of teaching real-world solutions by starting from a project with real-world problems.

➤ **Kevin Yank**
 Host, Elm Town Podcast

# Programming Elm

Build Safe and Maintainable Front-End Applications

Jeremy Fairbank

The Pragmatic Bookshelf

Raleigh, North Carolina

Many of the designations used by manufacturers and sellers to distinguish their products are claimed as trademarks. Where those designations appear in this book, and The Pragmatic Programmers, LLC was aware of a trademark claim, the designations have been printed in initial capital letters or in all capitals. The Pragmatic Starter Kit, The Pragmatic Programmer, Pragmatic Programming, Pragmatic Bookshelf, PragProg and the linking *g* device are trademarks of The Pragmatic Programmers, LLC.

Every precaution was taken in the preparation of this book. However, the publisher assumes no responsibility for errors or omissions, or for damages that may result from the use of information (including program listings) contained herein.

Our Pragmatic books, screencasts, and audio books can help you and your team create better software and have more fun. Visit us at *https://pragprog.com*.

The team that produced this book includes:

Publisher: Andy Hunt
VP of Operations: Janet Furlow
Managing Editor: Susan Conant
Development Editor: Brian MacDonald
Copy Editor: Sean Dennis
Indexing: Potomac Indexing, LLC
Layout: Gilson Graphics

For sales, volume licensing, and support, please contact *support@pragprog.com*.

For international rights, please contact *rights@pragprog.com*.

ISBN-13: 978-1-68050-285-5
Book version: P3.0—April 2020

# Contents

# Preface

Don't worry; you haven't picked up the latest gardening book (however, I can teach you how to grow some great tomatoes). Elm is a statically typed, functional programming language made for building safe front-end web applications. It compiles down to minimal JavaScript for easy deployment of your applications to the web.

If you're a front-end developer tired of the JavaScript framework churn or want to build more resilient and maintainable applications, then you need to learn Elm. This book will take you from no knowledge of Elm to creating complex single-page applications.

## Why Elm?

More and more front-end developers are choosing Elm to build applications for benefits such as:

- *No runtime exceptions in practice:* Elm's compiler catches problems early to prevent exceptions at runtime for your users.

- *No null or undefined errors:* Elm offers versatile types for representing null. The compiler also ensures you handle all possible nulls in your application.

- *No JavaScript fatigue:* You don't have to choose and wire up different frameworks and libraries to build an application. Elm has a built-in framework for creating applications, the Elm Architecture.

- *Predictable code:* All Elm code is free from side effects, you can trust your functions to always produce the same result based on their arguments.

- *Immutable data types:* You don't have to worry about your code or third-party code changing data unexpectedly and causing bugs. Your data will be consistent and safe.

- *Strong static types:* Elm's compiler uses static types to ensure you call functions with the right types of arguments. You won't run into subtle type-coercion bugs.

- *Custom types:* Elm's custom types let you create entirely new types for clearly modeling your business domain. Powerful pattern matching prevents undefined situations by ensuring you handle your custom types consistently.

- *Advanced tools:* Elm's Debug module makes it easy to inspect data to catch bugs, and add placeholders to your code until you're ready to implement it. Third-party tools such as create-elm-app let you quickly bootstrap Elm applications and offer powerful development servers for immediate development feedback.

## Who Is This Book For?

This book is for front-end developers new to Elm who want to quickly learn how to build maintainable applications with it. You'll start with basics such as Elm's syntax and creating functions and advance all the way to building a single-page application.

Before you read this book, you should know HTML and how to nest HTML elements. Elm's syntax for building UIs closely mimics HTML. You should also have a good grasp of JavaScript. This book compares some Elm code to JavaScript code—you should know basic JavaScript syntax, objects, arrays, and how to create functions.

In a later chapter, you'll add Elm code to an existing JavaScript application, so you should be familiar with how to process events with callbacks, bind functions to objects, interact with the DOM, deal with JSON, use promises, and add methods to ES2015 classes.

## What's In This Book?

The first five chapters of this book focus on how to build applications. You will create a photo sharing application called Picshare and add new functionality in each chapter.

Chapter 1, Get Started with Elm, on page 1 introduces you to Elm, explains some of the basics of functional programming, and lets you create a basic Picshare application.

Chapter 2, Create Stateful Elm Applications, on page 27 explains Elm's framework for building applications, the Elm Architecture. You'll use the Elm Architecture to manage state and events in the Picshare application.

Chapter 3, Refactor and Enhance Elm Applications, on page 47 expands on the Picshare application. You'll learn patterns for refactoring code and how to add new features to the Picshare application.

Chapter 4, Communicate with Servers, on page 61 lets you create a more realistic Picshare application. Front-end applications typically need to communicate with servers to be useful. You'll learn how to call APIs and safely decode JSON into static types.

Chapter 5, Go Real-Time with WebSockets, on page 85 takes Picshare's interactivity further. You'll use Elm subscriptions with WebSockets to receive updates in real time.

The next six chapters focus on advanced patterns for scaling, debugging, integrating, and maintaining Elm applications.

Chapter 6, Build Larger Applications, on page 103 addresses the problem of scaling complex applications containing lots of code. You'll use patterns such as reusable helper functions, extensible records, and message wrappers to refactor an application into a more maintainable state.

Chapter 7, Develop, Debug, and Deploy with Powerful Tooling, on page 131 introduces Elm's tooling. Although Elm's compiler prevents tons of bugs through static types, bugs can still occur from logic errors. You'll use Elm's Debug module to debug values at runtime. You'll also bundle and deploy an application with powerful third-party tools.

Chapter 8, Integrate with JavaScript, on page 153 covers interacting with JavaScript code, which is important for accessing impure APIs or migrating existing JavaScript applications to Elm. You'll learn how to add a new feature with Elm to an existing JavaScript application.

Chapter 9, Test Elm Applications, on page 175 introduces testing to ensure your code is correct. You'll use elm-test to create a module with test-driven development, test properties of your code with fuzz testing, and test an Elm application with elm-html-test.

Chapter 10, Build Single-Page Applications, on page 205 teaches you how to build modern single-page applications with Elm. You'll learn how to handle routes and coordinate different page components.

Chapter 11, Write Fast Applications, on page 235 concludes with speeding up your code. You'll learn about common performance issues, how to measure performance, and how to optimize applications with efficient algorithms, lazy design patterns, and the Html.Lazy module.

## How to Read This Book

If you're an Elm novice, then you should read chapters 1–5 in order to learn the basics and how to create applications with the Elm Architecture. Each of these chapters also builds upon the previous one by using the same application as an example.

If you already know the basics of building applications but want to learn how to interact with servers, then you could skip ahead to chapter 4. Each chapter has code downloads with a version of the application from the previous chapter, so you don't have to go through all of them to catch up.

This book is intended to be read from start to finish, but if you're already pretty familiar with Elm basics, you can skip around after chapter 5. If you're completely new to Elm, you can skip around too, but be forewarned: I introduce some general concepts and built-in Elm functions that might not make sense in later chapters if you skip a previous chapter.

## Online Resources

You can visit this book's web page[1] to download the source code examples from this book and provide feedback through an errata-submission form.

## Acknowledgements

I would like to thank the following people for reviewing this book and providing invaluable feedback to help improve it: Nick Capito, Jacob Chae, Joel Clermont, Elliot Davies, Zulfikar Dharmawan, Scott Ford, Matt Margolis, Nick McGinness, Luca Mezzalira, Nouran Mhmoud, Daivid Morgan, Eoghan O'Donnell, Emanuele Origgi, Will Price, Noel Rappin, Sam Rose, Dan Sheikh, Kim Shrier, Gianluigi Spagnuolo, Stefan Turalski, Mitchell Volk, and Stephen Wolff.

I would like to thank my editor Brian MacDonald for all his advice and direction on this book. You helped me become a better writer and teacher. This book wouldn't have been possible without you.

I would like to thank my wife Emily Fairbank for supporting me throughout this journey. You are the most compassionate and understanding person I

---

1. https://pragprog.com/book/jfelm/programming-elm

know. Thank you for bearing with me as I sacrificed so much time to write this book. I love you.

Thank you Tucker for being the most loving and loyal dog I ever knew and the inspiration behind many code samples in this book. Until we meet again.

Finally, thank you reader for choosing to explore this book. I'm humbled by all the kind words others have shared about it. I hope you find it useful and inspiring to embark on your own Elm journey.

Let's get this Elm party started.

# CHAPTER 1

# Get Started with Elm

Welcome to the world of Elm, a language that gets so much right. Although I had heard about Elm before, I finally tried it out in early 2016. And indeed, it amazed me. I arrived initially for the functional programming but stayed for the static types and no-nonsense Elm architecture. Elm breathed new life into front-end development for me. I hope you'll feel the same.

Because Elm is a functional, statically typed programming language, it boasts the awesome benefit of letting you create maintainable applications that are safe to refactor, plus no runtime exceptions and no "undefined is not a function" error messages. Don't worry if you're not familiar with functional programming or static types. I won't throw math and theory at you. Instead, we will focus on the practical applications.

In this chapter, we will lay the foundation for learning Elm. Elm is a functional language, so you will learn how to define and call Elm functions with Elm data types. Then, you will discover static types and create type annotations to document your code and harness the safety of the Elm compiler. Finally, you will use lists and the Html module to build your first static Elm application. Once you've completed this chapter, you will be able to create your own static applications with the versatile Html module.

## Get Started with Functions

Functions are the most key parts of Elm applications. Each piece of behavior in an Elm application lives inside a function. In this section, you will create and call functions. You will also learn about Elm's expressiveness and work with some of Elm's primitive data types such as strings and numbers.

## Explore with the Elm REPL

Before you begin, you will need a sandbox for interacting with Elm functions. If you haven't done so already, visit Appendix 1, Install Elm, on page 265 to install Elm on your system. After installing Elm, you will have several command-line tools at your disposal. Right now, we only care about the Elm *REPL* tool. REPL is an acronym for read-evaluate-print loop. The Elm REPL lets you interact with the Elm runtime without creating Elm files. This is perfect for getting immediate feedback.

Open your favorite terminal and run this command to start the Elm REPL:

```
elm repl
```

You should see a message and prompt similar to this.

```
---- Elm 0.19.1 -----------------------------------------------
Say :help for help and :exit to exit! More at
<https://elm-lang.org/0.19.1/repl>
--------------------------------------------------------------
>
```

You can type Elm code for the Elm runtime to evaluate right after the > symbol. Let's try a simple string message—"Hello Elm!" You can create Elm strings with double quotes like in JavaScript. Type this in the REPL. (Unlike JavaScript, single quotes don't create a string in Elm.)

```
> "Hello Elm!"
```

Below your string, you should see the REPL respond with this message:

```
"Hello Elm!" : String
```

When the REPL evaluates an expression, it returns the expression along with an *inferred* type. In this case, the REPL determined that the message "Hello Elm!" is a String type. You will explore types more thoroughly in a later section.

You can create variables in Elm similar to JavaScript too. Feeling ambitious? Answer all of life's questions by defining a meaningOfLife variable in the REPL:

```
> meaningOfLife = 42
```

The REPL will evaluate the assignment and return the number 42.

```
42 : number
```

Note that you don't need a keyword such as var to create variables in Elm. Unlike JavaScript, this inference won't create a global variable.

Elm variables also differ from regular JavaScript variables in this way: You can't change the value of a variable later in an Elm file. Elm variables are actually *constants*. This is common in functional programming languages and prevents subtle bugs from accidentally overwriting data. However, as a convenience, you can change the value of a constant inside the REPL.

Elm has typical arithmetic operators like JavaScript. Try these operations in the REPL. (Going forward, I will include the returned result inside REPL examples. Only type in the portion that begins with > when interacting with the REPL.)

```
> 1 + 2
3 : number
> 20 - 10
10 : number
> 3 * 3
9 : number
> 5 / 2
2.5 : Float
```

## Write Your First Function

Now that you have played with the REPL and some Elm data types, let's move on to functions. You will need functions to do useful work in Elm. Inside the REPL, create a friendly sayHello function like this:

```
> sayHello name = "Hello, " ++ name ++ "."
<function> : String -> String
```

Notice that you define functions in the same way as constants, except that functions have parameters. In this case, the sayHello function has one parameter called name. The return type is different from primitive data types too. It has two Strings and an arrow ->. You'll look at function types more closely later, but the -> separates the parameter and return value, which are both Strings in sayHello.

Elm functions don't use parentheses for parameters as in JavaScript. Creating a similar function in JavaScript might look like this.

```
function sayHello(name) {
  return "Hello, " + name + ".";
}
```

You don't need a return keyword either (unlike JavaScript) because Elm is an *expression-oriented* language. An expression is anything a programming language can evaluate to produce a value. Literals such as strings and numbers, math operations such as addition, and calling functions are examples of expressions in Elm.

Similar to how you define function parameters, you use whitespace to call functions with arguments. Call sayHello in the REPL with the string "Elm" as below. You should get back the result "Hello, Elm."

```
> sayHello "Elm"
"Hello, Elm." : String
```

You assign Elm functions to an expression that evaluates to the final result. For sayHello, you assign it to the expression "Hello " ++ name ++ ".". The ++ operator lets you concatenate strings together like the + operator does in JavaScript.

Functions with multiple parameters are similar too. Let's modify the sayHello function to accept a greeting argument. Inside the REPL, add this:

```
> sayHello greeting name = greeting ++ ", " ++ name ++ "."
<function> : String -> String -> String
```

Use whitespace rather than commas to delimit multiple parameters. Now, you can provide the particular greeting used inside sayHello. Calling a function with multiple arguments requires whitespace as well. Invoke the new sayHello function in the REPL:

```
> sayHello "Hi" "Elm"
"Hi, Elm." : String
```

Instead of "Hello, Elm.", you get "Hi, Elm." because you provided "Hi" as the greeting.

## Branch with Booleans

JavaScript functions conveniently allow you to add multiple statements such as if statements, for loops, and variable assignments. But, overusing these statements can lead to more lines of code and complexity.

Because Elm functions are expressive, they tend to be shorter than JavaScript functions. Surprisingly, this doesn't limit your possibilities for creating Elm functions. For example, Elm lacks if statements for conditional branching, but makes up for it with if *expressions*.

Let's create our first function with Boolean logic. Add this in the REPL:

```
> woodchuck canChuck = if canChuck then "Chucking wood!" else "No chucking!"
<function> : Bool -> String
```

The woodchuck function accepts a Boolean canChuck argument and branches with an if expression. If canChuck is true, then the function returns "Chucking wood!". Otherwise, it returns "No chucking!" in the else branch.

An if expression uses the following general format with three important keywords: if, then, and else.

```
if <boolean value> then <value when true> else <value when false>
```

Since if is an expression, you can set a function equal to it, just like any other expression. You can't do that with a JavaScript if *statement*. In fact, an Elm if expression is closer to a JavaScript ternary expression. An equivalent woodchuck function in JavaScript would look like this.

```
function woodchuck(canChuck) {
  return canChuck ? "Chucking wood!" : "No chucking!";
}
```

Let's try our woodchuck function out. Inside the REPL, call woodchuck with Elm's Boolean values, True and False:

```
> woodchuck True
"Chucking wood!" : String
> woodchuck False
"No chucking!" : String
```

As expected, calling woodchuck with True returns "Chucking wood!" and calling it with False returns "No chucking!".

Elm if expressions have two other advantages over JavaScript if statements. First, Elm makes you supply an else branch. The following function contains a syntax error.

```
woodchuck canChuck = if canChuck then "Chucking wood!"
```

Second, Elm makes you return the same type of value in each branch. Recall that woodchuck always returns a string. Thus, the version below is invalid.

```
woodchuck canChuck = if canChuck then "Chucking wood!" else 0
```

The above function is inconsistent and unpredictable because it returns a string in the if branch and a number in the else branch—you would need to inspect the return value at runtime to determine its type. But the Elm compiler ensures that all types are known at compile time.

The Elm compiler conveniently safeguards you. By making an if expression handle both branches and return the same type of value, the compiler protects you from undefined situations and type-related bugs.

## Compare Values

You've created Boolean values and conditionally branched using if expressions. More than likely, you'll need to branch on equality comparisons. Let's see how to compare values in Elm and branch multiple times in if expressions. Add the following function in the REPL. The REPL supports multiline functions. Hit Return to start a new line.

```
> tribblesStatus howMany =
|     if howMany == 1 then
|         "Its trilling seems to have a tranquilizing effect..."
|     else if howMany > 1 then
|         "They're consuming our supplies and returning nothing."
|     else
|         "I gave 'em to the Klingons, sir."
<function> : number -> String
```

In tribblesStatus, you check the value of the howMany number parameter. In the first if branch, you compare it to 1 with the equality operator ==. If the comparison is True, then you return a string. Otherwise, you compare with the > operator to see if howMany is larger than 1. Notice that you can branch again with else if, similar to JavaScript if statements. If the second comparison fails, then you finally return a default string in the else branch.

Call tribblesStatus with different numbers to see each branch's result:

```
> tribblesStatus 1
"Its trilling seems to have a tranquilizing effect..." : String
> tribblesStatus 1771561
"They're consuming our supplies and returning nothing." : String
> tribblesStatus 0
"I gave 'em to the Klingons, sir." : String
```

Thanks to the Elm if expression, you can still create complex functions with branching logic just like in JavaScript. Even more awesome, the Elm compiler guards you with type guarantees that JavaScript can't provide.

## Use Functions as Building Blocks

Not all functions need conditional branching. Since Elm lacks statements as in JavaScript, you will need other methods to make more complex Elm functions. Really, Elm calls for a new mindset. Instead of using multiple statements, Elm functions can call other functions to achieve similar results with less code. You can think of Elm functions as building blocks for other functions.

Let's build upon the modified sayHello function by creating a person function. The person function accepts a name argument and greets someone else with the sayHello function. Add this to the REPL:

```
> person name other = sayHello "Hi" other ++ " My name is " ++ name ++ "."
<function> : String -> String -> String
```

Call person with "Jeremy" and "Tucker" to test it out:

```
> person "Jeremy" "Tucker"
"Hi, Tucker. My name is Jeremy." : String
```

This is a great start, but you may want to control the way you greet other. You could accept an additional argument to pass to sayHello, but you really need something more flexible. The sayHello function always places the greeting before a name. Instead, you might want to say something like "Tucker, how are you? My name is Jeremy."

Rather than hardcode the way you greet another person, you can inject that behavior when you need it. Add this new definition for person in the REPL:

```
> person name greet other = greet other ++ " My name is " ++ name ++ "."
<function> : String -> (a -> String) -> a -> String
```

The person function takes a new greet argument. The greet argument is a function that accepts other as an argument to generate the actual greeting.

You are seeing something new: a function (person) that accepts another function (greet) as an argument. In functional programming speak, you would call person a *higher-order function.*

A higher-order function is basically a function that accepts another function as an argument or returns a function. Functions are first-class citizens in Elm. They are values just like strings, numbers, and Booleans. In fact, JavaScript functions are values too. That's why you can write functions that accept callback arguments.

Let's try the new, fancy person function out. Call it like this in the REPL:

```
> person "Jeremy" (\other -> sayHello "Hi" other) "Tucker"
"Hi, Tucker. My name is Jeremy." : String
```

You call the function with "Jeremy" and "Tucker" again, but between those arguments you use an *anonymous function.* An anonymous function is like a regular function with no name. Anonymous functions are great for creating functions on the fly.

To create an anonymous function, use \ and list the parameters. Then, use an arrow -> to separate the parameters from the body of the function. Although parentheses aren't a part of anonymous function syntax, you need them here to wrap this anonymous function and avoid a syntax error.

Notice that the anonymous function receives the other argument and lets you decide at call time how to greet other. In this instance, you use sayHello to say

"Hi" to other. Now person can greet in different ways. Run the following code in the REPL:

```
> person "Jeremy" (\other -> other ++ ", how are you?") "Tucker"
"Tucker, how are you? My name is Jeremy." : String
```

Here, you are using another anonymous function that receives other but returns a totally different greeting from sayHello.

## Partially Apply Arguments

Elm has one more trick up its functional sleeve. You can actually clean up how you call person from the previous section. Before you do that, let's revisit sayHello. Recall that sayHello accepts two arguments, a greeting and a name. Inside the REPL, call sayHello with just the first argument, like this:

```
> sayHello "Hi"
<function> : String -> String
```

Instead of an error, you get back another function. Elm isn't broken—this is how functions work in Elm. Elm functions are *curried*, which is a fancy way of saying they take one argument at a time.

When you call sayHello with two arguments, you are really calling it with one argument at a time. When you call it with the first argument, you essentially "fill in" the first greeting argument with the value "Hi". Then, Elm returns another function that is waiting on the value for the second name argument. When you call this new function with the second argument, Elm will know all arguments have values and so returns the final result.

Filling in one argument at a time is known as *partial application*. Calling a function with only some of its arguments is *partially applying* it. Calling a function with all its arguments is *fully applying* it. Try this in the REPL to understand what I mean:

```
> hi = sayHello "Hi"
<function> : String -> String
> hi "Elm"
"Hi, Elm." : String
```

Notice that you call sayHello with just "Hi" and assign the returned function to hi. Then, you call hi with the second argument "Elm" to get back "Hi, Elm."

Currying and partial application are incredibly useful tools in Elm and functional programming. Sometimes developers confuse the two concepts, so to keep them straight you can remember this phrase: create curried functions, partially apply arguments.

You can now use partial application to remove the need for anonymous functions. Recall how you called person with sayHello inside an anonymous function.

```
> person "Jeremy" (\other -> sayHello "Hi" other) "Tucker"
```

See how the anonymous function's other parameter becomes the second argument to sayHello. You just learned that when you call sayHello with its first argument, you get back a function that accepts the second argument. So you could instead call person as in the code below. In the REPL, try this:

```
> person "Jeremy" (sayHello "Hi") "Tucker"
"Hi, Tucker. My name is Jeremy." : String
```

Instead of passing an anonymous function, you call sayHello once with "Hi" to pass a function that accepts other as the next argument. Note that you have to wrap the function call in parentheses. If you don't, Elm will think you were trying to call person with four arguments. Since Elm uses whitespace to invoke functions, you may need parentheses to call functions in the correct order.

Partial application really shines for writing concise code. You could even partially apply the person function to create different people, like so:

```
> jeremy = person "Jeremy" (sayHello "Hi")
<function> : String -> String
> tucker = person "Tucker" (\other -> other ++ ", how are you?")
<function> : String -> String
> jeremy "Tucker"
"Hi, Tucker. My name is Jeremy." : String
> tucker "Jeremy"
"Jeremy, how are you? My name is Tucker." : String
```

You create jeremy and tucker by calling person with two out of three arguments. Each time you get back a function expecting the last argument. Later, you can call jeremy and tucker with the remaining argument to get a final result.

Great job! You can now write Elm functions and understand how expressive they are. You even know how to build complex functions out of simpler functions. Let's take your knowledge further in the next section by working with static types.

## Use Static Types

We've covered the first part of Elm's defining features: functions. In this section, we will explore the second part: *static types*. You will learn how Elm infers static types on its own, write your own *type annotations*, and see Elm's helpful compiler error messages. You will also create your first Elm file and compile it to HTML.

## Create an Elm File

Up to this point, you've used the Elm REPL to write Elm code. The REPL is perfect for experimentation, but you'll need Elm files to build applications. You'll also need Elm files to add type annotations to your code. Let's create our first Elm file as a great first step toward learning about static types.

Make a directory called elm-files. Inside that directory, run this command to initialize an Elm project:

```
elm init
```

The command should prompt you to create an elm.json file. Accept the prompt by typing y and Return. The elm.json file houses information about your Elm project such as the type of project (application or package), required Elm version, source directories, and dependencies.

```
{
    "type": "application",
    "source-directories": [
        "src"
    ],
    "elm-version": "0.19.1",
    "dependencies": {
        "direct": {
            "elm/browser": "1.0.2",
            "elm/core": "1.0.5",
            "elm/html": "1.0.0"
        },
        "indirect": {
            "elm/json": "1.1.3",
            "elm/time": "1.0.0",
            "elm/url": "1.0.0",
            "elm/virtual-dom": "1.0.2"
        }
    },
    "test-dependencies": {
        "direct": {},
        "indirect": {}
    }
}
```

By default, elm init creates a src directory and adds it to the source-directories property in elm.json. You can add additional directories to source-directories if you desire. You place all your source files in any directory listed in source-directories. elm init also adds elm/browser, elm/core, and elm/html as direct dependencies. The elm/core package contains all of Elm's core functions and data types.

The elm/browser and elm/html packages let you build applications for the browser. (You'll learn how to install additional packages in later chapters.)

Inside the src directory, create a file called Main.elm in your text editor. Add the following code at the top of the file:

get-started/elm-files/Main01.elm
```
module Main exposing (main)
```

Every Elm file is a *module*. Modules let you organize code into logical units. Every module contains one or more constants and functions that it can expose to other modules. For example, you could build a Math module that exposes functions for addition and subtraction.

When building Elm applications, you need a main, or entry point, module that exposes a special main constant. Elm needs the main module to compile your application into a JavaScript or HTML file for the browser.

In this case, the Main.elm file is a "main" module. You use the module keyword to create a new module called Main. Then, you use the exposing keyword to expose the main constant inside parentheses. You'll make the actual main constant in a moment.

 The name of the main constant is important but not the module's name. You could have called the module EntryPoint or Antidisestablishmentarianism if you wanted.

To print something in your file, you need to import the Html module. Add this code underneath your module declaration:

```
import Html exposing (text)
```

The import keyword lets you use another module's exposed items. Here you import the Html module and expose its text function via the exposing keyword. Exposing a function makes it available within the scope of the importing module.

Finally, let's create the main constant and put the text function to good use. Below the import, add the following:

```
main =
    text "Hello, Elm!"
```

The text function takes a string message to display in the browser. In this instance, you will display the message, "Hello, Elm!".

You could have also written this code as Html.text "Hello, Elm!". When you import a module, you can use its functions by prefacing them with the name of the module along with a dot. You don't have to use this *qualified* form, but it prevents ambiguity with other imported modules.

For example, you couldn't expose another module's text function because the Elm compiler wouldn't know which text function you want.

```
-- which text function should the compiler use?
import Html exposing (text)
import MyAwesomeModule exposing (text)
```

You can fix the ambiguity, however, by calling the functions in a qualified manner with their module names.

```
Html.text "hello"
MyAwesomeModule.text "hello"
```

You get Elm to compile the string message by assigning it to the exposed main constant. Notice that you added a newline and indented the function call too. This is a common formatting convention for Elm constants and functions. The Elm community has created a tool for automatically formatting code. Refer to Appendix 1, Install Elm, on page 265 to install it.

Compile this file and display your achievement in the browser. Inside the elm-files directory, run this command:

```
elm make src/Main.elm
```

You should see a success message similar to this.

```
Success! Compiled 1 module.
```

By default, the elm make command compiles your Elm file into an index.html file. It also generates an elm-stuff directory which contains intermediate files for compiling your Elm code.

Open up index.html in your browser. You should see the message "Hello, Elm!"

Good work. You've written your first Elm file. You're now ready to take over the world (OK, maybe not quite yet).

## Learn Static Types

Each Elm value has an associated static type. The static type describes the kind of data a value can be. Examples of static types in Elm are String, Int (integers), and Bool (Booleans). As the name suggests, a *static* type can't change.

Compare this to JavaScript's *dynamic* types, which can change. In the JavaScript example below, you can change the variable meaningOfLife from a number to a string.

```
var meaningOfLife = 42;
meaningOfLife = "forty two";
```

Since the JavaScript runtime makes no guarantees about a value's type, you can run buggy code like the below. The add function requires two numbers, but nothing stops you from calling it with strings.

```
function add(x, y) { return x + y; }
var result = add(1, "2"); // returns "12" instead of 3
```

Because Elm's types are static, the Elm compiler definitively knows every value's type at compile time. Elm can protect you from the type-coercion bugs that appear in JavaScript. For example, Elm won't even compile if you call the add function with a string.

```
add x y = x + y
result = add 1 "2" -- this won't compile
```

If you tried to compile the example above, you would get a compiler error message like this.

```
The 2nd argument to `add` is not what I expect:

7| result = add 1 "2"
                   ^^^
This argument is a string of type:

    String

But `add` needs the 2nd argument to be:

    number
```

Elm uses *type inference* to figure out static types on its own. Elm notices the + operator in the add function and determines that x and y must be numbers. Equipped with this information, the Elm compiler prevents you from calling add with strings (and anything else not a number).

Static types prevent a ton of bugs thanks to type inference. They're also super handy for documenting code through type annotations. In fact, that's what you will do next.

## Add Type Annotations

Now that you've created an Elm file and learned about static types, you're ready to add type annotations to your Elm file. Since Elm knows static types at compile time, you can leverage type annotations to document your code. Type annotations benefit you and your team by declaring the expected types of arguments and return values for functions. So, type annotations make your codebase less confusing and more approachable through documentation.

Let's start off by adding type annotations to some constants. Inside your Main.elm file, create a greeting constant:

get-started/elm-files/Main02.elm
```
greeting : String
greeting =
    "Hello, Static Elm!"
```

Notice the new syntax for type annotations above the greeting constant. A type annotation has two parts separated by a :, the identifier name (i.e., the constant or function name) and the static type. In this type annotation, you are showing that greeting is a String type.

Almost all static types in Elm use PascalCase.[1] This typically means that the first letter in the type is capitalized. If the static type has multiple words in it, then each word's first letter is capitalized. When you create your own types in later chapters, you'll use PascalCase to name them as well.

Back inside Main.elm, update main to display greeting:

```
main =
    text greeting
```

Then, compile your application and refresh index.html in your browser.

```
elm make src/Main.elm
```

You should see the message "Hello, Static Elm!". Granted, setting main equal to the text result of greeting would have displayed the message even without the type annotation. But, it's good to form a habit of adding type annotations to everything. For example, you might not be certain what the static type of greeting is in the code that follows without an explicit type annotation.

```
greeting : String
greeting = sayHello "Elm"
```

Let's peek at a few more primitive types before transitioning to function type annotations. Inside Main.elm, create annotations for other constants like so:

```
meaningOfLife : Int
meaningOfLife = 42
```

---

1. https://en.wikipedia.org/wiki/PascalCase

```
➤  pi : Float
   pi = 3.14

➤  canChuck : Bool
   canChuck = True
```

The Int type represents integers, the Float type represents floating point numbers, and the Bool type represents Booleans. You can update main to display these values by converting them to strings with the built-in Debug.toString function before passing them into text. For example, you display meaningOfLife like this:

```
main =
    text (Debug.toString meaningOfLife)
```

Now let's build upon type annotations for constants to create function type annotations. Add the first sayHello function you wrote in the REPL to Main.elm:

get-started/elm-files/Main03.elm
```
➤  sayHello : String -> String
   sayHello name =
       "Hello, " ++ name ++ "."
```

A function's static type depends on its arguments and return value. The sayHello function takes a String argument and returns a String value. In the sayHello type annotation, you separate the String argument and String return value with an arrow ->. The -> indicates a *mapping*, or *direction*. Thus, the sayHello function maps a String argument to a String result.

Now, update main to use sayHello:

```
main =
    text (sayHello "Functional Elm")
```

Compile and refresh your browser. You should see the message "Hello, Functional Elm".

You've handled the simplest function type annotation with one argument, but let's ramp up to multiple arguments. Add this function to Main.elm:

```
bottlesOf contents amount =
    Debug.toString amount ++ " bottles of " ++ contents ++ " on the wall."
```

The bottlesOf function accepts two arguments, contents and amount, and returns a string describing how many bottles of contents are on the wall. Notice that you need to convert amount to a string with Debug.toString.

I left out the type annotation for a moment to highlight another of its benefits. First, update main like so, then I'll explain further:

```
main =
    text (bottlesOf "juice" 99)
```

Compile and refresh your browser. You should see the message "99 bottles of juice on the wall." Now change 99 to True and recompile. You should see the message "True bottles of juice on the wall."

Something's not right. You intended for amount to be a number but you were able to pass in True. In fact, you could pass in anything for amount and the function would still return a result. The built-in Debug.toString function accepts any type of argument, so the Elm compiler believes amount can be any type.

You can fix this "bug" by adding a type annotation. Above bottlesOf, add the following type annotation:

```
bottlesOf : String -> Int -> String
```

Now you have explicitly declared that the contents argument is a String and the amount argument is an Int.

But wait a minute. We have *two* arrows in the type annotation. Recall that Elm functions are curried and that -> maps an argument to a return value. This type annotation doesn't say that bottlesOf takes two arguments. Instead, it says that bottlesOf takes a String argument and returns *another* function that takes an Int argument. The returned function returns a final String result.

The first arrow is pointing to a returned function. You can clarify this by wrapping the returned function type in parentheses, like this:

```
bottlesOf : String -> (Int -> String)
```

Digest how multiple arrows work for a moment because they can be confusing at first. I definitely scratched my head for a bit when I first learned function type annotations. A good rule of thumb is to remember to separate all arguments and the return value with ->. After a while, this becomes natural.

Now that you've fixed bottlesOf to only accept an integer amount, try compiling again to see the error message that Elm produces.

```
The 2nd argument to `bottlesOf` is not what I expect:

37|     text (bottlesOf "juice" True)
                                ^^^^
This `True` value is a:

    Bool

But `bottlesOf` needs the 2nd argument to be:

    Int
```

The Elm compiler recognizes that you only want Int, so it prevents you from calling the function with other types. You can fix your code by replacing True with 99.

You can fix this further by changing Debug.toString to String.fromInt, which converts integers to strings. It will then work correctly even without the type annotation. The Elm compiler only allows Debug.toString for local debugging. If you want to compile production-level code, you'll need to use more specialized conversion functions to convert to a string such as String.fromInt and String.fromFloat:

get-started/elm-files/Main04.elm
```
bottlesOf contents amount =
    String.fromInt amount ++ " bottles of " ++ contents ++ " on the wall."
```

Now you can document your code *and* help the compiler understand what types your functions take. Another perk of type annotations is that Elm's type inference can catch bugs as well. For example, take this buggy add function.

```
add : Int -> Int -> String
add x y = x + y
```

We want to return the sum of two Ints as a String, but we forgot to use String.fromInt to convert the result. The Elm compiler infers that add can only return an Int, so it prevents this code from compiling. The Elm compiler will direct us to the problem, showing that we forgot to call String.fromInt.

# Build a Static App

Great work so far! You've learned two foundational Elm concepts—functions and static types. You're now ready to bring those concepts together to create your first application. In this section, you will learn about the list data type and use lists to create HTML elements with the Html module. By the end, you will have a cool photo sharing application to show off.

## Create Collections with Lists

So far, you've worked with single data values such as strings and numbers. In Elm applications, you'll typically want to represent collections of data values, too. For example, to actually display an application, you'll need to represent multiple HTML elements. Elm lets you represent collections with the list data type. To create a list, you enclose zero or more values inside opening and closing braces [].

Open the Elm REPL and add this code:

```
> greetings = ["hi", "hello", "yo"]
["hi","hello","yo"] : List String
```

You just created a list called greetings that contains three strings, "hi", "hello", and "yo".

Although Elm lists look like JavaScript arrays, they differ in important ways. For example, you can't directly access members of a list as in the JavaScript array below.

```
var greetings = ["hi", "hello", "yo"];
var result = greetings[1]; // returns "hello"
```

In Elm, the equivalent code below would be invalid. Elm would think you're trying to call greetings like a function with the list [1] as an argument.

```
result = greetings[1] -- Elm thinks this is a function call
```

You can't access items in a list as you can in an array for a couple of reasons. First, lists are entirely different data structures from arrays. Arrays are special objects in JavaScript that associate indices with values.

Elm lists don't have a notion of indices. Lists work by letting each element reference the next element in the list, similar to the links in a chain. Lists are built for iteration. You traverse a list by visiting the first element and following its reference to the next element, and so on.

Second, Elm has to protect your code from potential undefined/null values. If you attempt to retrieve a value at an index that doesn't exist in an array, then you receive undefined. By not offering list indexing, Elm prevents null-like reference errors.

Elm lists also differ from JavaScript arrays by the types of values allowed inside them. A JavaScript array can contain a mix of types. The below array is completely valid.

```
var mixedBag = ["hi", true, 42];
```

A similar list in Elm would be invalid. Every value in an Elm list has to be the same type. If you traverse a list, you need to be sure it only contains values of a certain type. Recall that Elm has no way to determine a value's type at runtime. So really, Elm prevents unforeseen type errors that pop up in JavaScript from plaguing your Elm application.

Elm avoids these list type errors via *type variables*. Now that you understand static types and type annotations, let's examine the List static type to see what we are talking about. Inside the REPL, create an empty list like this:

```
> []
[] : List a
```

Look at the inferred type List a. That little a is a type variable. A type variable is a generic placeholder for a more specific type. When used with the List type, it refers to the type of values inside the list.

The empty list doesn't have any values, so the compiler isn't sure what its full static type is and leaves the type variable a. In the REPL, type greetings to retrieve the greetings list from earlier:

```
> greetings
["hi","hello","yo"] : List String
```

Notice that the static type is List String instead of List a. When you put strings inside the list, the Elm compiler inferred that the type variable should be the String type. This is similar to filling in a function argument with a value, except you fill in a type value.

With the type variable only having one possible type value, the Elm compiler will ensure that lists only contain one type of value.

## Create a Photo Sharing App

Now that you are armed with the list data type, let's build your first Elm application. You will create a photo sharing application called Picshare. Start by making a new directory called picshare. Inside picshare, initialize with elm init.

Inside the automatically generated src directory, create a new file called Picshare.elm. Declare the Picshare module at the top, similar to how you created the Main module earlier:

get-started/static-app/Picshare01.elm
```
module Picshare exposing (main)
```

Notice that you again expose a main constant. You will add it in a moment. Next, import the Html module, exposing a couple of new members like so:

```
import Html exposing (Html, div, text)
```

You expose text in the same way as Main.elm while also exposing Html and div.

Elm modules can expose types in addition to functions and constants. Here, you've exposed the Html *type* for representing HTML. Even though it shares the same name, it is different from the Html *module*.

The exposed div is a function for creating <div> elements. The Html module houses functions for creating other elements[2] as you'll see in a bit.

---

2. https://package.elm-lang.org/packages/elm/html/latest/Html

Let's put Html, div, and text to good use by creating the main constant. Add the following code at the bottom of Picshare.elm:

```
main : Html msg
main =
    div [] [ text "Picshare" ]
```

Let's examine the body of main first before talking about its type annotation.

You set main equal to div along with two lists. Recall that div is a function. It takes two arguments, a list of HTML attributes and list of HTML children.

The first argument is the empty list, so this div element has no attributes. Examples of attributes are id, class, src, and href. You'll add attributes a little later in this chapter.

The second argument is a list with one element, text "Picshare". The text function technically creates text nodes, so this div element will contain the text content "Picshare."

The text function is crucial here. You can't use a lone string because the Elm type system wouldn't accept it. Look at the type annotation for main to understand further.

Notice that you use the Html type imported earlier. The Html type represents something called the *virtual DOM*. Instead of directly manipulating the DOM, you use the virtual DOM to represent what the real DOM should look like. The virtual DOM is an actual data type in Elm similar to strings and lists. We'll talk more about the virtual DOM in the next chapter, but for now understand that it lets Elm efficiently update the real DOM on your behalf.

The Html type also has a type variable called msg, just like List has a type variable. We'll discuss msg in more depth in the next chapter too.

Let's compile what you have so far, but a little differently. Instead of compiling to HTML, you'll need to compile Picshare.elm to a JavaScript file. You'll want a JavaScript file so you can use your own HTML file to include custom CSS.

Run the elm make command with a new --output flag inside the picshare directory:

```
elm make src/Picshare.elm --output picshare.js
```

This command will compile Picshare.elm to picshare.js.

Next, inside this book's code downloads, find the index.html and main.css files in the get-started/static-app directory. Copy both files into your picshare directory. The index.html file loads main.css to customize the look of the Picshare application.

Since you're using a custom HTML file, you'll need to load your compiled Elm application inside of it. First, you'll need to mount your application into a real DOM element. Open index.html in your editor. Inside the <body> tag, replace the "REPLACE ME" comment with this <div> element:

get-started/static-app/index-completed.html
```
<div id="main" class="main"></div>
```

Next, load your compiled picshare.js file in a <script> tag and add some JavaScript code in a separate <script> tag below.

```
<script src="picshare.js"></script>
<script>
  Elm.Picshare.init({
    node: document.getElementById('main')
  });
</script>
```

A compiled Elm application creates a global Elm namespace variable. The Elm variable has properties for any top-level modules you compiled. In this case, it has a Picshare property.

Every compiled module has an init function that accepts a configuration object. The node property of the configuration object specifies a DOM node. The DOM node is where you want to display your Elm application. For the Picshare application, you display it inside the <div> tag you created earlier.

Open index.html in your browser, and you should see the text "Picshare." That's a great start, but let's put that custom CSS to work and display a photo in the Picshare application.

## Display a Photo

Before you display your first photo, you'll need to convert the "Picshare" text into a styled header. First, import the class function from the Html.Attributes module, like this:

get-started/static-app/Picshare02.elm
```
import Html.Attributes exposing (class)
```

The Html.Attributes module contains functions for adding attributes to virtual DOM nodes. You import class so you can style the top level div tag inside main.

The class function accepts class name(s) as a string argument. Add the header class name to the div's list of attributes (the first list argument):

```
main =
    div [ class "header" ] [ text "Picshare" ]
```

Next, import the h1 function from the Html module:

```
import Html exposing (Html, div, h1, text)
```

Wrap text "Picshare" in an h1 tag:

```
h1 [] [ text "Picshare" ]
```

Your main should now look like this. I recommend indenting the second list underneath div as in the example below to help with readability.

```
main =
    div [ class "header" ]
        [ h1 [] [ text "Picshare" ] ]
```

Compile and refresh your browser. The Picshare header should look like the following screenshot.

# Picshare

Now that you have a nifty looking header, let's add a photo to the mix. Begin by importing all members of Html:

```
get-started/static-app/Picshare03.elm
import Html exposing (..)
```

When you expose .. from a module, you bring in everything the module exposes. For the Html module, that includes Html, div, h1, and text as well as other HTML functions such as img and h2.

You'll use the img function in a moment, so also import the src function from Html.Attributes:

```
import Html.Attributes exposing (class, src)
```

The photo will live below the header, so you'll need to place another div tag underneath the div header. However, main can only have one root element. Fix this by wrapping the div header inside another div like this:

```
main =
    div []
        [ div [ class "header" ]
            [ h1 [] [ text "Picshare" ] ]
        ]
```

Next, add a child div for the photo to the new root div:

```
main =
    div []
        [ div [ class "header" ]
            [ h1 [] [ text "Picshare" ] ]
        , div [ class "content-flow" ]
            [ div [ class "detailed-photo" ]
                [ img [ src "https://programming-elm.com/1.jpg" ] []
                , div [ class "photo-info" ]
                    [ h2 [ class "caption" ] [ text "Surfing" ] ]
                ]
            ]
        ]
```

This new photo div is fairly complex, so let's unravel what's happening.

❶ The content-flow div is a wrapper div for all photos you'll display. Right now, you are only displaying one photo.

❷ This detailed-photo div represents an individual photo.

❸ The img function displays the photo just like an <img> element.

Note that you use the src attribute function in the attribute list and an empty list for the child elements. Even though img never contains children, all HTML functions have a consistent API in the Html module.

❹ You wrap the caption in the photo-info div. You will add more to this div in later chapters.

❺ You display the caption inside an h2 element.

> If you would prefer to serve the image locally, you can follow the instructions in Appendix 2, Run the Local Server, on page 267 to run the server on your computer. Then, replace https://programming-elm.com with http://localhost:5000.

Compile your application. Refresh your browser and you should see a surfer catching some waves.

Picshare

*Surfing*

Tubular job. Your application now displays its first photo.

## Display Multiple Photos

Now that you're getting the hang of static HTML in Elm, let's finish this chapter by introducing a couple more photos. You could duplicate the detailed-photo div to add another photo, but that would result in duplication and less maintainable code. Let's clean up our application with a reusable function that displays a photo. Above main, add this viewDetailedPhoto function:

```
get-started/static-app/Picshare04.elm
viewDetailedPhoto : String -> String -> Html msg
viewDetailedPhoto url caption =
    div [ class "detailed-photo" ]
        [ img [ src url ] []
        , div [ class "photo-info" ]
            [ h2 [ class "caption" ] [ text caption ] ]
        ]
```

Inside viewDetailedPhoto, you have the same HTML for a detailed photo. But instead of hardcoding the photo URL and caption, you accept them as url and caption arguments.

Before updating main, let's add a helper string to simplify generating photo URLs. Above viewDetailedPhoto, add this baseUrl constant:

```
baseUrl : String
baseUrl =
    "https://programming-elm.com/"
```

Recall that you can run the server locally (see Appendix 2, Run the Local Server, on page 267), so you can set baseUrl to http://localhost:5000/ instead.

Finally, use your new, fancy viewDetailedPhoto function to replace the single photo in main with three photos:

```
main =
    div []
        [ div [ class "header" ]
            [ h1 [] [ text "Picshare" ] ]
        , div [ class "content-flow" ]
➤           [ viewDetailedPhoto (baseUrl ++ "1.jpg") "Surfing"
➤           , viewDetailedPhoto (baseUrl ++ "2.jpg") "The Fox"
➤           , viewDetailedPhoto (baseUrl ++ "3.jpg") "Evening"
            ]
        ]
```

You avoided a ton of potential duplication and have cleaner code with viewDetailedPhoto. You can easily add some of your own photos if you like.

Compile one last time and refresh your browser. In addition to the surfing photo, you should see a photo of a fox and one of a sunset behind the clouds.

Fantastic work! You've built your first Elm application using Elm's awesome Html module and a reusable viewDetailedPhoto function.

## What You Learned

You achieved a lot in this chapter. You learned Elm syntax, played with different data types and functional programming concepts, and created Elm functions. You also learned about the safety guarantees from Elm's type system and wrote your own type annotations for constants and functions. Finally, you brought it all together to build your first Elm application. You learned about modules and used the Html module to construct a static photo sharing application. You even created a custom HTML file to mount your Elm application with JavaScript.

Now that you're familiar with the world of Elm, you can solve problems in a new language and build your own static Elm applications. You're also ready to forge ahead with deeper Elm concepts. Most Elm applications require state to be interactive for users. In the next chapter, you will discover the Elm Architecture for building stateful applications and will add new features to the Picshare application.

# CHAPTER 2

# Create Stateful Elm Applications

In the previous chapter, you learned how to define Elm functions and build the static Picshare application with the Html module. Most applications aren't going to be so simple, however. In this chapter, we'll introduce state to the Picshare application. State is important for creating interactive applications. For the Picshare application, you will add the ability to "like" photos. To do this, you will need application state to track if a photo is liked.

You'll learn how to use the Elm Architecture to create a model for application state, a view function for displaying the model, and an update function for making changes to the model. Along the way, you'll learn about records, custom types, and immutability—all important in creating Elm applications.

## Apply the Elm Architecture

The Elm Architecture is Elm's built-in framework for creating applications. In this section, you will learn about the architecture through adding a new feature to the Picshare application.

The Elm Architecture provides a standard way of building applications known as the *Model-View-Update pattern*. As its name suggests, this pattern has three important parts: a *model*, a *view*, and a method of *updating* the model. In the figure on page 28, you can see an overview of how the Elm Architecture works. You'll revisit later how all the pieces in the figure fit together. For now, we'll gain our understanding of a model by adding one to the application.

### Create a Model

In Elm applications, the *model* is responsible for containing all your application state. This is different from other architectures such as MVC (Model-View-Controller) and MVVM (Model-View-ViewModel), or stuffing data in the DOM via data-* attributes. Those approaches encourage spreading your state across

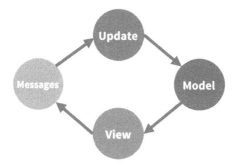

multiple models, making it hard to keep track of where state is located and how and when state changes. The Elm Architecture allows you to know where your state is located because it's consolidated in one place.

In Elm, the model can be whatever data type you want, such as a string or an integer. Typically, your model will be a *record* data type, which is what you'll use for the Picshare application.

## Work with Records

A *record* is similar to a plain old JavaScript object. It groups together related fields into key-value pairs. Elm developers typically refer to entries in a record as *fields*.

Let's learn more about records by creating a simple record to represent everyone's best friend, the dog. Fire up the Elm REPL from the command line with elm repl. Enter the following into the REPL:

```
> dog = { name = "Tucker", age = 11 }
{ age = 11, name = "Tucker" } : { age : number, name : String }
```

Notice that you use {} to create records, similar to creating JavaScript objects. The one difference from JavaScript objects is that you separate fields and their values with the = symbol instead of the : symbol.

After creating the dog constant, you get back a record instance with a record type of { age : number, name : String }. The record type looks similar to record values except it uses the : symbol to separate field names and their types.

You can access individual record fields with the dot operator, the same as with JavaScript objects. Try this out in the REPL:

```
> dog.name
"Tucker" : String
```

```
> dog.age
11 : number
```

Similar to lists in the previous chapter, accessing properties via bracket notation will not work, though. Elm will interpret the incorrect code below as a function call with a list argument. You can't access fields dynamically like you can in JavaScript. You'll see why in the next section.

```
> dog["name"]
-- TOO MANY ARGS ------------------------------------------------------- elm

The `dog` value is not a function, but it was given 1 argument.

5|    dog["name"]
```

## Create New Records

One significant difference between JavaScript objects and Elm records is that records are static. When you create a record instance, its type is set in stone. That means you won't be able to add new fields later or change the type of existing fields.

For example, the following code in the REPL will not work.

```
> dog.breed = "Sheltie"
-- PARSE ERROR --------------------------------------------------------- elm

I was not expecting this equals sign while parsing repl_value_3's definition.

4| repl_value_3 =
5|    dog.breed = "Sheltie"
              ^
Maybe this is supposed to be a separate definition? If so, it is indented too
far. Spaces are not allowed before top-level definitions.
```

Records are also *immutable*, which is a hallmark of many functional languages. An immutable data type can't change in place. In the case of a record, this means you won't be able to change the value of an existing field, so the following code will not work either.

```
> dog.name = "Rover"
> dog.age = 12
```

Changing values in place as in the previous example is known as *mutation* and would be valid in JavaScript. In Elm, you can't mutate values.

Not being able to mutate fields in a record might seem like a hindrance, but it's actually a great safeguard. You have a guarantee that no code can accidentally or intentionally change your record instance, meaning fewer bugs in your code.

Elm isn't going to leave you high and dry, however. Instead of mutating records, you can create *new* instances of records.

Let's write a function for the dog to have a birthday. You'll want to take a dog record as an argument and return a new dog with its age incremented by 1. Enter this into the REPL:

```
> haveBirthday d = { name = d.name, age = d.age + 1 }
<function>
    : { b | age : number, name : a } -> { age : number, name : a }
```

You get back a function with a very interesting-looking type annotation. It takes a record of type b that must have an age field of type number and a name field of type a. The types a and b are type variables similar to what you saw in the previous chapter. The number type is a special type variable that can only be an Int or Float type when filled in. (The "b-type" record is called an extensible record, which you'll learn more about in Chapter 6, Build Larger Applications, on page 103.)

Notice in the implementation that you reuse the d.name field and add 1 to the d.age field in the new record. You can use the haveBirthday function on the original dog record to create a new instance of a dog record. Try this in the REPL:

```
> olderDog = haveBirthday dog
{ age = 12, name = "Tucker" } : { age : number, name : String }
> dog
{ age = 11, name = "Tucker" } : { age : number, name : String }
```

You assign the new dog record to a constant called olderDog. If you inspect olderDog, you have a dog with the same name that is one year older. If you inspect the original dog reference, you see that it still has the same age.

## Use Record Update Syntax

Creating functions like haveBirthday might seem like a lot of boilerplate, especially when dealing with records with more fields. You have to make sure to copy all existing fields to return the same type. Elm provides some syntactical sugar for simplifying this process. Enter a new version of the haveBirthday function into the REPL like this:

```
> haveBirthday d = { d | age = d.age + 1 }
<function> : { a | age : number } -> { a | age : number }
```

We introduced the | symbol to record syntax. This is sometimes known as *record update* syntax. To the left of the | symbol, you provide an existing record reference, d. To the right, you specify any changes you want to make to values in the record reference. Elm will take all existing fields from the reference on the left and merge in changes from the right to create a new instance of the record with the changes. Try rerunning the examples from the code on page 30 in the REPL. You'll get back the same results from earlier.

One word of caution: the record update syntax might sound similar to the Object.assign function in JavaScript. Object.assign lets you merge together different JavaScript objects. Elm's record update syntax only allows you to create new values for *existing* fields in a record. You can't add new fields to the new record. Trying to add a breed field like this won't work.

```
> { dog | breed = "Sheltie" }
```

## Immutability Has Benefits

Creating new instances of data types is common in functional languages like Elm. If this concept still seems foreign or wrong to you, don't worry. It felt like that to me too when I first started with functional programming. Coming from an object-oriented programming (OOP) background, I didn't see how you could accomplish anything if you didn't mutate data.

With more experience, I realized that it's easy to get things done in a functional language and that immutable data has great perks.

1. It makes data flow explicit. If functions want to "change" a record, they have to return a new record instead of mutating an existing one.

2. Instances of data structures can share data internally because there is no risk of code accidentally or intentionally mutating the shared data.

3. In multithreaded languages, there is no risk of threads mutating the shared data.

## Create a Record Model

Now that you've learned about records, let's use one as the model for the Picshare application. In the last chapter, you statically displayed three images. To ease into making this a stateful application, you'll simplify the application to use one photo. Then, you can use a record model to represent the single photo.

For now, let's focus on displaying the single photo based on the fields of the model. You can jump into creating a *view* function in a moment. Open up the Picshare.elm file that you created in the last chapter and add this below the module imports and baseUrl constant:

```
stateful-applications/Picshare01.elm
initialModel : { url : String, caption : String }
initialModel =
    { url = baseUrl ++ "1.jpg"
    , caption = "Surfing"
    }
```

You create an initialModel record with two String fields, url and caption. Notice you also add a type annotation similar to the dog type annotation that the REPL printed earlier.

It's important for Elm applications to supply an initial state so there is something to initially display. That is why you named the record model initialModel. Using initialModel as the name for your initial state is common in Elm applications, but not required.

That's it as far as the model goes for right now. Let's turn our attention to displaying that model with a view function.

## Create the View

In the Elm Architecture, the *view* is responsible for displaying a model. In many JavaScript frameworks, the view layer not only displays state but can manage state of its own. Unfortunately, this leads to the same problem of spreading out state that I mentioned at the start of the previous section. The Elm Architecture enforces separation of concerns by preventing the view layer from storing state. The view is the visual representation of the model and nothing more.

In Elm, views are implemented as functions. They take a model as an argument and return a virtual DOM tree. Recall from Chapter 1, Get Started with Elm, on page 1 how you built a virtual DOM tree with the main constant by using the functions from the Html module. The virtual DOM tree describes what you want your application to display. Elm is responsible for converting the virtual DOM tree into real DOM nodes in the browser. You'll learn more about why and how Elm uses this virtual DOM tree later in this chapter.

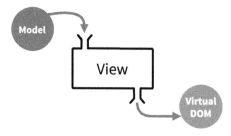

Create the view function by reusing the main constant at the bottom of Picshare.elm. Rename main to view and update it to take the model as an argument like so:

```
view : { url : String, caption : String } -> Html msg
view model =
    div []
        [ div [ class "header" ]
            [ h1 [] [ text "Picshare" ] ]
        , div [ class "content-flow" ]
            [ viewDetailedPhoto model ]
        ]
```

The type signature now takes the record type and returns Html msg. The function implementation takes the model and passes it into the viewDetailedPhoto function. You'll need to update the implementation of viewDetailedPhoto next.

## Display the Photo

The viewDetailedPhoto function currently takes the String arguments url and caption. You will want to condense those arguments down to just the record model because it contains fields for the url and caption. Update viewDetailedPhoto like this:

```
viewDetailedPhoto : { url : String, caption : String } -> Html msg
viewDetailedPhoto model =
    div [ class "detailed-photo" ]
        [ img [ src model.url ] []
        , div [ class "photo-info" ]
            [ h2 [ class "caption" ] [ text model.caption ] ]
        ]
```

The changes are minimal. You use model.url for the img src attribute and model.caption for the text content of the h2 tag.

Finally, you need to render the application in the browser. Create a new main constant for Elm to use:

```
main : Html msg
main =
    view initialModel
```

The main constant ties the model and view together by passing in initialModel to the view function. This allows Elm to display your view function in the browser.

Inside your directory with Picshare.elm, make sure you still have the index.html and main.css files from the previous chapter. If you don't, you can grab them from the book's code downloads inside the stateful-applications directory. Compile your application and open up index.html in your browser.

```
elm make src/Picshare.elm --output picshare.js
```

You should see this in your browser.

Picshare

*Surfing*

You now have a minimally stateful application. The difference between the static application and this one is that your view depends on state it receives as an argument instead of hard-coding in photo URLs and captions. State flows top down from main to view and finally to viewDetailedPhoto.

Try changing the caption in initialModel to something different or use one of the other images in the url (2.jpg or 3.jpg). After recompiling then refreshing your browser, you should see the changes reflected in what Elm displays.

You might say that you're still technically hard-coding in a photo via the initialModel, which is partially true. That is temporary. What you're really doing is setting up the application for later when the initial state can come from other sources like a server. Letting state flow through an application as a function argument is crucial to decoupling state from the view, and is also important when state can change—as you'll see when we introduce the update function in a bit.

## Handle State Changes

In MVC and MVVM applications, you can mutate models from almost anywhere in the codebase. This leads to the problem of not knowing where or when state changes. The Elm Architecture solves this with its update process. Just as all state is located in the model, all changes to the model have to take place in an update function.

The update function takes two arguments, a *message* and the *model*. The message argument comes from Elm's runtime in response to events such as mouse clicks, server responses, and WebSocket events. The message describes the type of state change. We'll discuss messages in the next section and the Elm runtime in more detail in a later section.

The update function is responsible for interpreting the message to change the state. Recall that data types in Elm are immutable, so the update function must return a new instance of the model with the changed state.

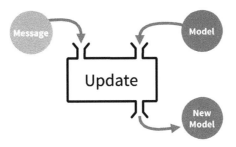

## Like a Photo

At the beginning of this chapter I mentioned adding the ability to like photos. Let's work through adding an update function to the application by implementing this feature. You'll need to update the model and view definitions first.

The change to the model will be straightforward. You'll need to add a new liked field with a type of Bool. Set the initial value to False. Update your initialModel definition in Picshare.elm to look like this.

stateful-applications/Picshare02.elm

```
initialModel : { url : String, caption : String, liked : Bool }
initialModel =
    { url = baseUrl ++ "1.jpg"
    , caption = "Surfing"
    , liked = False
    }
```

Likewise, update the type annotation for your view function to include the new liked field. Also, change the return type of the view function to Html Msg. The subtle change from Html msg to Html Msg means you're filling in the type variable msg with a concrete type Msg. We'll discuss this in more depth when you define the Msg type later. Your type annotation should look like this:

```
view : { url : String, caption : String, liked : Bool } -> Html Msg
```

We've taken care of some boilerplate with the model and view, but the real work lies ahead with the viewDetailedPhoto function. You'll need a way to display the liked field and allow it to trigger an event whenever a photo is liked or unliked. Let's do that next.

## Add a Love Button

We want the application to be friendly and welcoming, so let's use a heart icon for liking photos. We'll call it the "love button" (no affiliation with the "Love Shack").

You'll need a way to display a heart outline when the photo isn't liked and a filled heart when the photo is liked. You'll also need a way to handle mouse clicks in order to like and unlike the photo. To do all that, you need to introduce a let expression.

A let expression allows you to create local variables inside a function. This expression has four parts: a let keyword, one or more constant bindings or function definitions, an in keyword, and a body expression.

You'll use a let expression in this case to create two local variables based on the value of the model.liked field. Update your viewDetailedPhoto function like this:

```
viewDetailedPhoto :
    { url : String, caption : String, liked : Bool }
    -> Html Msg
viewDetailedPhoto model =
    let
        buttonClass =
            if model.liked then
                "fa-heart"

            else
                "fa-heart-o"

        msg =
            if model.liked then
                Unlike

            else
                Like
    in
    div [ class "detailed-photo" ]
        [ img [ src model.url ] []
        , div [ class "photo-info" ]
            [ div [ class "like-button" ]
                [ i
                    [ class "fa fa-2x"
                    , class buttonClass
                    , onClick msg
                    ]
                    []
                ]
            , h2 [ class "caption" ] [ text model.caption ]
            ]
        ]
```

❶ Update the type annotation to include the liked field and to return Html Msg. Note again that you use a concrete Msg type that you'll define in a moment.

❷ Create a local buttonClass constant based on the value of model.liked.

❸ Create a local msg constant based on the value of model.liked.

Like and Unlike are special values that you will introduce in a moment.

❹ Use the buttonClass string along with an i tag to create a heart icon in the body of the let expression. The i tag is available because you exposed all members of Html in the last chapter.

The possible values for buttonClass along with the class names "fa" and "fa-2x" come from the Font Awesome[1] library, which index.html references.

❺ Use the class attribute function here and at ❻. This is a clever feature of Elm that allows you to supply multiple dynamic class names without string concatenation. Elm will collapse together all calls to the class function to give your HTML element one class attribute.

❼ Provide the dynamic msg to the onClick handler.

 You can serve the Font Awesome locally for the love button if you prefer. Follow the instructions in Appendix 2, Run the Local Server, on page 267 and change the protocol and domain for the Font Awesome stylesheet in index.html from https://programming-elm.com to http://localhost:5000.

## Describe Events

After defining the classes for the i tag, you use an attribute function we hadn't covered yet, onClick. Elm views not only can describe HTML elements and attributes with functions but also events such as mouse clicks and keyboard input. You typically provide a message argument to an event function from the Html.Events module to listen for an event. These event functions produce attributes like the class and src functions you've already been using.

When you provide a message to an Elm event handler function, you give Elm a key to your update function. Elm wires up an event handler on your behalf and responds to the DOM event by calling your update function with the message you provided. Your update function is then responsible for responding to the message that you associate with the DOM event. This is different from JavaScript and the DOM API, which allows you to attach a

---

1.  http://fontawesome.io/

callback function directly in response to an event. We will cover Elm's handling of events and messages in more depth when you write the update function in a moment.

Returning to our specific example, onClick is the event function from the Html.Events module, and msg is the message you want to receive in response to a mouse click on the love button. Import onClick so you don't get a compiler error. Add this underneath your other module imports:

```
import Html.Events exposing (onClick)
```

## Create Messages with Custom Types

I've mentioned them several times, so let's finally clarify what messages are and how to create them in Elm. Inside the viewDetailedPhoto function, you set the local msg constant to two possible values, Like and Unlike. These are special values that come from something called a *custom type*.

In addition to its built-in types, Elm allows you to create your own types using custom types. Custom types let you constrain a set of values to a new type. Think of them as souped-up versions of *enumerations* from traditional languages like C++ or Java. Custom types go by other names such as union types, tagged unions, or discriminated unions in other programming languages.

You'll need to implement the custom type for the Like and Unlike values that the viewDetailedPhoto function references. Add this code below your view function:

```
type Msg
    = Like
    | Unlike
```

You create a custom type by using the type keyword and providing a name for your type. Here, you have a new custom type called Msg. Next, you declare the possible values of your custom type after the = symbol. Each value is separated by the | symbol. If you think of the | symbol as a stand-in for the word "or," then you can read the syntax as, "the custom type Msg can have the values Like or Unlike."

Most of the time, you'll hear Elm developers refer to the values of a custom type as *constructors*. You use constructors to *construct* an instance of the custom type. When you dynamically assign the local msg constant in the viewDetailedPhoto function, you're using the constructors Like and Unlike.

Notice the distinction here. The msg constant has a *type* of Msg but a *value* of either Like or Unlike. To make more sense of that statement, compare this to the liked constant, which has a *type* of Bool but a *value* of True or False. The only way to create a Msg type is to use either the Like or Unlike constructors. If you tried a third value such as Dislike without adding it to the custom type definition, then your code wouldn't compile.

```
-- This wouldn't compile. Dislike doesn't exist.
msg = Dislike
```

You'll learn the importance of custom types when you use the Msg type along with a case expression in the update function. Before you do that, let's view what you have so far. Update the type annotation for the main constant to use Html Msg:

```
main : Html Msg
```

Double-check to ensure that your code matches code/stateful-applications/Picshare02.elm from the code downloads and then recompile your application. You should see the heart outline underneath the photo.

Picshare

*Surfing*

## Add an Update Function

You now have a love button, but clicking on it does nothing. Clicking on the button should cause the heart to become filled. This visual change should come from a state change. Remember that the view only *displays* the model. As you saw earlier, state changes via an update function, so let's add that to the application.

Recall that the update function takes two arguments, a message and a model. The message is like an instruction. The update function needs to "interpret" the message to determine how to create new state.

One way to think about the update process is to imagine yourself as the update function. Let's say that your boss emails you or pings you on Slack about changing the background color of the header on the company website. We'll forgive your boss for not making a ticket this time around. At some level, the email or chat message is similar to the message argument of the update function. When you read the message, you interpret it and create a new version of the website with a different background color for the header.

In the case of this application, the update function needs to interpret the Like and Unlike messages. If the message is Like, then the update function needs to return a model with the liked field set to True. For the Unlike message, it needs to return a model with the liked field set to False.

Let's implement the update function. You might be tempted to use an if-else expression to check the message. You're going to use a more powerful Elm feature called *pattern matching* via case expression. Add the following code below your Msg type:

stateful-applications/Picshare03.elm
```
update :
    Msg
    -> { url : String, caption : String, liked : Bool }
    -> { url : String, caption : String, liked : Bool }
update msg model =
❶   case msg of
❷       Like ->
            { model | liked = True }

❸       Unlike ->
            { model | liked = False }
```

The type annotation shows that you take a Msg as the first argument and a record model as the second argument. You also return a record model. You might notice that the type annotation is quite long. You'll address that when you refactor the application in the next chapter.

Inside the body of the function, you use a case expression on the msg argument. In Elm, case expressions are similar to switch statements in JavaScript but are more versatile and robust.

❶ Designate the value to match by placing it between the keywords case and of. This is similar to switch (msg) in JavaScript.

❷ Try matching the Like constructor. This is similar to case Like: in JavaScript. If the msg value is Like, then use the expression to the right of the -> symbol. Notice the record update syntax to create a new model from the existing model, but with the liked field set to True.

❸ If the msg is instead Unlike, then match it and follow its branch to create a new model with the liked field set to False.

You'll notice that a couple of things are missing in the case expression when compared to switch statements in JavaScript. Remember that Elm is an expression-oriented language. Each branch of a case expression is itself an expression so you don't need a break statement. JavaScript switch statements don't implicitly return values like an Elm case expression, so they require a break statement or an explicit return statement inside branches to signal the end of that branch.

In a sense, you also don't need a default branch like a switch statement. This is where Elm case expressions and pattern matching really shine. Because Elm is strongly typed, when it matches on a custom type like Msg, it knows that the *only* values it can match are Like and Unlike. No other values are possible in this particular case expression, so there is no need for a default handler.

However, because Elm knows it must match either Like or Unlike, if you leave either of those branches out, your application will not compile. Let's intentionally break the application to see what I mean. Remove the Unlike branch from the case expression and try to compile. You should see a compiler error message like this:

```
-- MISSING PATTERNS ------------------------------------- src/Picshare.elm

This `case` does not have branches for all possibilities:

72|>    case msg of
73|>        Like ->
74|>            { model | liked = True }

Missing possibilities include:

    Unlike

I would have to crash if I saw one of those. Add branches for them!
```

The Elm compiler is a great safeguard if you accidentally forget to handle a value in a case expression. Technically, you can provide a "default" branch to handle any missing values. You could fix the intentional error you created by adding this under the Like branch.

```
_ ->
    { model | liked = False }
```

The underscore character serves as a wildcard in Elm pattern matching. In this instance, it would match the missing Unlike value. You should use underscores like this sparingly, though. Explicit code is easier to read and carries fewer assumptions.

Add the explicit Unlike branch back to your case expression.

## Create a Program

The ability to like photos is almost complete. Now that you've added an update function, you need to hook it up with your model and view function. You need a *program*.

A program in Elm ties together the model, view function, and update function. This is how Elm is able to subscribe to DOM events, dispatch messages to your update function, update your state based on the result of your update function, and display the changes in the browser. Let's add a program to the application and then walk through how the Elm runtime and the application will work together. You will need the Browser module to build programs, so import it above your other imports.

```
import Browser
```

Then, rewrite your main constant to look like this:

```
main : Program () { url : String, caption : String, liked : Bool } Msg
main =
    Browser.sandbox
        { init = initialModel
        , view = view
        , update = update
        }
```

The main constant is now equal to a program created from the Browser.sandbox function. This function takes a record argument with three required fields, init, view, and update. You match the init field with initialModel, the view field with the view function, and the update field with the update function. Browser.sandbox takes care of the rest.

Browser.sandbox returns a Program type. The definition for the Program type looks like this in Elm's internals.

```
type Program flags model msg = Program
```

Elm defines the Program type as a custom type with three type variables: flags, model, and msg. You've seen type variables in the context of lists and the Html type, but you can use them with custom types, too.

The flags type variable indicates the type of flags that you want to supply to an Elm program. Flags are similar to configuration data for initializing Elm applications. You'll learn more about flags in Chapter 8, Integrate with JavaScript, on page 153.

Look at the type annotation for main. You'll notice that you supply a () type for the flags type variable. The () type is the *unit type* and represents an empty value. You use it here to signal that this program receives no flags.

For the remaining Program type arguments, you supply the record model type for the model type variable and the Msg type for the msg type variable. You can think of the final type as a program with a model of your record type that produces messages of your Msg type.

With the main constant rewritten as a program, you can now like photos. Verify that your code matches code/stateful-applications/Picshare03.elm from the code downloads. Compile the application and click the love button. You should see the heart become filled as in the screenshot that follows.

Picshare

*Surfing*

## The Elm Architecture Life Cycle

If you continue clicking on the love button, the heart should toggle back and forth between being an outline and filled. To fully understand how your Elm program is working, let's walk through the life cycle of a mouse click on the love button within the context of the Elm Architecture. We'll start from the beginning when the model's liked field is False.

The Elm runtime takes your main program and bootstraps an initial application. It calls your view function with the initialModel to produce a virtual DOM representation of the HTML you want to be displayed. Elm interprets the virtual DOM and renders the correct HTML in the browser on your behalf as shown in the figure on page 44. At this point, Elm will display the unliked photo with a heart outline.

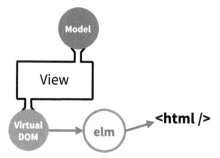

Recall from the viewDetailedPhoto function that if the model isn't liked, you use the Like constructor with the event function onClick.

Elm reads through the returned virtual DOM and encounters the event attribute, using the DOM API to wire up a click handler on the love button's DOM node. When you click on the love button, the click handler will dispatch the Like message to a queue in the Elm runtime.

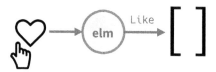

The Elm runtime will pick up the message from the queue and call your update function with the message and current model, which happens to be the initialModel at this moment. Your update function will use the case expression to return a new model with the liked field set to True.

The Elm runtime then calls your view function on the new model to retrieve a new virtual DOM representation. Elm compares the current virtual DOM with the new virtual DOM and computes what's called a *diff*. A diff is basically a list of differences between the old virtual DOM and the new virtual DOM. During the diff process, Elm creates a list of *patches* to apply to the real DOM in order to make it reflect the new virtual DOM. Diffs and patches are awesome because they give your application better performance. The Elm runtime can avoid *rerendering* your entire application and can instead add, remove, and replace DOM nodes *only where necessary*.

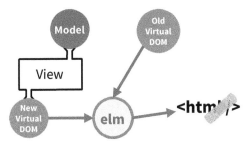

The cycle repeats when you click on the love button again, only this time it sends an Unlike message. Data flows in Elm applications are *unidirectional*. If you look back at the preceding figure, you'll see that data flows in one direction from model to view to messages to update and back to model. This structure sets the Elm Architecture apart and makes your life easier when building applications.

Even though Elm's update process might sound needlessly complex, I promise that it is beneficial. Let's summarize some of the key benefits we've covered.

- By using immutable data, you don't run the risk of state accidentally changing on you.

- By using messages, you know exactly how state changes.

- By using the update function, you know exactly where state changes.

- The virtual DOM gives your application better performance by avoiding unnecessary rerendering.

## What You Learned

You learned a lot in this chapter! You discovered language-level features and concepts such as records, custom types, and immutability. More importantly, you learned how to build a real-world application with the Elm Architecture. Well done. You now have the foundation to start creating stateful Elm applications on your own. You'll build on that foundation in the next chapter by learning how to refactor and enhance Elm applications with new features.

# CHAPTER 3

# Refactor and Enhance Elm Applications

In the previous chapter, you learned how to use the Elm Architecture to "like" a photo in the Picshare application. Unfortunately, you accumulated some technical debt in that process. Don't worry. Elm makes refactoring tech debt safe thanks to static types. In this chapter, you will refactor the application to simplify the code. Regardless of the language, refactoring is a common practice in programming and helps improve understanding and maintainability of codebases.

You will also enhance the application by allowing users to comment on the photo. In any real-world application, your boss will probably request new applications features from time to time, and Elm is well suited to new feature development. Thanks to Elm's type system and compiler, you can fearlessly refactor and improve your applications.

## Refactor with Good Practices

You wrote a lot of code in the previous chapter. Before forging ahead with new features, let's pause to clean up the code. In this section, you will refactor the code by using type aliases and simplifying how users like a photo.

### Create Type Aliases

We have a stinky code smell in the type annotations at the moment because we reused the record model { url : String, caption : String, liked : Bool } type in multiple places. In a larger code base, that will become annoying and hard to maintain. You can fix this problem by using a *type alias*.

A type alias allows you to associate a type name with another type. To create an alias, you use the type and alias keywords consecutively, followed by the name of the new type and the existing type to alias. Here is a common type alias that associates an Id type with the built-in Int type.

```
type alias Id = Int
```

If you added the above to your code, you could use the Id and Int types inter-changeably in your type annotations. You'll typically want to use type aliases to write more domain-specific code like the Id alias and to eliminate redundancy.

You can alias *any* type with a type alias. You can even create a type alias for record types. So let's create a type alias for the application's record model. Add a new type alias called Model above the baseUrl constant:

refactor-enhance/Picshare01.elm
```
type alias Model =
    { url : String
    , caption : String
    , liked : Bool
    }
```

Now you can use the Model type in place of every reference to the original record type. You'll need to update the following type annotations to use Model.

- Change initialModel to have a Model type.

  ```
  initialModel : Model
  ```

- Change viewDetailedPhoto to take Model as a parameter.

  ```
  viewDetailedPhoto : Model -> Html Msg
  ```

- Change view to take Model as a parameter.

  ```
  view : Model -> Html Msg
  ```

- Change update to take Model as a parameter and to return Model.

  ```
  update : Msg -> Model -> Model
  ```

- Change main to use Model as the second type argument to Program.

  ```
  main : Program () Model Msg
  ```

Double check that your code matches code/refactor-enhance/Picshare01.elm. Recompile with this command:

```
elm make src/Picshare.elm --output picshare.js
```

Your application should look the same as before, but now you've eliminated a lot of redundancy and made your code more explicit. This means you'll have an easier time maintaining your code in the future.

### Use a Type Alias Constructor

One neat feature of record type aliases that I didn't mention is that Elm also creates a *constructor function* with the same name as the type alias. Record constructor functions take values for each field of the record as arguments and create a new instance of the record. You could technically use a constructor function to create the initialModel like this.

```
initialModel =
    Model (baseUrl ++ "1.jpg") "Surfing" False
```

Here, you call the Model constructor function with values for the url, caption, and liked fields. Notice that the order of arguments matches the order you defined the fields in the Model type alias.

Record constructor functions are useful for creating records with less code, but use them with caution. Imagine what an initialModel might look like in a larger codebase if you used a constructor function.

```
initialModel =
    Model (baseUrl ++ "1.jpg") "Surfing" False [] "" True 42
```

The more fields you add to your record, the harder time you'll have remembering the number and order of fields. It is better in this case to be explicit and use the original record syntax to construct the initialModel. You'll have an easier time understanding and maintaining your code.

I'm not saying don't use constructor functions—but use them sparingly. If you only have one to three fields, then you're probably fine using a constructor function. If you have more fields than that, then you should pause before reaching for a constructor function. Ultimately, use your best judgement and choose whatever makes it easiest for you and the rest of your team to understand your code.

With my thought-leading out of the way, let's stick with the explicit record syntax in the Picshare application. Hint: you're going to add more fields soon.

## Simplify Liking a Photo

Another subtle code aroma you could fix is the way you like and unlike photos. Recall from the viewDetailedPhoto function that you determine which Msg constructor to use when clicking on the love button by checking the value of model.liked in an if-else expression. You can simplify the code to remove the need for the if-else expression.

You'll need a way for the viewDetailedPhoto function to still send a message to the update function. The update function will decide to like or unlike the photo based on the message and current model state.

Before you refactor the update function, let's update the Msg type. Since the viewDetailedPhoto function only needs to send one message, you can reduce the Msg values to one. Liking and unliking a photo is essentially toggling the value of the liked field between True and False. Update your Msg type to have one constructor called ToggleLike:

refactor-enhance/Picshare02.elm

```
type Msg
    = ToggleLike
```

Next, you'll need to update the viewDetailedPhoto function to use only the ToggleLike constructor. Before you do that, let's take this opportunity to tidy up the implementation of viewDetailedPhoto a little. You can extract the code for displaying the love button into its own function. That allows you to keep the love-button-related code together and make the viewDetailedPhoto code cleaner. Pull out the code for the love button into a separate function called viewLoveButton and update it to use the ToggleLike constructor with the onClick event function:

```
viewLoveButton : Model -> Html Msg
viewLoveButton model =
    let
        buttonClass =
            if model.liked then
                "fa-heart"

            else
                "fa-heart-o"
    in
    div [ class "like-button" ]
        [ i
            [ class "fa fa-2x"
            , class buttonClass
            , onClick ToggleLike
            ]
            []
        ]
```

Notice you no longer have the if-else expression for picking a constructor because you just pass ToggleLike directly to onClick. You need to update viewDetailedPhoto to use the new viewLoveButton function. The new function takes the model as an argument, so you need to be sure to pass in the model as well:

```
viewDetailedPhoto : Model -> Html Msg
viewDetailedPhoto model =
    div [ class "detailed-photo" ]
        [ img [ src model.url ] []
        , div [ class "photo-info" ]
            [ viewLoveButton model
            , h2 [ class "caption" ] [ text model.caption ]
            ]
        ]
```

Finally, you'll need to fix the update function to handle the lone ToggleLike constructor. The update function needs to update the liked field based on its current value. You could reuse the if-else logic from the previous version of viewDetailedPhoto to choose between True and False values. But remember that you just need to toggle a boolean value. You can use the built-in not function instead. Change the update function to look like this.

```
update : Msg -> Model -> Model
update msg model =
    case msg of
        ToggleLike ->
            { model | liked = not model.liked }
```

The not function is the counterpart to the ! operator in JavaScript. It negates Boolean values, so it flips True to False and False to True.

Make sure your Picshare.elm file matches what's in code/refactor-enhance/Picshare02.elm. Recompile and your application should still function the same but with cleaner code.

This is actually really awesome! The fact that your Elm application compiles is a good indication that your refactoring didn't break anything. The Elm compiler has your back when you need to refactor. Imagine refactoring important pieces of your codebase in a JavaScript application where there isn't a compiler to ensure the pieces still fit together. I'll admit that the Elm compiler doesn't prevent *all* bugs. Testing code is important too. You'll learn how to test Elm code later in Chapter 9, Test Elm Applications, on page 175.

You've drastically simplified your application. You learned how to create type aliases and how to find opportunities for refactoring. Granted, you could have written the original code to use the Model type alias, the ToggleLike constructor, and the viewLoveButton function, but I wanted you to see that you don't always land on the right abstraction immediately. And that's OK. You will find this type of refactoring process to be common in Elm development and, really, in development in general. As you're learning Elm, first strive to make it work and then make it right.

# Comment on Photos

In this section, you will take your knowledge of the Elm Architecture further and add another feature to the Picshare application. Any good photo sharing application not only allows you to like photos but also to leave comments on photos. In this section, you will work with input events and lists in order to add comments to photos. Let's get started.

## Update the Model

You'll first need to update your model to store multiple comments. A list will be a natural fit. You'll also need to add new comments to the list. As a teaser of what's to come, know that you're going to add an input element allowing a user to type in a new comment and save it. Because you're using the Elm Architecture to handle state, you'll need a way to temporarily store any comment a user is currently typing. You should also store the temporary comment in the model. Update the model alias to look like this:

```
refactor-enhance/Picshare03.elm
type alias Model =
    { url : String
    , caption : String
    , liked : Bool
    , comments : List String
    , newComment : String
    }
```

You now have a comments field, which is a list of strings, and a newComment field, which is a string. You'll need to add initial values to initialModel for these fields next. In the spirit of surfing and being corny, let's start with one comment, "Cowabunga, dude!" You should set the initial comments field to a list containing that string. For the newComment field, you can use the empty string. Make sure your initialModel looks like this:

```
initialModel : Model
initialModel =
    { url = baseUrl ++ "1.jpg"
    , caption = "Surfing"
    , liked = False
    , comments = [ "Cowabunga, dude!" ]
    , newComment = ""
    }
```

## Display a List of Comments

Now that you are storing comments in the model, the next step is displaying them in all their glory. Instead of jam-packing the view function with tons of new code, let's take a stab at writing a few helper functions up front. Before you start, expose the placeholder and type_ functions from the Html.Attributes module:

```
import Html.Attributes exposing (class, placeholder, src, type_)
```

When it comes to displaying lists, I like to take a bottom-to-top approach and figure out how to render each individual item before worrying about the whole list. So let's write a viewComment function for displaying an individual comment first. Add this code after your viewLoveButton function:

```
viewComment : String -> Html Msg
viewComment comment =
    li []
        [ strong [] [ text "Comment:" ]
        , text (" " ++ comment)
        ]
```

The function takes one String argument named comment, which you wrap with an li element. Inside the li element, you display a "Comment:" label via strong element and display the comment value via text node. Notice that you have to put an explicit space between the label and comment by concatenating the space with the comment value.

That takes care of an individual comment, but you need to display a list. Let's write a viewCommentList function next. The viewCommentList function should apply the viewComment function to every comment and wrap the list of rendered comments inside a ul element. Add the viewCommentList function below the viewComment function:

```
viewCommentList : List String -> Html Msg
viewCommentList comments =
    case comments of
        [] ->
            text ""

        _ ->
            div [ class "comments" ]
                [ ul []
                    (List.map viewComment comments)
                ]
```

The viewCommentList takes a list of strings as an argument and then uses a case expression on it. It turns out that pattern matching not only works on custom types but also other types like strings, integers, and even lists.

You use pattern matching on the list of comments to handle the empty list separately. Notice that when you match the empty list with [], you return an empty text node. You could technically get away with not handling the empty list separately, but I think it helps keep the final HTML and CSS cleaner by simply omitting the comment list when you have no comments. Another benefit of handling the empty list separately is that you could provide something similar to a "No Comments" message.

If you're wondering why you don't just check the length of the list in an if-else expression like JavaScript, it's because pattern matching is more versatile and faster. Elm lists are different from JavaScript arrays in that they don't have a length property. To get the length of a list, you have to use the List.length function which will traverse the list one item at a time. That could take a few hundred milliseconds on a large list and lead to a slow, unresponsive app for your users. *Always prefer pattern matching.*

Back to the function...if you don't match the empty list, you use the underscore wildcard to match lists with one or more comments. In this branch, you wrap the ul element with a div for styling purposes.

The most interesting part is how you render the actual list of comments. Notice that the second argument to ul is the result of calling List.map with the viewComment function and comments list. The List.map function creates a new list from an existing list by transforming every item in the list with a provided function.

For example, you can double every number in a list by using List.map as in this example.

```
> double n = n * 2
<function> : number -> number

> List.map double [1, 2, 3]
[2,4,6] : List number
```

Remember that the second argument to an Html node function is usually a list of other Html nodes. You can transform the list of comments into a list of Html nodes by applying the viewComment function to each comment with List.map.

## Display a Comment Input

The preceding code can display the comments list, but you also need to enable adding new comments. Let's create a function called viewComments to do that. Add the following definition below viewCommentList:

```
viewComments : Model -> Html Msg
viewComments model =
    div []
        [ viewCommentList model.comments
        , form [ class "new-comment" ]
```

```
            [ input
                [ type_ "text"
                , placeholder "Add a comment..."
                ]
                []
            , button [] [ text "Save" ]
            ]
        ]
```

The viewComments function takes the model as an argument and uses the view-
CommentList function to display the list of comments. More importantly, it uses
the form, input, and button element functions to allow adding a new comment.

Notice you use the type_ attribute function to create a text input and the
placeholder attribute function to provide a prompt to a user. If you're wondering
about the type_ attribute with a trailing underscore, it's to avoid a conflict with
the type keyword.

So far this function just displays the input. Users can't actually add comments
yet. You'll revisit that in a moment by adding some new Msg values. For now,
we're focused on making sure we can compile and display everything properly.

To finish up, you should use the new viewComments function inside the viewDetailedPhoto function to display the comments and input. Add it as the last child
to div [ class "photo-info" ]:

```
viewDetailedPhoto model =
    div [ class "detailed-photo" ]
        [ img [ src model.url ] []
        , div [ class "photo-info" ]
            [ viewLoveButton model
            , h2 [ class "caption" ] [ text model.caption ]
            , viewComments model
            ]
        ]
```

Make sure your code matches code/refactor-enhance/Picshare03.elm. Compile your
application, and you should see the screenshot on page 56 in your browser.

## Type New Comments

Now that the application can display comments, you can shift gears to actually adding comments. To start, let's expose a few more functions from the
imported modules. Expose the disabled and value functions from Html.Attributes
and the onInput and onSubmit functions from Html.Events.

Picshare

♡

*Surfing*

Comment: Cowabunga, dude!

Add a comment...                                    Save

refactor-enhance/Picshare04.elm
```
import Html.Attributes
    exposing
        ( class, disabled, placeholder, src, type_, value )
import Html.Events exposing (onClick, onInput, onSubmit)
```

You'll need to use these newly exposed functions inside the viewComments function you added in the last section. Before you do that, you'll need a couple of new Msg constructors. Modify your Msg type to look like this:

```
type Msg
    = ToggleLike
➤   | UpdateComment String
➤   | SaveComment
```

You now have two new message values, UpdateComment and SaveComment. You will use the UpdateComment value for storing typed comments into the model's newComment field and the SaveComment value for moving the stored newComment to the comments list. They look like straightforward additions except for the String type after UpdateComment. The String type here denotes a String parameter to the UpdateComment constructor.

Up to this point, you've treated constructors as static values, and this is technically correct when they have no parameters. However, constructors are really just functions that can take zero or more arguments. In this case, UpdateComment is a function that takes a single String argument to create an instance of a Msg type. You need the String argument to hold the value of the comment typed in the input field. You can think of the String value as the *payload* of this message.

You can now use the newly exposed functions and new message values to update the viewComments function. Modify your implementation to look like the following code:

```
viewComments model =
    div []
        [ viewCommentList model.comments
        , form [ class "new-comment", onSubmit SaveComment ]
            [ input
                [ type_ "text"
                , placeholder "Add a comment..."
                , value model.newComment
                , onInput UpdateComment
                ]
                []
            , button
                [ disabled (String.isEmpty model.newComment) ]
                [ text "Save" ]
            ]
        ]
```

❶ Add an onSubmit event handler with the SaveComment message to the form. This will allow users to click on the Save button or hit the Return key to save a comment.

❷ Let the value of the input field reflect what's currently in the model's newComment field. You'll need this when you clear the input later in the update function.

❸ Add an onInput event handler with the UpdateComment message to the input.

❹ Disable the button if the newComment field is currently empty. This prevents users from submitting empty comments.

Let's look more closely at the String argument of UpdateComment. Most of the event handlers such as onClick and onSubmit in the Html.Events module have the following type signature.

```
msg -> Attribute msg
```

These handlers take a type variable called msg and return Attribute msg. When you use onClick and onSubmit in the application, the msg type variable becomes the Msg type thanks to the static ToggleLike and SaveComment constructors, respectively. The type signature for onInput is different, though.

```
(String -> msg) -> Attribute msg
```

Instead of taking a static msg as an argument, it takes a function. The function itself takes a String argument and returns a msg type variable. That sounds a lot like the UpdateComment constructor.

Basically, Elm will use the onInput handler to wire up a DOM event handler in JavaScript that will capture the value of event.target.value and use *that* as the String argument to the UpdateComment constructor. This will happen every time the value changes in the input field, i.e., when you add or delete a character by typing.

When Elm invokes the UpdateComment constructor function, it creates a message value that it can send to the update function. You'll see what that message value looks like and how to extract the typed comment in the next section.

## Add Comments

Finishing up, you'll need to modify the update function to handle the fancy new message values. Add branches for UpdateComment and SaveComment to the case expression like so:

```
update msg model =
    case msg of
        ToggleLike ->
            { model | liked = not model.liked }

        UpdateComment comment ->
            { model | newComment = comment }

        SaveComment ->
            saveNewComment model
```

Notice what you're doing with the UpdateComment value. This is where pattern matching really starts to shine. When a custom type constructor receives its arguments, it constructs an instance of the custom type and also holds on to its arguments. Pattern matching allows you to match the constructor and bind the wrapped arguments to identifiers later. In the update function, you match UpdateComment and bind the String value to a constant called comment. The comment constant is then available in the expression to the right. You use the bound comment constant to update the newComment field. The state then reflects whatever you typed in the input field.

Moving on, when you match SaveComment, you call a separate function called saveNewComment and pass in the model. Using a separate function here keeps the update function tidy (and ensures the code doesn't extend past this book's margins). Add the saveNewComment function above the update function:

```
saveNewComment : Model -> Model
saveNewComment model =
    let
        comment =
            String.trim model.newComment
    in
    case comment of
        "" ->
            model

        _ ->
            { model
                | comments = model.comments ++ [ comment ]
                , newComment = ""
            }
```

In saveNewComment, you first use a let expression to remove trailing spaces from model.newComment via the String.trim function and bind the trimmed string to a constant called comment.

Then you use pattern matching with a case expression on the comment constant. Notice a *pattern* here? Sorry, I couldn't resist at least one pun.

When you pattern match on strings, you can match any string value. You start off by matching the empty string. Even though you disable the Save button when newComment is empty, you can still technically submit with the Enter key. You'll catch that here and ignore it by just returning the current model. This ensures you don't accidentally add an empty comment to the comment list.

If you don't have the empty string, then you use the wildcard to match *any other* string. Next, you update the model comments by using the concatenation operator to combine the old list with another list that contains the new trimmed comment. Lists are immutable like records, so concatenation creates a new list. You also reset the newComment field to the empty string, so users can type in another comment if they wish.

Make sure your code matches code/refactor-enhance/Picshare04.elm. Recompile and you should now be able to add comments to your application. Try typing "Totally tubular!" and clicking the Save button or hitting Enter. The new comment should appear below the initial comment as shown in the screenshot on page 60.

And that's it. You now have a simple application for liking and commenting on a photo. To recap how commenting works with the Elm Architecture: every time you type in the input field, the onInput handler will extract the value from the input field and supply it to the UpdateComment constructor. Then, Elm will

Picshare

♡

*Surfing*

Comment: Cowabunga, dude!
Comment: Totally tubular!

send the UpdateComment message to the update function. The update function will extract the comment value from UpdateComment and update the newComment field in the model. Finally, when you click the Save button or hit the Enter key, Elm will use the form's onSubmit handler to send a SaveComment message to the update function. The update function will retrieve the comment value from the model's newComment field and append it to the comments list.

## What You Learned

You have gained some important skills in this chapter. You saw how to approach refactoring an application and learned how the Elm compiler will prevent refactors from creating a broken application with runtime errors. During the refactoring process, you also learned about the useful type alias for simplifying working with record types.

Next, you saw how to enhance your application by introducing the ability to comment on photos. You learned how to take a step-by-step approach to add new features to Elm applications. Let's take that enhancement mindset further. Modern front-end applications typically need to interact with servers. In the next chapter, you will improve the Picshare application by fetching a list of photos from an API.

# CHAPTER 4

# Communicate with Servers

In the previous chapter, you learned how to build stateful Elm applications by applying the Elm Architecture to the Picshare application. You covered a range of concepts such as records, type aliases, custom types, models, view functions, messages, and update functions.

Your application's functionality is limited, though. You can only interact with one photo that is hardcoded into the initial state. Real-world front-end applications don't know the state of the world on their own. They must retrieve data from databases and other remote sources through HTTP REST APIs.

In this chapter, you will improve your Picshare application by retrieving the photo feed from an HTTP API. Along the way you will learn about JSON decoders, commands, and two special Elm types called Result and Maybe. By the end of this chapter, you will be able to create front-end applications that use real data from remote sources. Let's dig in.

## Safely Decode JSON

Prior to this point, you've been able to stay safely within the confines of Elm's magical world of static types. However, you're going to run into an interesting dilemma if you want to accept an arbitrary JSON payload from a server. Elm doesn't have a JSON.parse function like JavaScript because it can't dynamically create records like JavaScript can create objects. In this section, you're going to learn about *JSON decoders*, why they're important, and how to use them to safely convert JSON into a static type Elm can use.

### Understand the Problem

To understand why you need JSON decoders, let's look at a couple of example JSON payloads you could use with your application. Visit https://programming-elm.com/feed/1 in your browser. You should see this JSON payload.

```
{
  "id": 1,
  "url": "https://programming-elm.surge.sh/1.jpg",
  "caption": "Surfing",
  "liked": false,
  "comments": ["Cowabunga, dude!"],
  "username": "surfing_usa"
}
```

This JSON closely mimics the photo record type you created in the previous chapter. The only differences are that the JSON payload has an id property and a username property and lacks a newComment property. You could easily fix your static type to include id and username fields. The newComment property also isn't a problem because you only use it locally to temporarily store a typed comment.

Even with those changes, you still can't trust an arbitrary API payload. Elm is pure and safe, and some of its guarantees come from guarding your application from the outside world. If the JSON payload doesn't match what's expected in the record type, you will have a serious problem. For example, let's assume the API returned this JSON payload.

```
{
  "id": 1,
  "src": "https://programming-elm.surge.sh/1.jpg",
  "caption": null,
  "liked": "no"
}
```

This hardly matches your record type. The caption property is null instead of a string, the liked property is a string with the value "no" instead of the boolean false, and the comments property is missing.

Elm is caught in a catch-22. Elm requires the payload to have a specific *shape* but must protect your application from inconsistent, bad data. By shape, I mean a payload that contains specific properties with specific types.

Elm solves this dilemma with JSON decoders. When you create a JSON decoder, you describe the expected shape of the JSON payload and what static type to create from the payload. Elm uses your decoder to attempt to decode the JSON payload into your static type. You will work through creating a JSON decoder for your application over the next few sections.

## Initial Setup

Before you create a decoder, let's get a few prerequisite steps out of the way. Later in this chapter, you're going to change the Model type in your Picshare application from a photo to a record that contains the photo. This means you need to create a new type alias to represent a photo. You also need to add the id field to your record type because your application will fetch multiple photos (in the next chapter). You'll handle the username field in Chapter 10, Build Single-Page Applications, on page 205.

Open up your Picshare.elm file. Rename the Model type alias to Photo and then create a new Model type alias to the Photo type. The type alias rabbit hole can go as deep as you want, but be wary, there be dragons down that hole.

While you're at it, create a type called Id that aliases to Int. This will help make your later type annotations more readable when you want to treat an Int argument as an Id. Right underneath your imported modules, you should now have this code:

```
communicate/Picshare01.elm
type alias Id =
    Int

type alias Photo =
    { id : Id
    , url : String
    , caption : String
    , liked : Bool
    , comments : List String
    , newComment : String
    }

type alias Model =
    Photo
```

Because you added an id field to the Photo type, you'll need to add an initial id to your initialModel to ensure your application can still compile. Add an id of 1 at the start of the initialModel definition:

```
initialModel =
    { id = 1
    -- other fields you already defined
    }
```

The first step is out of the way. The next prerequisite step is to grab a couple of packages.

Elm has its own package manager that you can use to install additional dependencies.

Elm should have previously installed Elm's main JSON package elm/json as an indirect dependency when you ran elm init in the first chapter. An indirect dependency is a dependency of some other dependency in your application. You need to install elm/json as a direct dependency to let your application code use it. Make sure you're in your picshare directory and run this command:

```
elm install elm/json
```

The command should prompt you to move the dependency from indirect to direct dependencies. Accept the prompt.

```
I found it in your elm.json file, but in the "indirect" dependencies.
Should I move it into "direct" dependencies for more general use? [Y/n]:
```

Next, install a really helpful package called NoRedInk/elm-json-decode-pipeline, which has a lot of cool helper functions for building complex JSON object decoders:

```
elm install NoRedInk/elm-json-decode-pipeline
```

The command should prompt you to add the dependency to elm.json. Accept.

Great...you just learned how to install packages. You can browse all available Elm packages at https://package.elm-lang.org. You're also ready to build a photo decoder. But before you jump in, let's get your feet wet in the REPL with some simpler decoders.

## Play with Decoders

Writing a full-fledged decoder for the Photo type will be relatively easy and require little code. Understanding the code will be the challenging part. Let's get familiar with decoders by playing with some primitive decoders before you attempt to decode a photo object. Open up the Elm REPL and import the Json.Decode module.

```
> import Json.Decode exposing (decodeString, bool, int, string)
```

The Json.Decode module comes from the elm/json package and contains a few primitive type decoders as well as helper functions for building complex decoders. The primitive decoders you use here are bool, int, and string. As you might imagine, the bool decoder represents Bool types, the int decoder represents Int types, and the string decoder represents String types. Elm has one more primitive decoder called float.

Each of these primitive decoders has the type Decoder a. The type variable a refers to the static type that the decoder decodes to. For example, string has the type Decoder String, so it would decode to an Elm String.

The decodeString function uses a decoder to decode a raw JSON string into a static type. Let's create an int decoder and try it out with the number 42. Run this in the REPL:

```
> decodeString int "42"
Ok 42 : Result Json.Decode.Error Int
```

The first argument is the int decoder. The next argument is the JSON string "42". The return value is interesting, however. You didn't get back 42. Instead, you received Ok 42 with the type Result Json.Decode.Error Int. Before you investigate that further, run this snippet in the REPL:

```
> decodeString int "\"Elm\""
Err (Failure ("Expecting an INT") <internals>) : Result Json.Decode.Error Int
```

This time you received a value called Err with the same type as before, Result Json.Decode.Error Int. The Err value contains a Failure value with a string message "Expecting an INT". (The <internals> bit refers to the raw JavaScript that Elm parsed. Elm uses JavaScript's JSON.parse underneath the hood to initially parse to JavaScript before decoding to a type in Elm.)

The Result type is how Elm safeguards applications from bad JSON payloads. When you called decodeString, you declared that the payload was an integer, but you passed in the JSON string "\"Elm\"" instead of a number. The decode operation failed and gave back an error from the Result type.

The Result type is a built-in custom type with two constructors called Ok and Err. This is how it's defined in Elm.

```
type Result error value
    = Ok value
    | Err error
```

In the last chapter, you saw how custom type constructors could take arguments when you defined the UpdateComment String constructor. The argument type doesn't have to be set in stone, so you can use a type variable. If you use a type variable, then Elm's type system requires you to declare the type variable on the type itself too. The Result type has two type variables called error and value.

In Elm, you use the Result type to handle an operation that could succeed or fail. If the operation succeeds, you can use the Ok constructor to wrap the successful value. Conversely, if the operation fails, you can use the Err constructor to wrap an error.

The decodeString function returns the Result type to signal that the decoding process could fail, specifically if the JSON payload type doesn't match the decoder type. If the decoding process succeeds, then you get Ok with the actual decoded value. If the decoding process fails, then you get Err with a value explaining the error. You saw both of those scenarios just a moment ago when you tried decodeString with the JSON strings "42" and "\"Elm\"".

The Result type satisfies the type system so you can safely decode without any runtime errors. The Result type's two type variables indicate the static types it can contain. In the REPL example, the returned type was Result Json.Decode.Error Int. The Json.Decode.Error and Int types indicated that the result could contain a decoder error or a successful integer value.

The Json.Decode.Error type is another custom type defined in the Json.Decode module. You will work more with Json.Decode.Error in Chapter 7, Develop, Debug, and Deploy with Powerful Tooling, on page 131. You can also learn more about it from the docs.[1]

I know what you're probably thinking. It's all well and good that my application won't blow up, but I still need to access the successful value. That's what pattern matching is for. In fact, you'll see how to use pattern matching on the Result type later in this chapter when you actually fetch a photo from an API. For now, play with a few more primitive decoders in the REPL before you move on to decoding objects.

```
> import Json.Decode exposing (decodeString, bool, field, int, list, string)

> decodeString bool "true"
Ok True : Result Json.Decode.Error Bool

> decodeString string "\"Elm is Awesome\""
Ok ("Elm is Awesome") : Result Json.Decode.Error String

> decodeString (list int) "[1, 2, 3]"
Ok [1,2,3] : Result Json.Decode.Error (List Int)

> decodeString (field "name" string) """{"name": "Tucker"}"""
Ok "Tucker" : Result Json.Decode.Error String
```

The bool and string decoders are similar to the int decoder you used earlier. You also imported two helper decoders called field and list that build decoders from other decoders.

The list decoder lets you decode a JSON array. It accepts a decoder argument to decode each item in the array. This means every item in the array needs to be the same type, or decoding will fail.

---

1. https://package.elm-lang.org/packages/elm/json/latest/Json-Decode#Error

The field decoder lets you decode the value of a property in a JSON object. It takes two arguments, the property name and a decoder for the property. This decoder will fail if the JSON string doesn't contain an object, if the property is missing, or if the property type doesn't match the decoder property type. You generate the JSON string with triple quote """ syntax. This syntax allows you to create special strings that don't require escaping quotes inside the string. It also lets you create multiline strings like so.

```
myElmPoem =
    """
    Roses are red
    Violets are blue
    Elm is awesome
    And so are you
    """
```

Elm has more decoder helpers that you can explore in the docs.[2] For example, the at helper is great for extracting deeply nested object values, and the oneOf helper is great for trying multiple decoders until one succeeds. Try out a few other decoders on your own in the REPL.

## Pipe through Functions

Before we go further with decoders, we need to briefly detour to look at Elm's most useful operator, the *pipe operator*. You will need the pipe operator to create object decoders with elm-json-decode-pipeline.

One benefit of functional programming is that you can combine small, specialized functions to create more complex functions. Functional programmers call this *function composition*.

Let's say you need to write a function called excitedGreeting that accepts a String name and returns a greeting with the name in uppercase and ends with an exclamation point. You can create this function with smaller functions. Inside the REPL, add the greet and exclaim functions like the following:

```
> greet name = "Hello, " ++ name
<function> : String -> String

> exclaim phrase = phrase ++ "!"
<function> : String -> String
```

The greet function takes a String name and prepends the String "Hello, " to it. The exclaim function takes a String phrase and appends an exclamation point to it.

---

2. https://package.elm-lang.org/packages/elm/json/latest/Json-Decode

Now, along with the built-in String.toUpper function, create the excitedGreeting function like so:

```
> excitedGreeting name =
|   exclaim (greet (String.toUpper name))
<function> : String -> String
```

You compose the three functions together by passing in the result of one function as the argument to the next function. First, you call String.toUpper with name. This returns name in uppercase, which you then pass into greet. Finally, you pass the result of greet into exclaim. Try out excitedGreeting like so:

```
> excitedGreeting "Elm"
"Hello, ELM!" : String
```

Composition lets you build more complex functions but the syntax is awkward right now. Notice that you wrapped function calls in parentheses to enforce the order of operations. If you had left out parentheses, Elm would have thought you wanted to call exclaim with three arguments, greet, String.toUpper, and name.

The pipe operator fixes this problem by giving you more readable composition. Rewrite excitedGreeting in the REPL, like this:

```
> excitedGreeting name =
|   name |> String.toUpper |> greet |> exclaim
<function> : String -> String
```

The pipe operator |> takes the left operand and passes it in as the last argument to the function operand on the right. In this case, you take name on the left and pass it into String.toUpper on the right. Then, you pass the result of String.toUpper into greet on the right. You repeat this process, passing the next result into exclaim.

This style of composition simulates chaining or piping function calls together. You can think of the pipe operator as a chain link between each function. The pipe operator also points to the right, so you can clearly see the direction of applied functions to the previous result. You can even improve readability by placing each function call on a newline:

```
> excitedGreeting name =
|   name
|     |> String.toUpper
|     |> greet
|     |> exclaim
<function> : String -> String
```

Now you can scan from top to bottom to see each step you take to transform the name argument into the final result. Call excitedGreeting again with "Elm", and you should see the same return value as before.

## Decode an Object

Great. You're now familiar with the concept of decoders, know how to build some simple decoders, and know how to use the pipe operator. You're ready to go a step further and decode an entire JSON object. The elm-json-decode-pipeline package will come in handy here.

Let's revisit the dog record from the previous chapter to build a JSON dog decoder. Once you get a handle on that, you'll be ready to build a decoder for the Photo type in the Picshare application. Make sure your REPL is open and expose these members of the Json.Decode and Json.Decode.Pipeline modules:

```
> import Json.Decode exposing (decodeString, int, string, succeed)
> import Json.Decode.Pipeline exposing (required)
```

You've already seen the Json.Decode module. The Json.Decode.Pipeline module comes from elm-json-decode-pipeline. You expose a helper called required. Next, you need a helper function for creating a dog. Run this in the REPL:

```
> dog name age = { name = name, age = age }
<function> : a -> b -> { age : b, name : a }
```

You will need this function to build a dog decoder. Create the dog decoder by running this code in the REPL:

```
> dogDecoder =
|    succeed dog
|        |> required "name" string
|        |> required "age" int
<internals> : Json.Decode.Decoder { age : Int, name : String }
```

Here's where the fun begins, so let's dissect the dogDecoder piece by piece. On the first line, you call the succeed function from Json.Decode on the dog function. The succeed function creates a decoder literal. For example, if you call succeed on the string "Elm", then you get back a Decoder String. For the dog function, you get back a Decoder (a -> b -> { age : b, name : a }). Essentially, you get back a decoder of whatever you pass in, even if it's a function like dog.

On the next line, you use the pipe operator to feed the decoder into the required function. The required function comes from elm-json-decode-pipeline and resembles the field function you used earlier. It *requires* a property to exist in the JSON object just like field. It's different from field in that it not only extracts the property but also *applies* the value to the function inside the current decoder. Look at the type signature of required to see what I mean.

```
required : String -> Decoder a -> Decoder (a -> b) -> Decoder b
```

The first argument is a String, which is the name of the property. You used "name" for the property name in the dog example. The second argument is a Decoder a that expects the property to have a type of a. Recall that lowercase types such as a are type variables, so this can be a Decoder of anything. You used the string decoder in the dogDecoder example, so the concrete type you pass in will be Decoder String. The third argument is another decoder that contains a function. This inner function must translate the type a to the type b. This translation process allows required to return a Decoder b.

In this example, the third argument is the decoder that contains the dog function. If you had only run the first two lines from the example, your decoder would now have this type.

```
Decoder (a -> { age : a, name : String })
```

Compare that type to what you had previously from executing only the first line of the example.

```
Decoder (a -> b -> { age : b, name : a })
```

Notice that you filled in the first type variable to be a String. That is, you went from a function with two arguments to a function with one argument.

Moving to the third line in the example, you call the required function with the string "age", the int decoder, and the current dog decoder. The dog decoder can now extract the age property and apply it as the second argument to the original dog function, which gives you the following final decoder.

```
Decoder { age : Int, name : String }
```

The elm-json-decode-pipeline package makes decoders easy to read and write. The trick to understanding them is to remember that each pipe operation is applying an extracted value to a function inside a decoder. Once you satisfy all the arguments, you get back a decoder of the record you want to create. Let's try your newly minted dogDecoder on an actual JSON object. Run this code in the REPL:

```
> decodeString dogDecoder """{"name": "Tucker", "age": 11}"""
Ok { age = 11, name = "Tucker" }
    : Result Json.Decode.Error { age : Int, name : String }
```

Good job! You just grasped one of the trickiest concepts in Elm. Decoders are versatile and powerful. You can build some highly complex decoders in Elm.

## Create a Photo Decoder

Now that you're familiar with elm-json-decode-pipeline, let's use it to create a photo decoder. Switch back to editing Picshare.elm. First, import Json.Decode and Json.Decode.Pipeline underneath the other imported modules:

communicate/Picshare01.elm
```
import Json.Decode exposing (Decoder, bool, int, list, string, succeed)
import Json.Decode.Pipeline exposing (hardcoded, required)
```

These module imports look similar to what you had in the REPL. You import one additional function from Json.Decode.Pipeline called hardcoded. Next, add the decoder below the Model type alias:

```
photoDecoder : Decoder Photo
photoDecoder =
    succeed Photo
        |> required "id" int
        |> required "url" string
        |> required "caption" string
        |> required "liked" bool
        |> required "comments" (list string)
        |> hardcoded ""
```

This decoder resembles the dogDecoder you wrote in the REPL earlier with a couple of differences. First, you call succeed on Photo, which may seem confusing at first. You're not calling succeed on the Photo type but the Photo *constructor function*. Recall from Chapter 3, Refactor and Enhance Elm Applications, on page 47 that a type alias to a record also creates a constructor function for the record.

As you saw in the previous section, you can call succeed on a function and then pipe the decoder through elm-json-decode-pipeline helper functions to extract properties and apply them to the underlying function. Here you're doing exactly that, only you're capitalizing on the convenient constructor function that Elm creates for record type aliases.

You pipe the constructor function through several calls to required with different decoders. For the "id" property you use the int decoder. For the "url" and "caption" properties you use the string decoder. For the "liked" property you use the bool decoder. Finally, for the "comments" property you use list string. Remember that the list decoder takes another decoder as an argument to decode each item in the JSON array to that inner decoder's type.

At the end, you use the hardcoded function. The Photo record has six fields, which means the Photo constructor function takes six arguments. One of those fields is newComment, which the JSON payload on page 62 lacks. You can use the hardcoded function to tell the decoder to use a static value as an argument to the underlying decoder function instead of extracting a property from the JSON object. In this case, you use hardcoded to provide the empty string as the final newComment argument to the Photo constructor function.

Let's try out photoDecoder in the REPL to confirm it works. Temporarily expose photoDecoder from Picshare.elm:

```
module Picshare exposing (main, photoDecoder)
```

Make sure you're in the same directory as the Picshare.elm file and run this code in a new REPL session:

```
> import Picshare exposing (photoDecoder)
> import Json.Decode exposing (decodeString)

> decodeString photoDecoder """
|    { "id": 1
|    , "url": "https://programming-elm.surge.sh/1.jpg"
|    , "caption": "Surfing"
|    , "liked": false
|    , "comments": ["Cowabunga, dude!"]
|    } \
|    """
Ok { caption = "Surfing"
   , comments = ["Cowabunga, dude!"]
   , id = 1
   , liked = False
   , newComment = ""
   , url = "https://programming-elm.surge.sh/1.jpg"
   }
    : Result.Result Json.Decode.Error Picshare.Photo
```

You import photoDecoder from the Picshare module and import decodeString from the Json.Decode module. Then you apply the photoDecoder to a JSON object to get back an instance of the Photo record. Revert the Picshare module to only expose main.

Let's recap what you accomplished. You created a photo decoder by calling the succeed function from Json.Decode with the Photo constructor function and then piping the decoder through the required and hardcoded helper functions from Json.Decode.Pipeline. Each helper function applies the next argument to the Photo constructor function. The required function extracts a property from the JSON object and uses that as the argument to Photo. The hardcoded function uses whatever argument it receives as the argument to Photo. The successive application of each argument eventually builds up an entire Photo record.

One important note to add is that the order of the piping operations matters. The order needs to match the order of the arguments to the constructor function. For example, if you switched the order of the id and url field decoders, you would get a compiler error. That's because the decoder would think it needs to call the constructor function with a String first instead of an Int.

OK. You've learned a lot about decoders and why they're important. You've also successfully created a photo decoder. You're now ready to put it to use by fetching an initial photo from an API. Make sure your code matches code/communicate/Picshare01.elm at this point, and then let's get to work using HTTP in the application.

# Fetch from HTTP APIs

In this section, you will use the Http module to fetch an initial photo from an API endpoint. You will see how Elm treats HTTP requests differently from most JavaScript applications and learn why that's important. You will learn how to use commands to issue HTTP requests and how to represent missing information with another special type called Maybe. You will also discover how to use pattern matching on the Result type to extract a successful value or an error for error handling.

## Create a Command

The Http module does not ship with Elm's core library, thus the first order of business is to install it. Inside your picshare directory, run this command and accept the prompt:

```
elm install elm/http
```

Next, import the Http module with the rest of the imported modules. To avoid ambiguous function name usage, avoid exposing any members from Http. Your import should look like this.

communicate/Picshare02.elm
```
import Http
```

The Http package has many functions to create out-of-the-box HTTP requests and customized HTTP requests with custom headers, timeouts, etc. You can learn more about the Http package by visiting the docs.[3] We're going to keep it simple here and create a basic GET request for JSON data with the Http.get function. Add a constant called fetchFeed underneath the initialModel definition.

---

3. https://package.elm-lang.org/packages/elm/http/latest

```
fetchFeed : Cmd Msg
fetchFeed =
    Http.get
        { url = baseUrl ++ "feed/1"
        , expect = Http.expectJson LoadFeed photoDecoder
        }
```

You pass in a record with two fields, url and expect. You set the string url field to the baseUrl constant concatenated with the string "feed/1" to get the final photo URL. You set the expect field with the result of calling Http.expectJson with LoadFeed and the photoDecoder you created earlier. LoadFeed is a new Msg constructor that you'll add in a bit.

 Similar to the suggestion in Chapter 1, Get Started with Elm, on page 1, you can run the server locally to fetch from the /feed API endpoint. Follow the instructions in Appendix 2, Run the Local Server, on page 267, and change baseUrl to http://localhost:5000/.

You use the expect field to declare how you want to receive the request data. In this case, you expect JSON data via Http.expectJson. Http.expectJson uses the photoDecoder argument to decode the data into a Photo. Then, it wraps the decoded Photo Result with the to-be-written LoadFeed constructor.

Elm accomplishes this through *commands*. Notice that the type of fetchFeed is Cmd Msg. The Cmd type represents a command in Elm. Commands are special values that instruct the Elm Architecture to perform actions such as sending HTTP requests.

Elm HTTP requests differ from JavaScript HTTP requests. In JavaScript, web developers usually write applications that send HTTP requests when they are created. For example, you might see this equivalent JavaScript code for fetching an initial photo.

```
function fetchFeed() {
  return fetch(baseUrl + 'feed/1')
    .then(r => r.json())
    .then(photo => { /* handle photo */ });
}
```

The HTTP request here could succeed or fail any time based on the availability of the API. The JSON payload could also change without warning and break any code that depends on specific properties in the photo. This JavaScript function creates a problematic *side effect*, thus it is *impure*.

Elm functions instead are *pure* and generate no side effects. No matter how many times you call an Elm function, you can *always* expect the same execution and return value based on the provided arguments. Side effects break this expectation because they let functions affect the outside world. Side effects include fetching from an API, mutating some global state, and printing to the console.

Elm separates creating HTTP requests from sending HTTP requests through commands designed to solve this dilemma. That means that you only have to focus on the business logic of creating a request. Imagine that your application sits inside the Elm runtime as in the diagram below. To communicate with the outside world, your application gives commands to the Elm Architecture. Elm will handle the command and eventually deliver the result back to your application.

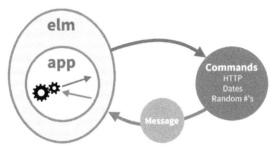

So, the command generated from Http.get contains all the instructions the Elm Architecture needs to send a request to the URL you desire and decode the data into the type your application needs.

Refer back to the Cmd type from fetchFeed. The Cmd type has one type variable called msg that represents the type of messages a command can produce. Commands can hook into your update function to notify you about the result of a command. The command here can produce the message LoadFeed whenever the HTTP request returns a result.

## Send a Command

In order to use the fetchFeed command, you must change how you build your Elm program. So far you've been using the Browser.sandbox function. You need the Browser.element function to be able to hand commands to the Elm Architecture.

Modify main to use Browser.element. Browser.element accepts a different record argument, so modify it to also have a subscriptions field, like this:

```
main =
    Browser.element
        { init = init
        , view = view
        , update = update
        , subscriptions = subscriptions
        }
```

You swap out Browser.sandbox for Browser.element and add the subscriptions field, setting it to a subscriptions value, which you will define in a moment.

The init field remains, but you now set it to an init value. The init value must be a function that returns the initial model and an initial command. Below your initialModel, add this definition for init:

```
init : () -> ( Model, Cmd Msg )
init () =
    ( initialModel, fetchFeed )
```

The init function accepts initialization flags when you embed your application from JavaScript code. You don't pass in any flags in this case, so you will receive the unit type () that you've seen previously. Notice that you use () in the type annotation and function definition. You can perform pattern matching in function arguments when a type has only one value. The unit type only has a () value. When you pattern match (), you don't bind the value to an argument name, so you effectively ignore the argument. You could also ignore the argument by using the _ wildcard instead.

```
init _ =
    ( initialModel, fetchFeed )
```

The init function returns a *tuple*. A tuple is a special data type that resembles lists and records. Tuples can hold multiple elements like a list, but those elements don't have to be the same type. You can think of tuples as records that organize values by position instead of a field label. You can create tuple literals similar to list literals by using parentheses instead of braces to surround the tuple members. The most commonly used type of tuple is the *pair*, which contains two items. In fact, the unit type is basically an empty tuple ().

 Elm limits tuple sizes to two or three items. Anything larger than that becomes hard to maintain, so you should use records if you need more than three items.

The Elm Architecture uses the pair that init returns to bootstrap the initial state and run any initial commands for your application. In this case, you provide initialModel and fetchFeed to fetch a photo when the application starts.

Let's ensure that Elm can fetch the photo by filling in a few more gaps. Currently, you won't be able to compile because you're missing three more changes. You need to define the LoadFeed message for Http.expectJson, fix the implementation of the update function, and define a subscriptions function.

Start by adding LoadFeed to the Msg type:

```
type Msg
    = ToggleLike
    | UpdateComment String
    | SaveComment
    | LoadFeed (Result Http.Error Photo)
```

The LoadFeed constructor takes one argument, a Result type. The inner Result type uses the Http.Error type for the error type variable and Photo for the value type variable. You'll learn how to handle LoadFeed and the inner Result type later in this chapter.

Next, you need to fix the update function. When you use Browser.element, the update function needs to return a tuple just like the init function. This allows your update function to hand off more commands to the Elm Architecture. Modify your update function to look like this:

```
update : Msg -> Model -> ( Model, Cmd Msg )
update msg model =
    case msg of
        ToggleLike ->
            ( { model | liked = not model.liked }
            , Cmd.none
            )

        UpdateComment comment ->
            ( { model | newComment = comment }
            , Cmd.none
            )

        SaveComment ->
            ( saveNewComment model
            , Cmd.none
            )

        LoadFeed _ ->
            ( model, Cmd.none )
```

You now return tuples where the first item is the same model update from before. The Elm Architecture knows to extract the first item in order to update your application state. The second item in every tuple in this case is a call to the function Cmd.none. The Cmd.none function produces—surprise—a command that does nothing. Cmd.none mainly satisfies the type constraint of always returning a tuple pair that contains Model and Cmd Msg. Finally, at the end of the update function, you have a placeholder for handling the new LoadFeed message. You ignore its inner result for now by matching with the wildcard underscore and returning the same model and no command.

The final missing piece is a subscriptions function. You won't deal with subscriptions until later, so you implement a no-op version. You'll still need this no-op implementation to create the correct type of record that Browser.element requires. Add this code below your update function:

```
subscriptions : Model -> Sub Msg
subscriptions model =
    Sub.none
```

In brief, the subscriptions function takes the model as an argument and must return a Sub msg type. You will eventually handle a stream of photos via subscriptions and WebSockets in Chapter 5, Go Real-Time with WebSockets, on page 85, which will make you fill in the msg type variable with the Msg type. So, you use Sub Msg in the type signature instead. Then you use the Sub.none function to return a no-op subscription just like Cmd.none returns a no-op command.

That should be enough to fetch the photo from the API endpoint. Make sure your code matches code/communicate/Picshare02.elm and then compile. Open up your browser and its network dev tools. When you visit your Picshare application, you should see a request to https://programming-elm.com/feed/1. Here is what I get in the Chrome dev tools' network tab.

OK, you are able to fetch the photo from the API, but still need to use it as the initial photo in your application. That will be our focus in the next sections.

## Safely Handle Null

Remember that the goal of fetching a photo is to make the application dynamic and not require a hardcoded initial photo. That poses a new challenge. Elm requires an initial model to bootstrap the application, but you don't have a photo until the HTTP request completes. The application is in a limbo state where it either has a photo or is waiting.

If you were to build this application in JavaScript, you might use null to represent a missing photo and then replace it with the photo once the API responds. Although null could work, I think it creates other issues by requiring you to be diligent about checking for null. If you forget to check somewhere, then it could lead to null reference errors. Also, having to check for null encourages overuse of if statements, which are not composable and add more code complexity. Even the creator of the null reference regrets bringing it into this world.[4]

Thankfully, Elm has your back when dealing with null-like situations. Instead of a null type, Elm has a Maybe type. The Maybe type is another built-in custom type with two constructors called Just and Nothing. Here is the definition of Maybe in Elm's core package.

```
type Maybe a
    = Just a
    | Nothing
```

If you squint just right, the Maybe type resembles the Result type. The Just constructor is the same as the Ok constructor, and the Nothing constructor is the same as the Err constructor minus an inner error value.

The Maybe type perfectly represents a value that may or may not exist. If the value exists, then you have *just* that value. If the value doesn't exist, then you have *nothing*. This solves the initial photo dilemma.

Let's integrate Maybe into the application before you work on actually receiving a photo from the API call. Restructure your model to be a record that maybe contains a photo. Update your Model type alias to look like this:

communicate/Picshare03.elm
```
type alias Model =
    { photo : Maybe Photo
    }
```

You now have a record with a photo field that has the type Maybe Photo. The Maybe type has one type variable, which refers to the type contained in the Just constructor. You need to update initialModel to reflect these changes. Change the initialModel into a record with a photo field. Pass the previously hardcoded photo into the Just constructor and assign it to the photo field:

```
initialModel =
    { photo =
```

---

4.   https://en.wikipedia.org/wiki/Tony_Hoare

```
        Just
            { id = 1
            , url = baseUrl ++ "1.jpg"
            , caption = "Surfing"
            , liked = False
            , comments = [ "Cowabunga, dude!" ]
            , newComment = ""
            }
    }
```

Next, you'll need to fix a few type annotations. The viewLoveButton, viewComments, viewDetailedPhoto, and saveNewComment functions currently take a Model as an argument. Update them to instead take a Photo. It's not required, but I also recommend changing the argument's name from model to photo to avoid ambiguity. If you do that, make sure to fix references to model inside each function too.

```
viewLoveButton : Photo -> Html Msg

viewComments : Photo -> Html Msg

viewDetailedPhoto : Photo -> Html Msg

saveNewComment : Photo -> Photo
```

You also need to fix the main view function. Deeply nested in view, you call viewDetailedPhoto on model. You might be tempted to change it to model.photo, but the types will be different. The viewDetailedPhoto function takes a Photo, but model.photo is a Maybe Photo.

You need a helper function to bridge between the type differences in view and viewDetailedPhoto. Recall that Maybe is a custom type. I bet you can guess what you need to use next: our good old friend pattern matching. Add a new function called viewFeed above view that looks like this:

```
viewFeed : Maybe Photo -> Html Msg
viewFeed maybePhoto =
    case maybePhoto of
        Just photo ->
            viewDetailedPhoto photo

        Nothing ->
            text ""
```

You pattern match over model.photo to access the underlying photo. If you have Just photo, you bind the photo to an identifier. Then, you pass the photo into the viewDetailedPhoto function and all is well. This is the benefit of Maybe over null. You can't have a null reference error because when you match Just, you definitely have a non-null value.

Remember that you have to handle all constructors in a case expression, so you also have a Nothing branch. The compiler ensures you deal with the null-like situation of Nothing, or your application won't compile. For the Nothing branch, you provide an empty text node in order to satisfy the compiler by returning Html Msg. Later, you'll provide a better message when you start using the photo from the API payload.

Now that you have the viewFeed function, use it instead of the viewDetailedPhoto function inside the main view function like so:

```
view model =
    div []
        [ div [ class "header" ]
            [ h1 [] [ text "Picshare" ] ]
        , div [ class "content-flow" ]
            [ viewFeed model.photo ]
        ]
```

Finally, you'll need to fix the update function to reflect the changes you've made with Maybe. Just like you learned with the view function, you can't access the photo record directly from model.photo. But you need to update the photo and the model while still wrapping the photo record inside Just.

You could try nesting case expressions over model.photo inside each branch of the update function, but that would become messy, redundant, and hard to maintain. Instead, create some helper functions so you can write a cleaner update function.

Start by extracting out the photo update logic for ToggleLike and UpdateComment into separate functions called toggleLike and updateComment, respectively. Place both functions above the update function:

```
toggleLike : Photo -> Photo
toggleLike photo =
    { photo | liked = not photo.liked }

updateComment : String -> Photo -> Photo
updateComment comment photo =
    { photo | newComment = comment }
```

Underneath these functions, you will need another function called updateFeed to bridge them to Maybe Photo. Before you add it, let's examine the implementation below.

```
updateFeed : (Photo -> Photo) -> Maybe Photo -> Maybe Photo
updateFeed updatePhoto maybePhoto =
    case maybePhoto of
        Just photo ->
```

```
        Just (updatePhoto photo)
    Nothing ->
        Nothing
```

The updateFeed function takes a function argument called updatePhoto that it applies to the unwrapped photo in the Just branch of the pattern match. Notice in the pattern match that the function wraps the updated photo with Just again. In the Nothing branch, it simply returns Nothing back. You can actually write this function in a cleaner way that avoids manually re-wrapping with Just or returning back Nothing again. Add the following updateFeed implementation underneath toggleLike and updateComment:

```
updateFeed : (Photo -> Photo) -> Maybe Photo -> Maybe Photo
updateFeed updatePhoto maybePhoto =
    Maybe.map updatePhoto maybePhoto
```

The cool Maybe.map function transforms whatever could be inside a Maybe type. It takes a transformation function as the first argument and the Maybe value as the second argument. If the Maybe value is a Just, then Maybe.map will create a new Just with the transformation function applied to the inner Just value. If the Maybe value is Nothing, then Maybe.map will return back Nothing.

If that sounds a little confusing, recall the List.map function that you use to apply a function to one or more values inside a List. A Maybe is kind of like a List that can only contain at most one value. So, Maybe.map will apply the function to the one value inside Just. The Nothing value is kind of like the empty list, so Maybe.map won't apply the function at all.

Now that you have new helper functions to update a photo, use them to fix the update function like so:

```
update : Msg -> Model -> ( Model, Cmd Msg )
update msg model =
    case msg of
        ToggleLike ->
            ( { model
                | photo = updateFeed toggleLike model.photo
              }
            , Cmd.none
            )

        UpdateComment comment ->
            ( { model
                | photo = updateFeed (updateComment comment) model.photo
              }
            , Cmd.none
            )
```

```
SaveComment ->
    ( { model
        | photo = updateFeed saveNewComment model.photo
      }
    , Cmd.none
    )
LoadFeed _ ->
    ( model, Cmd.none )
```

Instead of updating model.photo directly, you use updateFeed to pass in one of the helper functions to update the inner photo if it exists. For the UpdateComment branch, notice that you use partial application of the updateComment function to fill in the comment argument. The updateFeed function will supply the second photo argument later via Maybe.map.

Verify that your code matches code/communicate/Picshare03.elm and compile. You should be able to like and comment on the photo even though it's inside a Maybe.

## Receive the API Photo

OK...now that most of the setup work is out of the way, you can focus on actually receiving the photo from the API.

Set the initial photo inside initialModel to Nothing:

```
communicate/Picshare04.elm
initialModel =
    { photo = Nothing }
```

Next, modify the update function to handle the LoadFeed message. Inside update replace the wildcard match with these two new branches:

```
LoadFeed (Ok photo) ->
    ( { model | photo = Just photo }
    , Cmd.none
    )
LoadFeed (Err _) ->
    ( model, Cmd.none )
```

Recall that LoadFeed contains a Result type which itself contains either an Http.Error or a Photo. You can use a neat pattern matching trick to *destructure* values as deeply as you want. Destructuring is the Elm feature that lets you extract values out of constructors in pattern matching.

When you destructure LoadFeed to get the inner result, you can destructure the inner result at the same time. That's why you have two branches for LoadFeed (Ok photo) and LoadFeed (Err_). Note the necessary enclosing parentheses.

Then, you can easily access the inner photo from the API response and update the model.photo field. If there is an error, you ignore it for now by matching Err's inner value with the wildcard and returning the current model.

This is actually all you need to load the photo from the API, but let's spruce up the UX (user experience) a little. Go back to the viewFeed function and update the Nothing branch to return a loading message. You can assume for now that if you don't have a photo, it is still loading:

```
viewFeed maybePhoto =
    case maybePhoto of
        Just photo ->
            viewDetailedPhoto photo

        Nothing ->
            div [ class "loading-feed" ]
                [ text "Loading Feed..." ]
```

Compile your code and check your application in your browser. You should see the loading message for a moment and then see the photo load from the API.

Great work! You learned a lot in this section. You created an HTTP request and command with the Http module. You discovered how to issue commands with the Elm Architecture by learning about model-command tuples. You also used the powerful Maybe type for handling values that may not exist.

## What You Learned

We really covered a ton in this chapter. You learned how to create JSON decoders and how Elm safeguards applications from untrustworthy APIs. You learned how to use Maybe to deal with missing data and how to write elegant functional code with Maybe.map and function composition. Most importantly, you learned how to interact with HTTP APIs.

You can now build applications that use real data from servers. In the next chapter, you will take that knowledge further to update application state from servers in real time via WebSockets.

# CHAPTER 5

# Go Real-Time with WebSockets

In the previous chapter, you learned how to interact with servers by fetching JSON data from an HTTP API. This was an important step in creating a real-world application that can use data from remote sources. You also discovered the importance of safely converting JSON data into static types via JSON decoders.

Front-end applications are becoming increasingly real-time as well. Chat apps, stock tickers, and social media timelines depend on never-ending streams of data to stay current. Polling mechanisms and HTTP APIs cannot adequately satisfy these needs, so you need a different tool known as the WebSocket.

In this chapter, you will update the Picshare application to accept a stream of photos in real time via WebSockets and an Elm feature called subscriptions. You will need to change the application to use more than one photo, and also learn how to search the feed to like or comment on an individual photo. Let's go real-time.

## Load Multiple Photos

So far, you've used a single photo in the application, but it really should have many photos. In this section, you'll update the application to display multiple photos. You will learn how to search lists in a model and add error handling to the API calls from the previous chapter.

### Fetch Multiple Photos

In order to fetch multiple photos, you need to change the model to use a list of photos. First, create a helpful type alias for a list of photos called Feed:

```
real-time/Picshare01.elm
type alias Feed =
    List Photo
```

Then, replace the photo field in Model and initialModel with a feed field that has the type Maybe Feed:

```
type alias Model =
    { feed : Maybe Feed }

initialModel =
    { feed = Nothing }
```

Next, fix the initial API payload to receive multiple photos. Update fetchFeed to use a new URL and decoder like so:

```
fetchFeed =
    Http.get
➤       { url = baseUrl ++ "feed"
➤       , expect = Http.expectJson LoadFeed (list photoDecoder)
        }
```

Now you use the URL https://programming-elm.com/feed and a list decoder. Recall that the list decoder expects to receive a JSON array and in this case will apply the inner photoDecoder to every photo object in the array.

Fix the LoadFeed message as well because the inner Result value will now be a list of photos:

```
| LoadFeed (Result Http.Error Feed)
```

So far, so good. Now we're going to temporarily break some functionality in order to display a feed of photos. Inside the following functions, comment out event handlers like so:

- Comment out onClick in viewLoveButton with --. The double dash -- syntax comments out a single line.

  ```
  -- , onClick ToggleLike
  ```

- Comment out onSubmit and onInput in viewComments. Make sure to get the commas too. The {- some code -} syntax comments out a section of code in a line.

  ```
  ➤   , form [ class "new-comment" {- , onSubmit SaveComment -} ]
          [ input
              [ type_ "text"
              , placeholder "Add a comment..."
              , value photo.newComment
  ➤           -- , onInput UpdateComment
  ```

Inside the update function, comment out the branches for ToggleLike, UpdateComment, and SaveComment. You can create multiline comments with the {- some code -} syntax. Also fix the LoadFeed branch to use the feed field, and add a temporary wildcard match at the bottom to handle the branches you just commented out:

```
{-
ToggleLike ->
    ( { model
        | photo = updateFeed toggleLike model.photo
      }
    , Cmd.none
    )

UpdateComment comment ->
    ( { model
        | photo = updateFeed (updateComment comment) model.photo
      }
    , Cmd.none
    )

SaveComment ->
    ( { model
        | photo = updateFeed saveNewComment model.photo
      }
    , Cmd.none
    )
-}
LoadFeed (Ok feed) ->
    ( { model | feed = Just feed }
    , Cmd.none
    )
LoadFeed (Err _) ->
    ( model, Cmd.none )

_ ->
    ( model, Cmd.none )
```

To actually display the photos, you need to let viewFeed handle a list of photos. Let viewFeed take a Maybe Feed as an argument. Inside the Just branch, use List.map to apply the viewDetailedPhoto to each photo in the unwrapped feed list. Your viewFeed function should look like this:

```
viewFeed : Maybe Feed -> Html Msg
viewFeed maybeFeed =
    case maybeFeed of
        Just feed ->
            div [] (List.map viewDetailedPhoto feed)

        Nothing ->
            div [ class "loading-feed" ]
                [ text "Loading Feed..." ]
```

Finally, fix the view function to pass model.feed into viewFeed:

```
[ viewFeed model.feed ]
```

Make sure your code matches code/real-time/Picshare01.elm. Compile it and check your application. Your application should now load three photos from the API: the surfing photo you've been using, a photo of a fox, and a photo of a field.

## Update Multiple Photos

We're fetching multiple photos like a real photo application but we broke the ability to like and comment on photos. Let's walk through adding back that functionality, which will require updating specific photos in the list of photos.

In order to update only a specific photo, you need a way of identifying photos. Hey…the photos from the API include an id field! Let's use that. Go back to your Msg type definition and update ToggleLike, UpdateComment, and SaveComment to take an additional Id argument like so:

real-time/Picshare02.elm
```
type Msg
    = ToggleLike Id
    | UpdateComment Id String
    | SaveComment Id
    | LoadFeed (Result Http.Error Feed)
```

You can uncomment the event handlers from the last section to now use the modified constructors:

- Fix onClick and ToggleLike in viewLoveButton like so.

  ```
  , onClick (ToggleLike photo.id)
  ```

- Fix onSubmit, SaveComment, onInput, and UpdateComment in viewComments like so.

  ```
  , form [ class "new-comment", onSubmit (SaveComment photo.id) ]
      [ input
          [ type_ "text"
          , placeholder "Add a comment..."
          , value photo.newComment
          , onInput (UpdateComment photo.id)
  ```

In each of these examples, you wrap the constructor with parentheses because you fill in the id of the photo ahead of time. Later on, Elm will dispatch the message containing the id of the photo you want to actually update.

In order to update a specific photo, you'll also need an immutable approach to updating a record inside a list. Create a new helper function called updatePhotoById above the updateFeed photo, like this:

```
updatePhotoById : (Photo -> Photo) -> Id -> Feed -> Feed
updatePhotoById updatePhoto id feed =
    List.map
        (\photo ->
            if photo.id == id then
                updatePhoto photo

            else
                photo
        )
        feed
```

You take a function argument called updatePhoto to transform a photo, an Id argument, and a Feed argument. Then, you map over the feed with List.map. You pass in an anonymous mapping function to inspect each photo's id. If the photo.id matches the id argument, then you apply updatePhoto to the matching photo and return the transformed photo. Otherwise, you return the photo with no change. You effectively update the photo by creating a new list where the matching photo is replaced by an updated version.

Let's modify updateFeed to use the new updatePhotoById function. Fix the type annotation to use Maybe Feed instead of Maybe Photo and then use updatePhotoById as the mapping function passed into Maybe.map like so:

```
updateFeed : (Photo -> Photo) -> Id -> Maybe Feed -> Maybe Feed
updateFeed updatePhoto id maybeFeed =
    Maybe.map (updatePhotoById updatePhoto id) maybeFeed
```

You use partial application on updatePhotoById to pass in the updatePhoto function argument and the id argument. The Maybe.map function handles passing in the final feed argument if maybeFeed is a Just. A List.map within a Maybe.map is mind-bending at first but really elegant and clean.

Finally, fix the update function to reflect the changes you've made. Uncomment the ToggleLike, UpdateComment, and SaveComment branches. Then, update each pattern match to bind the id value, and replace the usage of the old photo field with feed. Also, remove the wildcard match at the end:

```
ToggleLike id ->
    ( { model
        | feed = updateFeed toggleLike id model.feed
      }
    , Cmd.none
    )
```

```
UpdateComment id comment ->
    ( { model
        | feed = updateFeed (updateComment comment) id model.feed
      }
    , Cmd.none
    )

SaveComment id ->
    ( { model
        | feed = updateFeed saveNewComment id model.feed
      }
    , Cmd.none
    )

LoadFeed (Ok feed) ->
    ( { model | feed = Just feed }
    , Cmd.none
    )

LoadFeed (Err _) ->
    ( model, Cmd.none )
```

Verify that your code matches code/real-time/Picshare02.elm and then compile and run your application. You should now be able to like and leave comments on individual photos without affecting other photos. Great job! Your application works like a real photo-sharing application.

## Handle Errors

Before we conclude this section, let's improve the application further by handling errors. Currently in the update function, you ignore the Err constructor by returning the existing model.

```
LoadFeed (Err _) ->
    ( model, Cmd.none )
```

Let's actually do something with the error value inside Err in order to give users helpful error messages. Update your Model and initialModel to hold Maybe Http.Error, like this:

real-time/Picshare03.elm
```
type alias Model =
    { feed : Maybe Feed
    , error : Maybe Http.Error
    }

initialModel =
    { feed = Nothing
    , error = Nothing
    }
```

Just as with the feed, you may or may not have an error. You need to check for that in the view layer. Create a helper function called viewContent that takes the Model as an argument and pattern matches on the model.error field like so:

```
viewContent : Model -> Html Msg
viewContent model =
    case model.error of
        Just error ->
            div [ class "feed-error" ]
                [ text (errorMessage error) ]

        Nothing ->
            viewFeed model.feed
```

If you have an error, you create a div for displaying an error message. Otherwise, you call the viewFeed function with the model.feed field. Notice that if you do have an error, you use a function called errorMessage. You still need to write errorMessage, but it will convert the error into a string for the text function. Add errorMessage above viewContent like so:

```
errorMessage : Http.Error -> String
errorMessage error =
    case error of
        Http.BadBody _ ->
            """Sorry, we couldn't process your feed at this time.
            We're working on it!"""

        _ ->
            """Sorry, we couldn't load your feed at this time.
            Please try again later."""
```

Recall that the Err constructor will contain an Http.Error. The Http.Error type is a custom type with a few constructors. We're primarily concerned with the BadBody constructor that Elm uses when JSON decoding fails. You can learn about the other constructors by checking the docs.[1]

The BadBody constructor has one type argument, an error message explaining why decoding failed. But you ignore it here. Instead, you provide a more user-friendly error message that says the application couldn't process the JSON body, but you're working on it (I'm sure you want to be on call for another application, right?). For all other error values, you return a generic error message.

Hook the viewContent and errorMessage functions into the main view function. Swap out viewFeed with viewContent inside the view function like so:

```
[ viewContent model ]
```

---

1. https://package.elm-lang.org/packages/elm/http/latest/Http#Error

Finally, accept the error in the update function. Alter the appropriate LoadFeed branch to add the error to the model, like this:

```
LoadFeed (Err error) ->
    ( { model | error = Just error }, Cmd.none )
```

That's all you need. Check your code against code/real-time/Picshare03.elm and compile your application. Your application should still work fine. Let's try displaying the error messages.

Go back to the fetchFeed command and change the string "feed" to "badfeed". The "badfeed" URL path will respond with an array that contains the incorrect payload on page 62.

Compile your application and refresh your browser. After the HTTP response comes back, you should see the error message for the BadBody constructor. Try changing the string to something like "notfound" and you should see the other error message after recompiling.

Great. Now you can provide error messages to users so they don't see a blank screen when something fails. Make sure to change the string in fetchFeed back to "feed" before moving on.

Let's recap what you accomplished in this section. You learned how to easily create a list decoder from another decoder. You used a list in a model and learned how to include identifying payloads like the id field in a message. Then, you used the id to update a specific photo with List.map. Now that you know how to work with lists in your update function, you can build upon this knowledge to update the application in real time with WebSockets and subscriptions.

## Receive Photos from WebSockets

Now that the application handles multiple photos, you can update it in real time with new photos via WebSockets. A WebSocket is a network protocol that allows a client application and a server to communicate back and forth. WebSockets are great for applications, such as chat apps, that require real-time notifications. WebSockets allow a server to effectively push data to a client, perfect for updating the photo feed in real time. If you'd like to learn more about WebSockets, I recommend checking out *WebSocket: Lightweight Client-Server Communications [Lom15]*.

In this section, you will hook the application up to a WebSocket server, connecting to the server with JavaScript while using Elm ports to communicate WebSocket data to the Elm application. Then, you will apply previous concepts such as JSON decoding and manipulating lists to easily add new photos to the feed.

## Connect to a WebSocket Server

As of this writing, the Elm core team has not updated Elm's WebSocket package to Elm 0.19. To connect to the server, you'll need to use JavaScript and Elm *ports* instead. You'll learn more about ports in Chapter 8, Integrate with JavaScript, on page 153. Basically, ports allow Elm and native JavaScript code to communicate asynchronously. The JavaScript code will connect to the WebSocket server then pass along WebSocket data to Elm via ports.

Once the Elm WebSocket package becomes available, it should let you connect to a WebSocket server and receive events without ports. Feel free to come back and update the application to use the WebSocket package when Elm's core team releases it.

Start by creating a file in picshare/src named WebSocket.elm. Name the module WebSocket and expose two functions, listen and receive, which you'll define in a moment:

real-time/WebSocket.elm
```
port module WebSocket exposing (listen, receive)
```

Note the addition of the keyword port in front of the module keyword. This signals to Elm that this module is a port module. Port modules expose public interfaces (ports) for JavaScript code to interact with an Elm application.

Next, define the listen and receive functions as ports like so:

```
port listen : String -> Cmd msg
```

```
port receive : (String -> msg) -> Sub msg
```

You create ports with the port keyword, a port name, and function type definition. The listen port takes a String and returns a Cmd msg. The receive port takes a function that accepts a String, returns a msg, then returns a Sub msg. The Sub type is short for subscription. You'll learn more about subscriptions later in this section.

Ports such as listen that return a Cmd are *outgoing* ports. They send data to JavaScript. You will use listen to send the server URL to JavaScript so it can connect to the server.

Ports such as receive that return a Sub are incoming ports. They receive data from JavaScript. You will use receive to—well—receive WebSocket event data from JavaScript.

That's all you need on the Elm side for the moment. Now, let's write the JavaScript portion. Open up picshare/index.html in your editor. Replace the contents of the bottom <script> tag with this:

```javascript
(function() {
  var app = Elm.Picshare.init({
    node: document.getElementById('main')
  });
})();
```

You create and call an immediately-invoked-function-expression (IIFE). The IIFE lets you create variables inside the scope of the function instead of polluting the browser's global namespace. Inside the IIFE, you call Elm.Picshare.init but now assign its return value to a variable called app. The init function returns an application object, which you'll use next.

Below the call to init but still inside the IIFE, add this line:

```javascript
app.ports.listen.subscribe(listen);
```

The application object has a ports property that holds any ports your Elm application defines. For outgoing ports such as listen, JavaScript can subscribe to the port via the subscribe method. You subscribe to the listen port, passing in a reference to a listen function that you'll write next.

Add the listen function below the port subscription (still inside the IIFE):

```javascript
function listen(url) {
  var socket = new WebSocket(url);

  socket.onmessage = function(event) {
    app.ports.receive.send(event.data);
  };
}
```

WebSocket is a built-in JavaScript constructor function for connecting to Web-Socket servers. You receive the url from the port and create a new instance of WebSocket with it. Then, you define the WebSocket's onmessage callback, which will receive events from the server. The actual photo data you'll need resides in the data property, so you pull that out and pass it into app.ports.receive.send. Ports that receive data, such as receive, provide a send method for JavaScript to forward data to Elm.

## Use the WebSocket Ports

Now, go back to Picshare.elm and import the provided WebSocket module:

real-time/Picshare04.elm
```
import WebSocket
```

Create a string constant for the WebSocket server URL called wsUrl. Place it underneath baseUrl:

```
wsUrl : String
wsUrl =
    "wss://programming-elm.com/"
```

 You can run the WebSocket server locally. Follow the instructions in Appendix 2, Run the Local Server, on page 267, and set wsUrl to ws://localhost:5000/.

Next, you need to connect to the WebSocket server at wsUrl from Elm. Modify the successful LoadFeed branch inside the update function like so:

```
LoadFeed (Ok feed) ->
    ( { model | feed = Just feed }
    , WebSocket.listen wsUrl
    )
```

You replace Cmd.none with a call to the WebSocket.listen port function. Recall that WebSocket.listen accepts a String URL and returns a Cmd. The Cmd essentially wraps the URL and passes it to the JavaScript code in index.html via ports to connect to the server. You call WebSocket.listen in this branch of update to ensure you have an initial feed of photos before attempting to connect to the Web-Socket server for more photos.

Finally, at the bottom of the application, change the implementation of the subscriptions function to use the WebSocket.receive port function like so:

```
subscriptions model =
    WebSocket.receive LoadStreamPhoto
```

The function argument to WebSocket.receive is basically a message constructor argument. You use a new LoadStreamPhoto message that you'll create in a moment. The WebSocket.receive function returns a subscription which has the type Sub Msg. Subscriptions let your application interact with the outside world, similar to commands.

Subscriptions differ from commands in that commands tell the Elm Architecture to *do something* to the outside world while subscriptions tell the Elm Architecture to *receive information* from the outside world. The Elm Architecture will listen for events related to subscriptions, and notify your application's update function with whatever message constructor you provide at subscription time. In this case, WebSocket.receive expects the message constructor to take a string argument which will become the raw string data from the WebSocket event. Recall that the JavaScript code will call the receive port with event.data, which will trigger the subscription on the Elm end to receive the data.

Elm provides other subscriptions that don't depend on ports such as period-ically getting the current time[2] or receiving certain browser events.[3]

To finish up, add LoadStreamPhoto with a String argument to the Msg type:

```
| LoadStreamPhoto String
```

Then, handle LoadStreamPhoto in your update function at the bottom like so:

```
LoadStreamPhoto data ->
    let
        _ =
            Debug.log "WebSocket data" data
    in
    ( model, Cmd.none )
```

You bind the raw WebSocket event string data to a variable called data and then use a debugging technique to inspect data. The Debug.log function prints its arguments to the JavaScript console. The first argument is a string label that identifies your message in the console, and the second argument is any data type you want to print. This technically means that Debug.log bends the rules on function purity by printing to the console. We'll forgive this since it's main use is for local debugging.

Because you can't have statements in Elm, you "hack" a let expression in order to print out data. The Debug.log function returns whatever its second argument is, but you ignore the return value by setting it equal to the underscore character.

Make sure your code matches code/real-time/Picshare04.elm and recompile. Open the application in your browser with your dev tools console open. Wait a few seconds. Now you should begin to see the WebSocket data printed out like the screenshot that follows. Notice that your application receives JSON strings of new photos.

```
WebSocket data: "{\"id\":6,\"url\":\"https://programming-elm.surge.sh/
6.jpg\",\"caption\":\"Pretty Flowers\",\"liked\":false,\"comments\":
[],\"username\":\"the_botanist\"}"

WebSocket data: "{\"id\":5,\"url\":\"https://programming-elm.surge.sh/
5.jpg\",\"caption\":\"Contemplation\",\"liked\":false,\"comments\":
[],\"username\":\"be_still\"}"

WebSocket data: "{\"id\":4,\"url\":\"https://programming-elm.surge.sh/
4.jpg\",\"caption\":\"Tree Canopy\",\"liked\":false,\"comments\":
[],\"username\":\"elpapapollo\"}"
```

---

2. https://package.elm-lang.org/packages/elm/time/latest/Time#every
3. https://package.elm-lang.org/packages/elm/browser/latest/Browser-Events

And that's it. Hooking up to a WebSocket server in Elm was pretty easy. Granted, most of the JavaScript code is simple too, but even with the eventual first-class WebSocket Elm package, you should be able to connect with minimal effort and little boilerplate.

The real challenge is to do something useful with the WebSocket data. Let's shift gears to decode the data and add it to the feed.

## Process WebSocket Data

You need to convert the JSON photos into the Photo type as with the photos you receive via HTTP. Then, you need to add each new photo to the top of the feed. You will queue up photos instead of immediately adding them to the feed, though. If you started popping photos into the feed right away, you would push old photos down and disrupt users if they're already looking at a photo. Instead, you will provide a banner to notify users that they can view new photos. If users click on the banner, you will flush the photos from the queue and add them to the main feed.

### Update the Model and Subscriptions

Create a new field called streamQueue on the Model and initialModel for queueing photos. Because the streamQueue is a list of photos, you can use the Feed type:

```
real-time/Picshare05.elm
type alias Model =
    { feed : Maybe Feed
    , error : Maybe Http.Error
    , streamQueue : Feed
    }

initialModel =
    { feed = Nothing
    , error = Nothing
    , streamQueue = []
    }
```

You'll focus on decoding the JSON data next. Expose the decodeString function from the Json.Decode module:

```
import Json.Decode exposing (Decoder, bool, decodeString,
                             int, list, string, succeed)
```

The Http module automatically decoded JSON payloads with your decoder. You will need to decode manually in the subscriptions function. Update it like so:

```
subscriptions model =
    WebSocket.receive
        (LoadStreamPhoto << decodeString photoDecoder)
```

The argument to WebSocket.receive has become more interesting.

The << operator is the *backward composition operator*. It combines two functions into one function. It chains the functions together by passing in the return value of one function as the argument to the next function. The first function in the chain receives the initial argument. Because the operator points to the left, it calls functions from right to left.

You use function composition to create a function that takes a string argument and decodes it to a Result Json.Decode.Error Photo. Then, the function passes the result into LoadStreamPhoto to create a message. The code is the same as this explicit version with an anonymous function.

```
WebSocket.receive
    (\json -> LoadStreamPhoto (decodeString photoDecoder json))
```

Remember, the WebSocket.receive function really just needs a *function* as its argument, so you can technically pass in any function here. However, subscriptions won't type check if the function doesn't return a Msg. Using LoadStreamPhoto by itself worked before because it does return a Msg. Since LoadStreamPhoto is a function, you can use function composition to still return a Msg but process the data beforehand. This means that LoadStreamPhoto will now contain a Result Json.Decode.Error Photo to handle in the update function.

### Queue Photos

Update the LoadStreamPhoto constructor to use its new Result argument. Also, add another constructor called FlushStreamQueue, which you will need later for flushing the queue:

```
| LoadStreamPhoto (Result Json.Decode.Error Photo)
| FlushStreamQueue
```

Now you can modify the update function to start receiving photos from the LoadStreamPhoto message. Replace the LoadStreamPhoto branch in the update function like so:

```
LoadStreamPhoto (Ok photo) ->
    ( { model | streamQueue = photo :: model.streamQueue }
    , Cmd.none
    )

LoadStreamPhoto (Err _) ->
    ( model, Cmd.none )
```

You repeat the nested pattern matching you used with LoadFeed to check if you have a successful value or error. You cheat again and ignore any errors, but if you have a photo, you add it to model.streamQueue with the :: operator.

The :: operator is known as the *cons* operator. It creates a new list by prepending the left operand to the list on the right.

You will temporarily ignore the FlushStreamQueue branch, so return the current model for now:

```
FlushStreamQueue ->
    ( model, Cmd.none )
```

Great. Now you're queuing up photos. Let's work on the banner to notify users of new photos.

### Add a Notification Banner

The banner needs to display the number of new photos to users and allow users to click on the banner to add the photos to their feed. Create a new function called viewStreamNotification above viewContent like so:

```
viewStreamNotification : Feed -> Html Msg
viewStreamNotification queue =
    case queue of
        [] ->
            text ""

        _ ->
            let
                content =
                    "View new photos: "
                        ++ String.fromInt (List.length queue)
            in
            div
                [ class "stream-notification"
                , onClick FlushStreamQueue
                ]
                [ text content ]
```

If the queue is empty, you hide the banner. If you have photos in the queue, you display the message "View new photos: " along with the number of photos. You use the List.length function to obtain the number of new photos. You also add an onClick handler with FlushStreamQueue to allow users to flush the queue to the feed.

You need to make sure the banner displays above the feed, so tie viewStreamNotification into your view layer by updating the Nothing branch of viewContent like so:

```
Nothing ->
    div []
        [ viewStreamNotification model.streamQueue
        , viewFeed model.feed
        ]
```

OK...let's ensure that the notification banner works. Double-check your code with code/real-time/Picshare05.elm and compile. Open up your application and you should see the notification banner pop up after a few seconds. Clicking won't work yet because you need to handle FlushStreamQueue properly in update. And what better time than now.

# Picshare

View new photos: 3

## Flush the Queue

You only need to add a tiny bit of code to handle FlushStreamQueue, but I want to walk through the code slowly. When you flush the queue, you need to combine model.streamQueue and model.feed together. The ++ operator can concatenate lists together, similar to concatenating strings, but recall that model.feed is a Maybe of a list. You could solve this dilemma by using Maybe.map like so.

```
Maybe.map (\feed -> model.streamQueue ++ feed) model.feed
```

Elm has another trick up its sleeve to help you avoid writing a separate anonymous or named function. In Elm, when you wrap an operator in parentheses, you convert it into a function. For example, these two lines of code are equivalent.

```
[ 1, 2 ] ++ [ 3, 4 ]    -- returns [ 1, 2, 3, 4 ]
(++) [ 1, 2 ] [ 3, 4 ] -- returns [ 1, 2, 3, 4 ]
```

When you convert an operator into a function, the left operand becomes the first argument to the function and the right operand becomes the second argument to the function. An operator function is curried like any other Elm function, so you can partially apply it. That means you could partially apply the left operand like this.

```
prepend1And2 = (++) [ 1, 2 ]
prepend1And2 [ 3, 4 ] -- returns [ 1, 2, 3, 4 ]
```

Let's use this nifty feature in the update function. Update the FlushStreamQueue branch like so:

```
real-time/Picshare06.elm
FlushStreamQueue ->
    ( { model
        | feed = Maybe.map ((++) model.streamQueue) model.feed
        , streamQueue = []
      }
    , Cmd.none
    )
```

You use partial application with the function version of ++ to make the model.streamQueue the left operand. Then, the Maybe.map function supplies the feed as the second operand if model.feed is a Just. Order is important here—you want model.streamQueue to be the left operand because these are the newest photos that need to be on the top. After adding the queue to the feed, you also make sure to empty the queue so you don't have duplicate photos.

Recompile your application and refresh your browser. When the notification banner pops up, click on it. New photos should pop into the top of the feed. You should see a photo of trees, a photo of candles, and a photo of flowers, but not necessarily in that order.

Well done. You learned how to apply your knowledge of JSON decoding and lists to make a real-time application with WebSockets. Your application works like a real photo application.

## What You Learned

You accomplished a lot in this chapter. You learned useful methods for updating individual photos in a list. Then, you learned how to use Elm ports and subscriptions along with WebSockets to update the photo feed in real time.

You now have an amazing base of knowledge and experience to write your own Elm applications. You can build upon that base to start investigating more advanced concepts. Real-world applications are typically larger than a couple hundred lines of code. In the next chapter, you will learn techniques for organizing code and managing larger codebases.

# CHAPTER 6

# Build Larger Applications

Over the past few chapters, you built a stateful Elm application complete with server interaction. Although complex, that application was small and straightforward to build. Not every application is a cakewalk, unfortunately. As Elm applications grow, they can quickly become unmaintainable if you're not careful. Large applications process many messages, which can lead to long, unreadable update and view functions with lots of code duplication.

In this chapter, you will shift gears to refactor a seemingly simple application suffering from scaling pains. This application isn't large when measured by lines of code. However, you will see that maintaining it would be a problem in a truly large application.

You will split up and organize functions to make code more readable. Then, you will consolidate messages to simplify the update function. Next, you will use nested state and extensible records to make the application more modular. Then, you will remove code duplication from the view layer with reusable helper functions. Finally, you will prevent invalid state configurations by combining view state fields into a single custom type. With these patterns, you will be able to build easily maintainable and scalable Elm applications.

## Organize the View

In this section, you will learn about the application and discover the problems with its view function. The previous developer put all the application's markup inside one view function, creating tons of duplication and hard-to-read code. You will spend extra development time adding new features unless you organize the view function first. Let's fix this dilemma. You will divide the view function into separate functions to make the code more understandable.

## Build a Salad

A large chain of restaurants known as Saladise needs help with a new salad-builder application. Customers can customize a salad with their favorite greens, toppings, and dressing. Then, they can supply contact information to receive an alert to pick up their salad.

But not all is well in the Saladise paradise (sorry). Saladise needs to add new features to the application but already feels overwhelmed by its complexity. They want the application to be more manageable before they'll feel comfortable with adding features—so they've brought you on to help.

To start, create a directory called salad-builder. From this book's code downloads, copy the contents of code/larger/salad-builder into your salad-builder directory.

Prior to this point, you've manually compiled Elm applications to run them. This application uses the create-elm-app and Webpack tools to manage developing and building the application. You'll learn more about these tools for faster Elm development in the next chapter. For now, go into your salad-builder directory and install dependencies with npm.

```
npm install
```

After installation finishes, start the application with this command.

```
npm start
```

A development server will start listening at http://localhost:3000. Note: If another program is listening on port 3000, the start command will suggest a different port. When the application boots up, it will open a new tab in your browser:

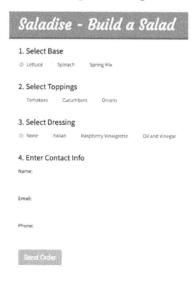

Try the application out. Build a salad, enter some contact info, and submit the order. Note that the application requires all contact info, validates the format of the email address, and validates the phone number as a ten-digit number. After submitting, you should see a "Sending Order…" message and an order confirmation, similar to this.

# Woo hoo!

Thanks for your order!

| | |
|---|---|
| Base: | Spinach |
| Toppings: | • Cucumbers<br>• Tomatoes |
| Dressing: | Oil and Vinegar |
| Name: | Jeremy |
| Email: | hello@example.com |
| Phone: | 1231231234 |

You can cause a submission to fail by appending a fail query parameter to the sendUrl constant https://programming-elm.com/salad/send?fail and submitting the same data. Make sure you remove the parameter before proceeding.

 You can run the server locally to fetch from the /salad/send API endpoint. Follow the instructions in Appendix 2, Run the Local Server, on page 267, and change sendUrl to http://localhost:5000/salad/send.

## Examine the Model

Now that you're familiar with the application, let's dive into the code. Open src/SaladBuilder.elm in your editor.

Model-related code lives at the top of the file after the imported modules. Model is a type alias to a record with several fields. The building, sending, success, and error fields represent the application's different view states.

```
type alias Model =
    { building : Bool
    , sending : Bool
    , success : Bool
    , error : Maybe String
    , -- other fields
    }
```

The base field holds the selected salad base, or green. Notice that base's type is Base, which is a custom type of three values, Lettuce, Spinach, and SpringMix.

```
type Base
    = Lettuce
    | Spinach
    | SpringMix

...

type alias Model =
    { -- other fields
    , base : Base
    , -- other fields
    }
```

Model also has fields for the salad toppings and dressing along with respective custom types, Topping and Dressing.

```
type Topping
    = Tomatoes
    | -- other values

type Dressing
    = NoDressing
    | -- other values

type alias Model =
    { -- other fields
    , toppings : Set String
    , dressing : Dressing
    , -- other fields
    }
```

Note that toppings' type is Set String instead of Topping. Because a user can select and deselect toppings, you need a type that can easily add and remove multiple toppings. You could use a list, but you would have to write custom code to add toppings, remove toppings, and check if a user already added a topping. Set's API can do all of that for you.

Set[1] is a built-in Elm type that holds multiple items like a list. Unlike lists, it prevents duplicate values, automatically sorts values, and lets you easily look up values. Set's only caveat is that values have to be *comparable*. Comparable values include Int, Float, Char, and String. List and Tuple are also comparable if they contain comparable values. Elm represents comparable values with the built-in—wait for it—comparable type variable. Based on the name, Elm can compare comparable values with one another if they're the same concrete type (e.g. both values are Int).

---

1.  https://package.elm-lang.org/packages/elm/core/latest/Set

Since Set requires comparable values, you have to convert Topping custom type values into String before storing them in the Model toppings field. Look at the ToggleTomatoes branch inside the update function to see how we insert a topping as a String. We convert toppings with a custom toppingToString function defined near the Topping type.

```
{ model | toppings = Set.insert (toppingToString Tomatoes) model.toppings }
```

Finally, Model has name, email, and phone fields for storing contact information.

## Split the View

Skip over the remaining model-related code and go to the view function. The view function has two parts, a header and content. The header is a simple h1 tag. The content is definitely not simple and where we will focus on refactoring.

```
view : Model -> Html Msg
view model =
    div []
        [ h1 [ class "header" ]
            [ text "Saladise - Build a Salad" ]
        , div [ class "content" ]
            [ if model.sending then
                -- display a sending message
              else if model.building then
                -- display the salad builder
              else
                -- display a confirmation message
            ]
        ]
```

The content section stretches almost 200 lines inside a behemoth if-else expression. It is extremely unreadable and duplicates a ton of code. Now you see why Saladise has hired you. The view function alone is unmaintainable. Imagine trying to find a bug in it. You would need a few minutes to thoroughly scan through it. Now picture a larger application with an even longer view function. Good luck with that.

To get a grip on this codebase, you will need to refactor it piece by piece. You can get a quick win by organizing view into separate functions. You'll address code duplication later in this chapter.

Look closely at the if-else expression. When model.sending is True, you display a sending message. When model.building is True, you display the salad builder. And when both fields are False, you display a confirmation message. You don't even check the model.success field. These fields and this if-else expression are smelly code, but you'll come back to them later.

So you have three important parts inside the content: sending, building, and confirmation. Additionally, you display errors with model.error and pattern matching inside the building section. That makes four parts. Let's pull these parts out into separate functions to organize view.

Start by creating a viewSending constant above view. Move the code under if model.sending then into viewSending:

larger/examples/SaladBuilder01.elm
```
viewSending : Html msg
viewSending =
    div [ class "sending" ] [ text "Sending Order..." ]
```

Unlike view, viewSending does not need a Model argument, so you can give viewSending a simple Html msg type. This will make it much easier to scan code when you are searching for a bug's source. If the bug is related to a model field, you immediately know it can't occur in viewSending because it does not use the model.

Underneath viewSending, create a viewError function to display errors. Move only the case expression under else if model.building then to viewError:

```
viewError : Maybe Error -> Html msg
viewError error =
    case error of
        Just errorMessage ->
            div [ class "error" ] [ text errorMessage ]

        Nothing ->
            text ""
```

Notice that viewError takes a Maybe Error argument instead of the entire model. Just as I explained with viewSending, simplifying the type makes it easier to know where to look for bugs.

The Error type doesn't exist yet, so let's make it. Create a type alias to String above the Base custom type. Using the Error type alias clarifies in type annotations when you expect a string Error:

```
type alias Error =
    String
```

Next, move the remaining code underneath else if model.building then to a new viewBuild function after viewError. The viewBuild function will need several model fields, so accept the entire model as an argument. Also, viewBuild produces Msg values from input events, so ensure the type annotation returns Html Msg.

Inside viewBuild, add the display of errors back by calling viewError as the first child of the container div. The first few lines of viewBuild should look like this:

```
viewBuild : Model -> Html Msg
viewBuild model =
    div []
        [ viewError model.error
        , section [ class "salad-section" ]
            [ -- more code not displayed
            ]
```

There's one branch left. Move the code underneath the final else into a new function called viewConfirmation after viewBuild like so:

```
viewConfirmation : Model -> Html msg
viewConfirmation model =
    div [ class "confirmation" ]
        [ h2 [] [ text "Woo hoo!" ]
        , p [] [ text "Thanks for your order!" ]
        , -- table code not displayed
        ]
```

Just like viewBuild, viewConfirmation accepts the entire model as an argument because it needs to access multiple model fields.

Fantastic! You've created four functions to better organize the view layer. Creating these four functions has given you another debugging benefit, too. They all return Html msg except for viewBuild, which returns Html Msg. Recall that Html msg means you haven't supplied a type value to the msg type variable. Therefore, you shouldn't expect functions with that return type to produce any messages. If you encounter a bug from a click handler, you likely don't have to bother looking at those functions during debugging.

Now that you have helper functions for the separate view states, let's organize the main view function a little more. Currently, you should have an empty if-else expression inside div [ class "content" ].

```
if model.sending then
else if model.building then
else
```

You need to use the new helper functions inside the if-else expression. But before that, let's move it into a separate function. The inlined if-else expression makes view hard to read. Move the if-else expression into a new function called viewStep above view. Accept the model as an argument and call the view helper functions in the correct branches. Also, return Html Msg in the type annotation because viewBuild returns Html Msg:

```
viewStep : Model -> Html Msg
viewStep model =
    if model.sending then
        viewSending
```

```
else if model.building then
    viewBuild model
else
    viewConfirmation model
```

You're almost finished with view. Call viewStep inside the child list of div [ class "content" ]. You should now have a view function like this:

```
view : Model -> Html Msg
view model =
    div []
        [ h1 [ class "header" ]
            [ text "Saladise - Build a Salad" ]
        , div [ class "content" ]
            [ viewStep model ]
        ]
```

Be sure your code matches SaladBuilder01.elm from the code/larger/examples directory in this book's code downloads. Start the application and check your browser to verify the application compiles and still works.

You have completely organized view. By dividing it into smaller functions, you have made the codebase easier to read and scan for sources of bugs. You still have some duplication in viewBuild and viewConfirmation, but you'll fix them later. Let's move on to the Msg type and update function.

## Simplify Messages

The update function suffers from code duplication and unnecessary complexity. In this section, you will simplify it by reducing the messages it handles. You will learn how to collapse multiple message values into one parameterized message value.

Look for the update function near the bottom of SaladBuilder.elm. This function is over 100 lines, so we have a problem.

```
update : Msg -> Model -> ( Model, Cmd Msg )
update msg model =
    case msg of
        SelectLettuce ->
            ( { model | base = Lettuce }
            , Cmd.none
            )
        -- other branches
```

Notice the duplication where we handle the ToggleTomatoes, ToggleCucumbers, and ToggleOnions messages. Surprisingly, we have duplication with the other salad-related messages for selecting a base and dressing.

One problem is that the Msg type has 15 values.

```
type Msg
    = SelectLettuce
    | SelectSpinach
    | SelectSpringMix
    | -- 12 more values
```

The Msg values should use the Base, Topping, and Dressing custom types to their advantage.

Here's what I mean: take the SelectLettuce, SelectSpinach, and SelectSpringMix Msg values, for example. Each of these messages maps to updating the model.base field with a specific Base value. SelectLettuce maps to setting model.base to Lettuce and so on.

Instead of mapping a message to a value, you can make the message wrap the value you want to set. You can collapse SelectLettuce, SelectSpinach, and SelectSpringMix into one message called SetBase. Then, SetBase can wrap over a Base value. Let's try that out to understand. Replace those three messages with SetBase like this:

```
type Msg
    = SetBase Base
    | -- other Msg values
```

Remember that custom type values are constructor functions, so SetBase accepts a Base argument. Update the radio buttons in viewBuild to use the new SetBase message with the correct Base value. Make these replacements:

- Replace SelectLettuce with SetBase Lettuce
- Replace SelectSpinach with SetBase Spinach
- Replace SelectSpringMix with SetBase SpringMix

For example, the lettuce onClick handler should look like this once you're done.

```
, onClick (SetBase Lettuce)
```

You give onClick a SetBase message that contains the inner Base value. Then, you can use the Base value in the update function when a user selects the radio button.

Speaking of update, let's now combine the SelectLettuce, SelectSpinach, SelectSpringMix branches into one. Replace them with a SetBase branch like this:

```
SetBase base ->
    ( { model | base = base }
    , Cmd.none
    )
```

Instead of mapping a particular Msg value to a particular Base value, you unwrap the selected base from SetBase and update model.base with it. Not only do you have fewer update branches but also less code duplication. This is a great win.

Let's apply the previous exercise to dressing and topping selection to reduce code duplication further. Fixing dressing selection will closely mirror what you did with base selection. Follow these steps:

1. Combine SelectNoDressing, SelectItalian, SelectRaspberryVinaigrette, and SelectOilVinegar into one SetDressing constructor that accepts a Dressing argument.

   ```
   SetDressing Dressing
   ```

2. Update viewBuild to use SetDressing. Call SetDressing with the appropriate Dressing argument. For example, the onClick handler for selecting no dressing should look like this.

   ```
   , onClick (SetDressing NoDressing)
   ```

3. Combine the dressing branches in update into one SetDressing branch. Unwrap the selected dressing and update model.dressing with it. Your code should look like this.

   ```
   SetDressing dressing ->
       ( { model | dressing = dressing }
       , Cmd.none
       )
   ```

Fixing topping selection will mimic the previous examples but will require a little more work. Follow these steps:

1. Combine ToggleTomatoes, ToggleCucumbers, and ToggleOnions into one ToggleTopping constructor. The new ToggleTopping value needs to accept a Topping argument and a Bool argument to know if the user selected or deselected a topping. ToggleTopping should look like this.

   ```
   ToggleTopping Topping Bool
   ```

2. Update viewBuild to use ToggleTopping. Call ToggleTopping with the appropriate Topping argument. Recall that custom type constructor functions are curried, so you need to partially apply the Topping argument. The onCheck handler will later provide the Bool argument when a user clicks on the checkbox. For example, the onCheck handler for toggling tomatoes should look like this.

   ```
   , onCheck (ToggleTopping Tomatoes)
   ```

3. Combine the topping branches in update into one ToggleTopping branch. Make sure you unwrap the Topping and Bool arguments. The previous code had some duplication in how model.toppings is updated. Move the if-else branch into a let expression and branch on the Bool argument to select a Set function for updating toppings. If you're adding a topping, you want Set.insert. Otherwise, you want Set.remove. Use this code in the ToggleTopping branch.

```
ToggleTopping topping add ->
    let
        updater =
            if add then
                Set.insert

            else
                Set.remove
    in
    ( { model
        | toppings = updater (toppingToString topping) model.toppings
      }
    , Cmd.none
    )
```

Wow, that was a huge improvement! You went from 15 Msg values to eight. You also reduced the number of branches in update and eliminated a lot of code duplication. You're making great progress with this codebase. Before you go to the next section, check that your code matches SaladBuilder02.elm from the code/larger/examples directory in this book's code downloads. Also, make sure the application still compiles with npm start. Now, on to the model.

## Use Nested State

The Model currently has fields for different application concepts including view state, salad options, and contact information. This has produced an update function with too many responsibilities. You need modular patterns to manage the Model state so the application can scale. Otherwise, the update function will grow even more cumbersome over time.

In this section, you will use nested state to manage the salad portion of Model. You will modularize the application by creating a separate update function and message type for updating salad state. You will also learn the pros and cons of nested state.

## Extract the Salad

One way to manage salad state is to create a Salad record type that has base, toppings, and dressing fields. Then, Model can replace those fields with a salad field of type Salad.

Let's try this approach. Create a Salad type alias above Model:

larger/examples/SaladBuilder03.elm
```
type alias Salad =
    { base : Base
    , toppings : Set String
    , dressing : Dressing
    }
```

Then, replace the three salad-related fields in Model with the salad field like this:

```
type alias Model =
    { -- view state fields
    , salad : Salad
    , -- contact fields
    }
```

Inside initialModel, move the three salad-related field values inside a nested salad field record:

```
initialModel =
    { -- view state values
    , salad =
        { base = Lettuce
        , toppings = Set.empty
        , dressing = NoDressing
        }
    , -- contact values
    }
```

At this point, the application won't compile. The viewBuild, viewConfirmation, encodeOrder, and update functions are trying to access salad-related fields directly from the model instead of through the nested salad field. Before you fix those functions, let's modularize Msg and update first.

You want to give Salad its own messages and update function. Then, you can simplify the main update function by removing salad-related branches.

You'll still need the main update function to know about salad messages, but it will behave like a router to the salad update function. You'll see what that looks like in a moment. For now, let's make a separate salad message type and update function.

Above the main Msg type, add a SaladMsg type. Move the SetBase, ToggleTopping, and SetDressing values from Msg to SaladMsg:

```
type SaladMsg
    = SetBase Base
    | ToggleTopping Topping Bool
    | SetDressing Dressing
```

Create an updateSalad function that accepts SaladMsg and Salad and returns Salad:

```
updateSalad : SaladMsg -> Salad -> Salad
updateSalad msg salad =
    case msg of
```

Move the SetBase, ToggleTopping, and SetDressing branches from update to updateSalad. Make sure you rename model to salad in the branches. Also, since updateSalad doesn't need to return Cmd, you remove the tuples and just return the updated salad. For example, the beginning of updateSalad's case expression should look like this.

```
case msg of
    SetBase base ->
        { salad | base = base }
    -- other branches
```

Now you have an isolated updateSalad function that updates a salad according to SaladMsg values.

## Wire Up the Salad

The SaladMsg type and updateSalad function do not work until you wire them into update and viewBuild. Basically, viewBuild must dispatch SaladMsg values when a user builds a salad. Then, update must route SaladMsg values to updateSalad so it can update the nested salad state.

Look back at viewBuild. Technically, it already dispatches SaladMsg values. For example, the first radio button dispatches SetBase with the onClick handler. Recall that SetBase now belongs to SaladMsg instead of Msg.

Examine viewBuild's type, though, and you'll notice a problem. The return type is Html Msg, which means viewBuild must dispatch Msg values. But you're trying to dispatch SaladMsg values also. Elm's type system won't allow this.

You can fix the issue by making a new Msg value that *wraps over* SaladMsg values. Add a new SaladMsg value to Msg like so:

```
type Msg
    = SaladMsg SaladMsg
    -- other Msg constructors
```

You're probably confused why SaladMsg appears twice, so let's break it down. The first SaladMsg is a *new constructor* for the Msg *type*. The second SaladMsg is the SaladMsg *type* you created a moment ago. You can give each the same name because one is a *value* and the other is a *type*.

Many Elm developers use this same name convention, but you can give the Msg value a different name such as SaladMsgWrapper if you want.

Now that you've added a SaladMsg wrapper, let's fix viewBuild with it. While we're in the neighborhood, we'll fix accessing salad-related fields through model.salad as well. Update the first radio button's checked and onClick attributes like so:

```
, checked (model.salad.base == Lettuce)
, onClick (SaladMsg (SetBase Lettuce))
```

Now you access the salad base through model.salad.base. Also, you wrap the SetBase Lettuce value inside the SaladMsg wrapper. Repeat this process for the other salad base radio buttons.

Skip over salad toppings for a moment and repeat the previous steps for the dressing radio buttons. For example, the first dressing radio button should now have these checked and onClick attributes:

```
, checked (model.salad.dressing == NoDressing)
, onClick (SaladMsg (SetDressing NoDressing))
```

Return back to salad toppings. You'll wrap the ToggleTopping values with the SaladMsg wrapper differently. Update the first topping checkbox to have these checked and onCheck attributes:

```
, checked (Set.member (toppingToString Tomatoes) model.salad.toppings)
, onCheck (SaladMsg << ToggleTopping Tomatoes)
```

You use the backward composition operator << to chain together the Toggle-Topping and SaladMsg constructor functions. The << operator calls ToggleTopping first. Remember that ToggleTopping accepts two arguments, a Topping and a Bool. You've partially applied Topping, so you receive back a function waiting on a Bool. When a user checks the checkbox, Elm supplies the Bool argument. This creates a ToggleTopping value which the << operator pipes into the SaladMsg wrapper function to create a final Msg.SaladMsg value. The << operator essentially builds a function like this for you.

```
toggleToppingMsg : Topping -> Bool -> Msg
toggleToppingMsg topping add =
    SaladMsg (ToggleTopping topping add)
```

Fix the remaining topping checkboxes similarly. Now you can address the update function. Insert this branch at the top of update's case expression:

```
SaladMsg saladMsg ->
    ( { model | salad = updateSalad saladMsg model.salad }
    , Cmd.none
    )
```

Remember I said that update will still know about salad messages. You give the Elm Architecture the update function through the main constant at the bottom of the file. update receives all dispatched messages and must route messages to updateSalad, which doesn't directly receive its messages. So, update unwraps the SaladMsg *wrapper* to store the underlying SaladMsg *value* in a saladMsg constant.

Then, update passes saladMsg and model.salad into updateSalad. The updateSalad function returns a new Salad which you use to update model.salad.

Finally, let's address the broken viewConfirmation and encodeOrder functions. Fix each function by accessing salad fields through model.salad. Replace model.base with model.salad.base, model.toppings with model.salad.toppings, and model.dressing with model.salad.dressing.

Verify your code matches SaladBuilder03.elm from the code/larger/examples directory in this book's code downloads. Start the application to make sure it still compiles and runs correctly.

## Nested State: An Epilogue

Using nested salad state helped you clean up the code in many ways. You could reason about the separation between the main model and the salad state. You could also create a separate SaladMsg type and updateSalad function to simplify the update function's responsibilities.

You encountered some issues, though. View functions such as viewBuild and viewConfirmation have to display salad- and contact-related info together in a common layout. You couldn't separate responsibilities easily and had to reach into model.salad to access salad-related fields. That can get annoying.

If you continue using nested state as this application grows, that annoyance could multiply. You could also run into worse problems. Imagine if Saladise wanted to let users request delivery and provide payment details. You could end up with deeply nested fields like model.delivery.payment.address.line1.

If you had an updateDelivery function, you might become stuck with code like this just to update line1.

```
updateDelivery msg delivery =
    case msg of
        SetLine1 line1 ->
```

```
let
    payment = delivery.payment
    address = payment.address
in
{ delivery
    | payment =
        { payment
            | address = { address | line1 = line1 }
        }
}
```

You would have to pull each nested record into a separate constant for record update syntax to work. Nested record update syntax is awkward and hard to understand. You could fix it with more nested update* helper functions, but that introduces more indirection that could make the code harder to follow.

My advice is to avoid nesting state or use it sparingly like you did with Salad. If you have to nest state, try not to go more than one level deep.

# Use Extensible Records

Now that you've organized the salad state, you need to handle the contact-related state. You've seen the pitfalls of nested state. In this section, you will learn a different approach by using extensible records to create a Contact type without nesting state. Yet, you will still build a separate updateContact function that only changes contact-related fields.

## Extract the Contact

You need to make a Contact type alias, but it will differ from the type aliases you've made previously. Below the Salad type alias, add this code:

larger/examples/SaladBuilder04.elm
```
type alias Contact c =
    { c
        | name : String
        , email : String
        , phone : String
    }
```

This is an *extensible record type*. An extensible record resembles an interface. Any record that has all of the extensible record's fields is an instance of the extensible record type. For example, the Contact extensible record declares that *any record* with name, email, and phone String fields is a Contact.

The beginning { c | syntax says that any other fields in the record have a collective type of c. Since c is lowercase, it's a type variable. Note that you have to include the type variable in the type alias portion too: type alias Contact c.

This record is a Contact.

```
{ name = "Jeremy", email = "j@example.com", phone = "123" }
```

This record with an additional age field is also a Contact.

```
{ name = "Tucker", email = "t@example.com", phone = "123", age = 11 }
```

This record *isn't* a Contact because it lacks the phone field.

```
{ name = "Sally", email = "s@example.com" }
```

Recall that you must modularize contact information in the salad builder application. You need to create separate contact-related message values and an updateContact function to handle a Contact record. The Contact record will actually be the Model itself. Because the Model has name, email, and phone String fields, it is technically a Contact. Using extensible records instead of nested state might seem counterintuitive to modularizing the application. You'll see why it's useful in a second.

For now, let's make the separate contact message values. Create a ContactMsg type below SaladMsg and move SetName, SetEmail, and SetPhone from Msg to ContactMsg:

```
type ContactMsg
    = SetName String
    | SetEmail String
    | SetPhone String
```

Similar to what you did with salads, create a ContactMsg *wrapper* inside Msg to wrap over ContactMsg *values*:

```
type Msg
    -- other Msg values
    | ContactMsg ContactMsg
    -- other Msg values
```

## Wire Up the Contact

Now let's explore why we want an extensible record for contact state. Add the updateContact function definition above update like so:

```
updateContact : ContactMsg -> Contact c -> Contact c
updateContact msg contact =
    case msg of
```

The updateContact function takes ContactMsg and Contact c arguments and returns Contact c. Note that you must include the c type variable with Contact. Based on the type annotation, updateContact accepts any record that is a Contact. That means you can pass in a Model record. You'll do that in a moment, actually.

Finish defining updateContact by moving the SetName, SetEmail, and SetPhone branches from update. Rename model to contact and remove the tuples and commands. Your case expression should look like this inside updateContact:

```
case msg of
    SetName name ->
        { contact | name = name }
    -- other branches
```

Next, wire up updateContact inside update. Add a ContactMsg branch under the SaladMsg branch like so:

```
ContactMsg contactMsg ->
    ( updateContact contactMsg model
    , Cmd.none
    )
```

You call updateContact with the unwrapped contactMsg and the model. Then, you use the return value of updateContact as the new model. The updateContact function only changes contact-related fields. It won't modify or remove other model fields.

Extensible records come from the concept of *narrowing types*. Narrowing types means limiting functions to only the arguments they really need. You didn't have to make a Contact type. The updateContact function could instead receive Model in its type annotation. But then it could access non-contact-related fields, which would violate separation of concerns.

Instead, you narrowed updateContact's type to only what it needs, a Contact record. Extensible records offer the benefits of modularization and separation of concerns without the awkwardness of nested fields.

Let's finish this section by fixing viewBuild. Similar to the SaladMsg values, you need to wrap ContactMsg values with the ContactMsg wrapper. Wrap SetName, SetEmail, and SetPhone with ContactMsg by using the << operator. For example, the onInput handler for the name text input should look like this:

```
, onInput (ContactMsg << SetName)
```

You need the << operator because Elm supplies the String argument when a user types in the text input. So, Elm calls SetName with the String argument and passes the result on to ContactMsg to satisfy the Html Msg type.

And that's it. You don't have to fix any other functions because you didn't nest the contact state. Flat state avoids many of the nested state problems you discovered earlier.

Extensible records and flat state still have a minor downside. The Model had to know it was also a Contact by designating its own name, email, and phone fields.

Creating flat Model types and initial state with many fields can be cumbersome. But I think that's a fair trade-off to avoid nested state code complexity.

Regardless, in larger applications, you might find that a balance of nested state and extensible records works best for you. Feel each option out and choose the least awkward approach that encourages readability and reduces code complexity.

Ensure your code matches SaladBuilder04.elm from the code/larger/examples directory in this book's code downloads and that your application still runs. Onward to eliminate code duplication.

## Remove View Duplication

Now that you've split Msg, Model, and update into manageable pieces, you need to return to the view layer. In this section, you will create reusable helper functions to eliminate the excessive code duplication in viewBuild and make it easier to create new form inputs in the future.

### Create a Reusable Section

Removing the input duplication will be tricky, so let's start with the form sections. Notice that you repeat a section tag with a "salad-section" class name. Each of these sections has an h2 heading and form input content. First, you extract the creation of a form section into a reusable function. Add a viewSection function above viewBuild like so:

```
larger/examples/SaladBuilder05.elm
viewSection : String -> List (Html msg) -> Html msg
viewSection heading children =
    section [ class "salad-section" ]
        (h2 [] [ text heading ] :: children)
```

The viewSection function accepts two arguments, a String heading and a List of Html msg children. Then, it creates the section tag and uses the children argument as the list of child elements. Notice that you prepend the h2 tag to the list of children with the :: operator. This allows viewSection to display the h2 tag as a sibling of the other child elements.

Next, modify viewBuild to use viewSection. Replace every section tag with a call to viewSection. Make sure you remove the h2 tag and use its text as the first argument to viewSection. For example, the first section should become this:

```
, viewSection "1. Select Base"
    [ label [ class "select-option" ]
        [ input
            -- remaining code for selecting base
```

## Create a Reusable Topping Option

Now let's work on the form inputs. You'll start with the simplest case, the topping checkboxes. Each checkbox repeats the same pattern. It has a label with a "select-option" class. Inside the label is the actual checkbox input and the topping name passed into text. The checkbox input duplicates the same logic for the checked and onCheck attributes.

Pull all the duplication out into a reusable function. Create a viewToppingOption function above viewBuild like so:

```
viewToppingOption : String -> Topping -> Set String -> Html Msg
viewToppingOption toppingLabel topping toppings =
    label [ class "select-option" ]
        [ input
            [ type_ "checkbox"
            , checked (Set.member (toppingToString topping) toppings)
            , onCheck (SaladMsg << ToggleTopping topping)
            ]
            []
        , text toppingLabel
        ]
```

You accept a String toppingLabel argument and pass it into the label's text. For the checked attribute, you use the topping and toppings arguments to determine if the topping is selected. Finally, for the onCheck attribute, you call ToggleTopping with the topping argument and compose the partially applied function into the SaladMsg wrapper like before.

Before you update viewBuild, let's create another helper function to use viewToppingOption to consolidate the topping options in one place. Add a viewSelectToppings function below viewToppingOption:

```
viewSelectToppings : Set String -> Html Msg
viewSelectToppings toppings =
    div []
        [ viewToppingOption "Tomatoes" Tomatoes toppings
        , viewToppingOption "Cucumbers" Cucumbers toppings
        , viewToppingOption "Onions" Onions toppings
        ]
```

You accept the Set of toppings as an argument and call viewToppingOption for each topping. Replace all the content in viewBuild's topping section with one call to viewSelectToppings:

```
, viewSection "2. Select Toppings"
    [ viewSelectToppings model.salad.toppings ]
```

You just eliminated a huge chunk of code and made viewBuild slightly easier to navigate. Now you can quickly find where you display topping options.

## Create a Reusable Radio Button

You will apply the previous solution to radio buttons. However, you will create a more general reusable function that can accommodate salad base and dressing options.

Look at one of the radio buttons in viewBuild. Each radio button closely mimics a checkbox. It has a label with text and contains an actual radio button input with duplicated logic for the checked and onClick attributes. Remove the duplication by creating a reusable viewRadioOption function. Add its definition below viewSection like so:

```
viewRadioOption :
    String -> value -> (value -> msg) -> String -> value -> Html msg
viewRadioOption radioName selectedValue tagger optionLabel value =
    label [ class "select-option" ]
        [ input
            [ type_ "radio"
            , name radioName
            , checked (value == selectedValue)
            , onClick (tagger value)
            ]
            []
        , text optionLabel
        ]
```

OK, viewRadioOption's type annotation is a doozy. Let's process it one argument at a time:

- radioName is a String that you pass into the name attribute. Recall that an HTML radio button uses the name attribute to group related radio buttons.

- selectedValue is the currently selected value for the group of related radio buttons. Its type is value, which is a type variable, so it can be whatever you want. You compare selectedValue with the value *argument* to check or uncheck the radio button.

- tagger is a function that accepts a value type and returns a msg type. The msg type is also a type variable, so you can use whatever type of message you want. You call tagger with the value argument to create a message for the onClick handler. This mirrors calling SetBase with Lettuce.

- optionLabel is the String argument to the text node inside the label tag.

- value is the radio button's value. It uses the value *type variable* for its type.

- Html msg is the return type where msg is a type variable. The msg type variable depends on whatever type of message tagger produces.

The viewRadioOption might seem complex, but it's highly reusable. Because you added the value type variable, you can use this function with Base and Dressing values. You can even use this function in the future with other values or message types.

Similar to your code for toppings, add functions to co-locate the radio button options for the salad base and dressing. Create a viewSelectBase function under viewRadioOption like this:

```
viewSelectBase : Base -> Html Msg
viewSelectBase currentBase =
    let
        viewBaseOption =
            viewRadioOption "base" currentBase (SaladMsg << SetBase)
    in
    div []
        [ viewBaseOption "Lettuce" Lettuce
        , viewBaseOption "Spinach" Spinach
        , viewBaseOption "Spring Mix" SpringMix
        ]
```

The viewSelectBase function accepts the currently selected base as a currentBase argument. You use a let expression and partially apply viewRadioOption with a few arguments to create a viewBaseOption function. Essentially, you're configuring viewRadioOption into a reusable viewBaseOption function that only works with salad base options.

First, you pass in a radio name of "base". Then, you pass in currentBase as selectedValue and (SaladMsg << SetBase) as tagger. This configuration lets you avoid retyping the same arguments, especially the radio name which you could mistype. Finally, you call viewBaseOption with unique arguments to make each radio button.

Repeat this process to create a viewSelectDressing function:

```
viewSelectDressing : Dressing -> Html Msg
viewSelectDressing currentDressing =
    let
        viewDressingOption =
            viewRadioOption
                "dressing" currentDressing (SaladMsg << SetDressing)
    in
    div []
        [ viewDressingOption "None" NoDressing
        , viewDressingOption "Italian" Italian
```

```
            , viewDressingOption "Raspberry Vinaigrette" RaspberryVinaigrette
            , viewDressingOption "Oil and Vinegar" OilVinegar
            ]
```

Note how viewSelectDressing mirrors viewSelectBase with the difference being you use dressing-related values and messages.

Replace the appropriate radio buttons inside viewBuild with viewSelectBase and viewSelectDressing. The salad base section should look like this:

```
, viewSection "1. Select Base"
    [ viewSelectBase model.salad.base ]
```

The dressing section should look like this:

```
, viewSection "3. Select Dressing"
    [ viewSelectDressing model.salad.dressing ]
```

You're making this code look really nice. You've transformed viewBuild into a very readable function.

## Create a Reusable Text Input

The remaining duplication in viewBuild lives in the contact section. Let's apply what you've done with checkboxes and radio buttons to build a reusable text input function. Under viewSelectToppings, add a viewTextInput function:

```
viewTextInput : String -> String -> (String -> msg) -> Html msg
viewTextInput inputLabel inputValue tagger =
    div [ class "text-input" ]
        [ label []
            [ div [] [ text (inputLabel ++ ":") ]
            , input
                [ type_ "text"
                , value inputValue
                , onInput tagger
                ]
                []
            ]
        ]
```

The viewTextInput function accepts three arguments. You use the inputLabel argument with the nested div tag to display a descriptive label. Then, you pass the inputValue argument into the text input's value attribute to display the current value.

Lastly, you have a tagger argument. The tagger argument resembles viewRadioOption's tagger argument. It's a function that accepts a String argument and returns a msg. You use it with onInput; it receives whatever text the user types in.

Use viewTextInput input to consolidate the text inputs inside a new viewContact function above viewBuild:

```
viewContact : Contact a -> Html ContactMsg
viewContact contact =
    div []
        [ viewTextInput "Name" contact.name SetName
        , viewTextInput "Email" contact.email SetEmail
        , viewTextInput "Phone" contact.phone SetPhone
        ]
```

This function differs from the other field-consolidating functions. You take contact as an argument but return Html ContactMsg instead of Html Msg. You call viewTextInput with a label, value, and ContactMsg value. You no longer compose the ContactMsg values into the ContactMsg wrapper with the << operator. Let's integrate viewContact into viewBuild to see why we're doing this.

Replace the text inputs inside the contact section of viewBuild with a call to viewContact: You can pass in the whole model because it accepts a Contact argument. Make sure you don't accidentally delete the send button inside the contact section. The contact section should look like this:

```
, viewSection "4. Enter Contact Info"
    [ viewContact model
    , button
        [ class "send-button"
        , disabled (not (isValid model))
        , onClick Send
        ]
        [ text "Send Order" ]
    ]
```

If you left this code unaltered, you would have a type error. The viewBuild function produces messages of type Msg, but viewContact produces messages of type ContactMsg. You could fix this by composing the ContactMsg values into the ContactMsg wrapper. But, I want to highlight another option to fix this via the Html.map function. Update the viewContact call to look like this:

```
Html.map ContactMsg (viewContact model)
```

You pass the ContactMsg wrapper and the Html ContactMsg result of viewContact into Html.map.

The Html.map function accepts a function argument and applies the function to the message values of Html. Essentially, when a user types in one of the contact fields, Html.map will intercept the ContactMsg *value* and pass it into the ContactMsg *wrapper*. Then, it passes the wrapped message on to your update function.

Think of Html.map in terms of List.map. Imagine that the Html type is like a list. If the list contained ContactMsg values, then you would wrap them like so.

```
List.map ContactMsg [ SetName "Jeremy", SetEmail "j@example.com" ]
-- returns [ ContactMsg (SetName "Jeremy")
--         , ContactMsg (SetEmail "j@example.com")
--         ]
```

Html.map enables you to write more modular code. It allowed you to write a viewContact function that only cared about contact-related code. It didn't need to know about the Msg type. The main application code had to integrate view-Contact with other code through Html.map to satisfy the type system.

You could apply this approach to other functions such as viewSelectBase if you wanted. Instead of directly composing SaladMsg values with the SaladMsg wrapper, you could call Html.map with the SaladMsg wrapper and the result of viewSelectBase.

Great work! You cleaned up and organized viewBuild immensely. Now you can easily add new features in the future. Also, because you narrowed types with the helper functions you wrote, you won't struggle to pinpoint the source of bugs when debugging. For example, if there's a problem with contact fields, you can focus on functions that accept a contact argument only.

Check your code matches SaladBuilder05.elm from the code/larger/examples directory in this book's code downloads, and verify your application still compiles.

# Prevent Invalid States

You can drastically improve the salad builder's maintainability with one final tweak. The application uses four fields to represent view state: building, sending, success, and error. In this section, you will see how invalid configurations of these fields could lead to ambiguity and bugs. Then, you will fix the issue by consolidating the fields into one.

## Combine the Fields

Here's the problem: the *four* view state fields encapsulate *one* possible view state. Inside viewStep, you check the fields in an arbitrary order with if-else to pick what to display. First, you check sending and then building. You never bother checking the success field and you assume it's True in the else branch.

That means you could display viewConfirmation if sending, building, and success were all False. Nothing stops the Model from that configuration. It's up to you to prevent invalid configurations in initialModel and the update function.

This could be a huge problem in a larger codebase. You would have to write thorough tests to verify invalid states can't occur. That puts a lot of pressure on you as a developer. Instead of inviting possible human error and bugs, you can create a better view state representation with the type system and make invalid states impossible. Above the Base custom type, add this Step custom type:

larger/examples/SaladBuilder06.elm
```
type Step
    = Building (Maybe Error)
    | Sending
    | Confirmation
```

The Step type represents each view state as a separate value. Building represents building a salad, Sending represents sending the order, and Confirmation represents the order confirmation. Building also includes a Maybe Error parameter because you only display errors when building a salad.

Replace the four view state fields with a new step field in the Model type:

```
type alias Model =
    { step : Step
    , -- salad and contact fields
    }
```

Do the same with initialModel. Give the step field an initial Building Nothing value because the application starts off building without an error:

```
initialModel =
    { step = Building Nothing
    , -- salad and contact values
    }
```

Now change viewStep to pattern match on model.step like so:

```
case model.step of
    Building error ->
        viewBuild error model

    Sending ->
        viewSending

    Confirmation ->
        viewConfirmation model
```

You call viewBuild when step is Building, viewSending when step is Sending, and viewConfirmation when step is Confirmation. In the Building branch, you also unwrap the error and pass it into viewBuild as a new argument. Update viewBuild to use the error argument:

```
viewBuild : Maybe Error -> Model -> Html Msg
viewBuild error model =
    div []
        [ viewError error
        , -- sections
        ]
```

Next, modify the Send and SubmissionResult message branches in the update function to only change the step field:

```
Send ->
    let
        newModel =
            { model | step = Sending }
    in
    ( newModel, send newModel )

SubmissionResult (Ok _) ->
    ( { model | step = Confirmation }
    , Cmd.none
    )

SubmissionResult (Err _) ->
    let
        errorMessage =
            "There was a problem sending your order. Please try again."
    in
    ( { model | step = Building (Just errorMessage) }
    , Cmd.none
    )
```

You greatly simplified those branches. For Send, you set step to Sending. For SubmissionResult (Ok _), you set step to Confirmation. For SubmissionResult (Err _), you set step back to Building along with an error message inside Just.

That's all you need to do. You reduced four fields to one and created a custom type that encodes the exact possible view states. You prevented possible bugs. And you can more easily test and scale this code. Whenever possible, use the type system to prevent invalid states from happening.

Verify your code matches SaladBuilder06.elm from the code/larger/examples directory in this book's code downloads. Start the application to check that it still compiles and works.

## What You Learned

Whoa, what a whirlwind of changes. You drastically improved the salad builder. Saladise compliments you on your changes and wants you to help with future features.

Let's recap what you accomplished. You organized the view function into separate functions. Then, you simplified the number of messages by combining them into parameterized messages. You used nested state and extensible records to modularize handling salad and contact state. You created form input helper functions to eliminate code duplication. Finally, you consolidated separate fields to prevent invalid state configurations. Using these patterns, you can now easily scale and maintain large Elm applications of your own.

You could improve the salad builder even more. We didn't address the table duplication in viewConfirmation. Try fixing it on your own. Write a helper function for creating a table row. Then, write a helper function for building a table from a list of labels and values. (Hint: you'll probably want a list of tuple pairs.) If you need some help, peek at the SaladBuilderFixed.elm file from the code/larger/examples directory in this book's code downloads.

Now that you can manage applications of any size, we can explore debugging and deploying those applications. In the next chapter, you will learn how to speed up your development time and debug and deploy Elm applications with fantastic tooling.

# CHAPTER 7

# Develop, Debug, and Deploy with Powerful Tooling

In the previous chapter, you used helper functions, message wrappers, nested state, and extensible records to create a more maintainable application that will easily scale in the future. Your productivity increases with more maintainable applications because you spend less time refactoring. However, your productivity can only go so far with application structure.

In this chapter, you will master tools and concepts that will help you debug code more easily, develop faster, and deploy your own Elm applications without hesitation.

The Elm compiler provides invaluable feedback at compile time, but you need meaningful feedback for debugging runtime bugs too. You will use the Debug module to inspect values at runtime. Manually compiling code also steals valuable development time. You will speed up your development time with tools such as Elm Reactor and Create Elm App. Finally, you will automate building and deploying production-ready Elm code with Create Elm App.

## Debug Code with the Debug Module

Using Elm prevents tons of common bugs that normally pop up in JavaScript. In JavaScript, you can call functions with the wrong number and types of arguments, leading to runtime exceptions and type-coercion bugs. The Elm compiler safeguards you from those problems through static types.

However, not all bugs come from static type mismatches. Incorrect business logic can also lead to bugs, even in Elm applications. We can't ship buggy applications to our users, so an ability to debug bad code is critical.

Debugging code in Elm differs from most other languages with traditional debuggers. Debuggers that pause the world make sense in imperative languages. In imperative languages, functions and methods typically have more responsibilities; data mutates, and side effects are common. Imperative languages require a debugger that can step through each statement to digest how application code progresses.

In Elm, debugging is simpler. Elm code is mostly a string of function calls. Because Elm is expressive, functions tend to be smaller and have fewer responsibilities. We also don't have to worry about side effects or mutation. And honestly, most bugs are type mismatches and null reference errors, which the Elm compiler prevents. We don't need to pause the world for Elm.

Most bugs in Elm applications will originate from incorrect logic, so you only need tools to inspect data. In this section, you will start with the Debug module, which lets you inspect values inside functions. You will use the Debug.log and Debug.todo functions to debug a simple application for printing a dog's description.

## Log Info with Debug.log

You already used Debug.log in Chapter 5, Go Real-Time with WebSockets, on page 85 when you printed raw WebSocket data to the console. Just to refresh, the Debug.log function takes a String label and a value to print to the JavaScript console. The value can be any type. The Debug.log function also returns the value so you can inspect it and continue to use it later.

Open up the Elm REPL and run these commands to try the Debug.log function out:

```
> Debug.log "hello" "world"
hello: "world"
"world" : String

> Debug.log "dog" { name = "Tucker" }
dog: { name = "Tucker" }
{ name = "Tucker" } : { name : String }

> Debug.log "maybe" (Just 42)
maybe: Just 42
Just 42 : Maybe number
```

Notice in each example that Debug.log prints both arguments to the console and returns the second argument back. For example, when you call Debug.log with "hello" and "world", it prints hello: "world" and returns back the string "world".

The Debug.log function is incredibly useful for printing intermediate results with the pipe operator too. Try this example in the REPL:

```
> list = List.range 1 10
[1,2,3,4,5,6,7,8,9,10] : List Int

> list
|    |> List.map (\n -> n * 2)
|    |> Debug.log "doubled"
|    |> List.filter (\n -> n > 6)
|    |> Debug.log "filtered"
|    |> List.map (\n -> n * n)
doubled: [2,4,6,8,10,12,14,16,18,20]
filtered: [8,10,12,14,16,18,20]
[64,100,144,196,256,324,400] : List Int
```

You create a list from 1 to 10 via the List.range function. Then, you double every number in the list with List.map, keep numbers greater than 6 with List.filter, and square the remaining numbers. The List.filter function keeps or removes values in a list. It takes a function that returns True or False for every item in the list. If the function returns True, then it keeps the value. If the function returns False, then it drops the value. Finally, it returns the new filtered list.

With Debug.log, you can ensure that the intermediate lists are in fact doubled and filtered as you expect. The intermediate lists pass into Debug.log as the second argument, thanks to the pipe operator.

## Inspect Decoded JSON

The Debug.log function really shines for inspecting JSON decoder results. Recall that decoding JSON returns a Result type which can succeed (Ok) or fail (Err). You can use Debug.log to discover why decoding failed by inspecting the Err value of Result.

Let's build a simple application that decodes a JSON representation of a dog and use Debug.log to inspect the Result. Start by creating a new directory called debugging. Inside the debugging directory, initialize a new Elm project.

```
elm init
```

Then, install the elm/json and NoRedInk/elm-json-decode-pipeline packages.

```
elm install elm/json
elm install NoRedInk/elm-json-decode-pipeline
```

Create a new file called Debugging.elm inside the src directory generated by elm init. Declare the Debugging module and import the necessary dependencies like so:

develop-debug-deploy/Debugging01.elm
```
module Debugging exposing (main)

import Html exposing (Html, text)
import Json.Decode as Json
import Json.Decode.Pipeline exposing (required)
```

The import...as syntax lets you import and shorten long module names. Here, you import Json.Decode and rename it to Json. This lets you use qualified function calls with Json instead of typing out Json.Decode. You can alias a module to whatever name you prefer, so you could have renamed Json.Decode to something shorter like J.

Next, you'll need a static type alias and decoder for a dog record type. Add them below the imported modules:

```
type alias Dog =
    { name : String
    , age : Int
    }

dogDecoder : Json.Decoder Dog
dogDecoder =
    Json.succeed Dog
        |> required "name" Json.string
        |> required "age" Json.int
```

To keep the application straightforward, you will use a static JSON string to represent a dog. Add a jsonDog constant under the dogDecoder:

```
jsonDog : String
jsonDog =
    """
    {
      "name": "Tucker",
      "age": 11
    }
    """
```

Underneath the jsonDog constant, add a decodedDog constant which actually decodes jsonDog with the dogDecoder:

```
decodedDog : Result Json.Error Dog
decodedDog =
    Json.decodeString dogDecoder jsonDog
```

Note that decodedDog has the type Result Json.Decode.Error Dog. Recall that the first type variable of Result is the error type wrapped by the Err constructor. If decoding fails, you will receive a Json.Decode.Error inside Err.

Finally, let's render the decodedDog. Below decodedDog, add a function called viewDog that displays the dog's name and age:

```
viewDog : Dog -> Html msg
viewDog dog =
    text <|
        dog.name
```

```
        ++ " is "
        ++ String.fromInt dog.age
        ++ " years old."
```

Notice that you use a new operator <| known as the *backward pipe operator*. It passes in the right operand as the last argument to the left operand. It has a lower associativity than the ++ operator, so the concatenated string to the right will be the entire argument to the text function.

The <| operator is mainly useful as an alternative to grouping expressions together with parentheses to avoid associativity problems. You could have written the viewDog function like this.

```
text
    (dog.name
        ++ " is "
        ++ String.fromInt dog.age
        ++ " years old."
    )
```

Grouping multiline expressions with parentheses is arguably harder to read and write, so most Elm developers opt for the <| operator in these situations.

To bridge the gap between decodedDog and the viewDog function, create the final main constant. Add the following code underneath the viewDog function:

```
main : Html msg
main =
    case Debug.log "decodedDog" decodedDog of
        Ok dog ->
            viewDog dog

        Err _ ->
            text "ERROR: Couldn't decode dog."
```

You call Debug.log with the label "decodedDog" and the decodedDog constant. Remember that Debug.log returns its second argument, so you use pattern matching on decodedDog. If decoding succeeds, then you call viewDog with the decoded dog record. Otherwise, you display a generic error message.

Be sure your file matches code/develop-debug-deploy/Debugging01.elm from the book code downloads. Compile Debugging.elm to a file called debugging.html and open it in your browser with dev tools open:

```
elm make --output debugging.html src/Debugging.elm
```

Decoding the dog should succeed, and you should see the message "Tucker is 11 years old." Inside your console, you should see the Debug.log message decodedDog: Ok { age = 11, name = "Tucker" }.

## Inspect Failed Decodings

The Debug.log function is fine for inspecting successful values, but you really want to use it for debugging failures. Let's intentionally break the JSON and decoder to see what types of messages Debug.log will print.

Model a scenario where you accidentally create the wrong decoder and record type. Assume that you thought the age field was a String instead of an Int. Change the age field in the Dog type alias to be String and the age field in dogDecoder to be string. Also, temporarily remove String.fromInt in viewDog.

```
type alias Dog =
    { name : String
    , age : String
    }

dogDecoder =
    decode Dog
        |> required "name" Json.string
        |> required "age" Json.string

viewDog dog =
    text <|
        dog.name
            ++ " is "
            ++ dog.age
            ++ " years old."
```

Recompile your application and refresh your browser. Now you should see "ERROR: Couldn't decode dog." in the browser. More importantly, you should see something like decodedDog: Err (Field "age" (Failure "Expecting a STRING" <internals>)) in the console.

With Debug.log, you can inspect the error message wrapped by the Err constructor to see *why* a decoder failed. In this case, the error message states that the decoder expected a String for the age field.

This is immensely useful if you happen to misread an API's documentation and build the wrong decoder. While you are developing an application, you can use Debug.log to help you fix problems with a decoder. To fix the problem here, you would revert the changes to Dog and dogDecoder to make age an Int field.

An API could also send unexpected data that lacks an expected field, or is even invalid JSON altogether. For these scenarios, the decoding process will create other helpful error messages for Debug.log to display.

Try some other situations to see the messages that Result and Debug.log can provide. Use these suggestions to change the jsonDog constant and inspect the console messages from Debug.log after recompiling. Your error messages may differ depending on your chosen browser. The error messages shown came from Chrome.

- Remove the "name" field

  - Expected message: decodedDog: Err (Failure "Expecting an OBJECT with a field named `name`" <internals>)

- Wrap the object in an array

  - Expected message: decodedDog: Err (Failure "Expecting an OBJECT with a field named `age`" <internals>)

- Remove the closing curly brace }

  - Expected message: decodedDog: Err (Failure "This is not valid JSON! Unexpected end of JSON input" <internals>)

- Remove the quotes surrounding "Tucker"

  - Expected message: decodedDog: Err (Failure "This is not valid JSON! Unexpected token T in JSON at position 21" <internals>)

These messages mostly help you pinpoint the exact problem with your decoder or with an API. I admit that some of them are definitely not as enlightening as others. For example, when you wrapped the JSON object in an array, the error message did not indicate that the JSON was an array instead of an object.

Alternatively, you can transform the Json.Decode.Error into a String with Json.Decode.errorToString. This function inserts newlines into the returned string, so you may find it difficult to parse in the console from Debug.log. In that case you can temporarily print the error inside a <pre> tag like this.

```
main =
    case decodedDog of
        Ok dog ->
            viewDog dog

        Err error ->
            Html.pre []
                [ text (Json.errorToString error) ]
```

Feel free to try out the previous error-generating changes to the jsonDog with the above suggestion to see more detail in the error messages.

## Iterate with Debug.todo

The Debug.todo function is another great tool for debugging Elm applications. It lets you add placeholders to parts of your application before you're ready to implement them. This allows you to test the rest of your application without worrying about one particular function or branch in a case expression.

One caveat here is that Debug.todo intentionally crashes your program. I know I said that Elm has no runtime exceptions, but this is an—uh— exception. Debug.todo crashes your application in order to provide valuable information about the context at the crash site, which you'll see in a moment.

This probably sounds a lot like throwing an error in JavaScript, but I'll reiterate that Debug.todo is *only* for debugging during development. Instead of throwing errors, you should model failures with pure values like Result and Maybe. You can't even catch errors created with Debug.todo in Elm anyway.

Let's try out Debug.todo by having it decode a new breed field for the dog. A dog breed is mostly a finite representation, so you could implement it with a custom type. We'll keep it simple by only introducing two breeds. Add a Breed custom type above the Dog type alias like so:

```
type Breed
    = Sheltie
    | Poodle
```

Then, add a breed field to the Dog type:

```
type alias Dog =
    { name : String
    , age : Int
    , breed : Breed
    }
```

Inside jsonDog, you'll have to represent the breed with a string because JSON doesn't have custom types. Update jsonDog, like this:

```
{
  "name": "Tucker",
  "age": 11,
  "breed": "Sheltie"
}
```

To convert the string breed into a static constructor, you'll need a new decoder for Breed. Underneath the Dog type alias, create a decodeBreed function that takes a String and returns a Decoder Breed:

```
decodeBreed : String -> Json.Decoder Breed
decodeBreed breed =
```

```
    case Debug.log "breed" breed of
        "Sheltie" ->
            Json.succeed Sheltie

        _ ->
            Debug.todo "Handle other breeds in decodeBreed"
```

Inside decodeBreed, the case expression checks the String breed and returns an appropriate decoder. You also inspect the breed with Debug.log.

In the first branch, decodeBreed returns Json.succeed Sheltie. succeed creates a literal decoder with the provided value.

Notice that decodeBreed only handles Sheltie right now. It ignores other breeds with a wildcard match and Debug.todo. Debug.todo takes a string message to print to the console after crashing your application to provide some context around the todo. This lets you focus on ensuring that Sheltie works before adding any other breeds.

Let's integrate decodeBreed with dogDecoder next. Add this new piping operation to the bottom of dogDecoder:

```
|> required "breed" (Json.string |> Json.andThen decodeBreed)
```

Note that the decoder you pass into required is wrapped in parentheses. The JSON breed value starts off as Json.string and then pipes into the decodeBreed function via the Json.andThen function. Here's the type signature for Json.andThen.

```
andThen : (a -> Decoder b) -> Decoder a -> Decoder b
```

Json.andThen lets you *replace* the current decoder with a new decoder. It takes a function that returns a Decoder, which is the decodeBreed function in this case. Then, it takes an existing Decoder, unwraps the decoded value, and passes the value into the previously provided decoder function. Whatever the provided decoder function returns becomes the new decoded value. In this case, Json.andThen passes the String breed into the decodeBreed function and then uses the return value as the final decoded value for the JSON breed field.

Update viewDog to display the breed in the dog description:

```
text <|
    dog.name
        ++ " the "
        ++ breedToString dog.breed
        ++ " is "
        ++ String.fromInt dog.age
        ++ " years old."
```

You add in the string " the " and dog.breed converted to a string via breedToString. The breedToString function doesn't exist yet. Add it below the Breed custom type, like this:

```
breedToString : Breed -> String
breedToString breed =
    case breed of
        Sheltie ->
            "Sheltie"

        _ ->
            Debug.todo "Handle other breeds in breedToString"
```

Here you only handle the Sheltie constructor, thanks to Debug.todo.

Make sure your code matches code/develop-debug-deploy/Debugging02.elm and recompile. You should see the updated dog description "Tucker the Sheltie is 11 years old." You should also see breed: "Sheltie" in the console from the Debug.log you added in decodeBreed.

Let's have Debug.todo run in decodeBreed now. Change the breed field in jsonDog to "Poodle". Recompile and check your console. You should see breed: "Poodle" from Debug.log and message. (I have manually formatted the message to limit the line length.)

```
decodedDog: Err (
  Failure "This is not valid JSON!
  TODO in module `Debugging` on line 37
  Handle other breeds in decodeBreed" <internals>
)
```

Notice the decodedDog tag in the message. The message you see actually comes from Debug.log in the main constant. Debug.log informs us that the "Poodle" breed value got through, and Debug.todo lets us know that you're in the context of handling other breeds in decodeBreed on line 37 (or whatever line number your message included).

When Elm's native JavaScript code decodes JSON, it uses JSON.parse to parse the string into an object and then uses your decoder to decode the object. Because JSON.parse can throw an error with malformed JSON, Elm wraps that part of its code in a try-catch block to prevent runtime errors for your application code. This means it caught the error thrown from Debug.todo here and failed the decoding with an Err Result. Inside the message, it captured the output from the TODO tag along with the line number from the source code.

The Debug.log and Debug.todo combo provides great value. You can know what values get through a case expression while putting off implementing some branches. Imagine you're playing with a dog API. You could quickly notice other breeds you hadn't considered supporting in your application.

You might also see misspellings or different capitalizations that you hadn't considered. For example, try changing the breed field to a fully lowercase "sheltie". After you recompile, you'll still see the previous messages because "sheltie" got to the TODO. Pattern matching is case-sensitive with strings so the first branch won't match.

You could consider supporting multiple capitalizations or simply decide to call String.toLower before pattern matching. The point is that the Debug module provides visibility into what values might come through your case expression. Ideally, the API should provide good documentation about its payloads.

 Previously in Elm 0.18, Debug.todo's predecessor, Debug.crash, provided more context inside a case expression such as the wildcard match that passes through, meaning you would not need an extra Debug.log. If the Elm core team adds that functionality back into Elm 0.19 or a future version, feel free to use Debug.todo alone for debugging.

Let's say through using Debug.log and Debug.todo you've discovered some inconsistent capitalization in the breed and also seen beagle as another common breed. Clean up the code and make it production-ready by adding a new Beagle value to the Breed custom type like so:

develop-debug-deploy/Debugging03.elm
```elm
type Breed
    = Sheltie
    | Poodle
    | Beagle
```

Then, remove Debug.log and Debug.todo and handle Poodle and Breed in decodeBreed like so:

```elm
case String.toLower breed of
    "sheltie" ->
        Json.succeed Sheltie

    "poodle" ->
        Json.succeed Poodle

    "beagle" ->
        Json.succeed Beagle

    _ ->
        Json.fail ("Unknown breed " ++ breed)
```

Likewise, remove Debug.todo and handle the other breeds in breedToString:

```
breedToString breed =
    case breed of
        Sheltie ->
            "Sheltie"

        Poodle ->
            "Poodle"

        Beagle ->
            "Beagle"
```

Finally, remove Debug.log from the case expression in main:

```
case decodedDog of
```

You now officially support shelties, poodles, and beagles. For all other breeds, the Json.fail function creates a failing decoder with the message "Unknown breed " ++ breed so you can still know if other breeds get through. The failed decoder will become an Err value during the actual decoding process.

Note that the Json.fail function will fail the entire dog decoding process too, so you could alternatively add a fourth Breed value called Unknown and return that with Json.succeed instead. That way you can display other dogs without officially supporting their breed.

Great job with the Debug module. You now know how to inspect values with Debug.log and partially implement functions with Debug.todo—most importantly for working with tricky JSON decoders. You also learned the useful Json.Decode functions andThen and fail. Next, you will learn how to speed up your development process with some different tools.

## Rapidly Develop and Deploy Elm Applications

The Elm compiler is a critical tool for developing Elm applications. However, our current development cycle suffers from a couple of drawbacks. First, the development feedback loop is slow. You have to manually recompile code and refresh the browser to see changes. Second, your application isn't exactly production-ready. Your compiled JavaScript code is unoptimized in its current state, and it's not minified. Elm offers ways to optimize compiled code but it doesn't minify. Minification is a process that removes extra bytes from JavaScript code by removing insignificant whitespace, shortening variable names, and eliminating dead code. Unminified code adds extra download time to browsers due to the extra bytes in human-readable code.

To combat these problems, you need to introduce tooling to accelerate your development cycle and generate production-worthy code. In this section, you will briefly look at the built-in Elm development server and then turn your attention to a more powerful third-party tool known as Create Elm App. You will also explore platforms such as Surge for hosting Elm applications. These examples will help you choose the right tools for rapidly developing and deploying Elm applications in your environment.

## Boot Up Elm Reactor

Elm actually comes with a built-in development server called Elm Reactor. Elm Reactor makes it easier to compile and view your application in the browser. Let's try it out with your Picshare application from previous chapters. If you don't have the complete Picshare application, copy the code/develop-debug-deploy/picshare-complete directory from this book's code downloads to your computer. Inside your picshare-complete directory, run this command:

```
elm reactor
```

The server will start and print the URL where it's running. You should see a message similar to this.

```
Go to http://localhost:8000 to see your project dashboard.
```

By default, Elm Reactor attempts to run on port 8000. If it fails because another program is using 8000, you can specify a different port such as 8001, like this:

```
elm reactor --port 8001
```

In your browser, open the URL where Elm Reactor is running, and there you should see a listing of the files in the picshare-complete directory, as shown in the following figure.

Elm Reactor is essentially a static file web server with some extra logic for .elm files. If you click on an .elm file, Elm Reactor will compile and display the application instead of serving its source code.

Click on the src directory and then on Picshare.elm. Your Picshare application should load and begin displaying the photo feed. However, you should notice one problem. All of the application styles are missing. Elm Reactor generated HTML that does not include the CSS files you used previously.

You could overcome this problem by loading CSS from within Elm. Temporarily add this code to your view function:

```
view model =
    div []
        [ div [ class "header" ]
            [ h1 [] [ text "Picshare" ] ]
        , div [ class "content-flow" ]
            [ viewContent model ]
        , Html.node "link"
            [ Html.Attributes.rel "stylesheet"
            , Html.Attributes.href "../main.css"
            ]
            []
        ]
```

The Html.node lets you create any arbitrary HTML tag. Here you create a <link> tag with a rel attribute of "stylesheet" and a href of "../main.css".

Refresh your browser and you should see a nicer-looking application. Unfortunately, the love button is missing. Create a similar <link> tag for the Font Awesome CSS file in index.html. You only have to worry about the rel and href attributes. Refresh again and you should see the love button.

Elm Reactor's greatest feature is semi-automatic compilation on file changes. Notice that with Elm Reactor you are able to make code changes and see them after you refresh the browser. You didn't need to manually compile the file.

Elm Reactor is a great tool for ramping up with an Elm application in development, but it has limitations. You couldn't render CSS <link> tags inside the <head> tag where they belong. Plus, you may have noticed that the WebSocket feed of photos didn't work. You had no way to wire up the JavaScript portion for the ports. Also, you'll eventually find that the manual process of refreshing your browser can be tedious.

Let's shift gears to a third-party tool that fully automates the compilation process, refreshes the browser for you, allows you to have custom HTML with CSS in the <head> tag, and lets you use ports. You can close Elm Reactor in the terminal with Ctrl-c.

## Create Elm App

To overcome some of the caveats with Elm Reactor, let's introduce the more versatile tool, Create Elm App.[1] Create Elm App is a command-line tool that removes the boilerplate of starting new Elm projects. It lets you scaffold new applications, offers a development server for rapid development feedback, and bundles your application and other assets for production deployment via Webpack.[2]

Bundling is a popular method for building front-end applications because it combines source code files and assets, such as CSS and images, into one (or more depending on your need) file for the browser to download. This improves performance for browsers and servers that still use HTTP 1.1 by reducing the number of HTTP requests to fetch an application and its assets. HTTP 2 mostly solves this dilemma by allowing a server to send multiple files in one connection.

Let's try Create Elm App's development server with the Picshare application. Then you will use it to bundle and deploy the application. First, start by installing v4.2.1 of Create Elm App globally via npm. (You're welcome to install the latest version instead, but I recommend sticking to the version I used when writing this book to avoid bugs or inconsistencies.)

```
npm install -g create-elm-app@4.2.1
```

After you install, you should have two new binaries on your path, create-elm-app and elm-app. Use the first binary to generate a new application folder structure. Create a new picshare-elm-app directory. Run the following command inside the directory:

```
create-elm-app picshare
```

The command will create a new picshare directory and install a few Elm packages. When the command finishes, you should see a success message along with example commands you can run with the elm-app binary. For now, go inside the picshare directory.

```
cd picshare
```

Inside the directory you should see a few files and subdirectories. The src directory holds Elm, JavaScript, and CSS files along with other assets you might want to bundle with your application. The public directory holds an index.html file for displaying your application in the browser. You may also

---

1.  https://github.com/halfzebra/create-elm-app
2.  https://webpack.js.org/

include assets in the public directory that you'd prefer to not bundle. The tests directory holds your test files. You will learn how to test Elm in Chapter 9, Test Elm Applications, on page 175.

The application's main entry point resides in the src/index.js file.

```
import './main.css';
import { Elm } from './Main.elm';
import * as serviceWorker from './serviceWorker';

Elm.Main.init({
  node: document.getElementById('root')
});

// If you want your app to work offline and load faster, you can change
// unregister() to register() below. Note this comes with some pitfalls.
// Learn more about service workers: https://bit.ly/CRA-PWA
serviceWorker.unregister();
```

Create Elm App uses the most modern version of JavaScript and compiles it using Babel.[3] Don't worry if you're unfamiliar with the newer JavaScript syntax; this is the most JavaScript you'll deal with here. Basically, this entry file imports CSS from src/main.css, imports the Elm application as Elm from src/Main.elm, imports a serviceWorker module for registering and unregistering a ServiceWorker,[4] and initializes the Elm application inside a div element with an id of root.

It might seem odd that you can import CSS and Elm directly into JavaScript. Create Elm App's underlying Webpack configuration allows Webpack to detect when you import non-JavaScript files and do special work with them. For example, importing CSS will cause Webpack to generate a style tag during local development and an actual stylesheet for production deployment.

More importantly, importing Elm will make Webpack use the Elm tooling to compile the Elm file and return a compiled JavaScript module. The compiled JavaScript module includes the init() method, which Create Elm App uses to embed the Elm application in the DOM. The actual DOM layout comes from public/index.html, which Create Elm App will serve to the browser.

Boot up the development server by running this command with the elm-app binary from Create Elm App:

```
elm-app start
```

---

3. http://babeljs.io/
4. https://developer.mozilla.org/en-US/docs/Web/API/Service_Worker_API

Create Elm App should display a message that your server is running at http://localhost:3000/. The command should also open the application in a new tab in your browser. Inside your browser, you should see a default application as shown in the figure on page 147.

**Your Elm App is working!**

Let's see what the development server can do by tweaking the default Elm application. Open up src/Main.elm in your editor. The file structure should be similar to what you built in Picshare. There is a Model, a Msg type, an init tuple, an update function, a view function, and a main program.

Change the text inside the view function to "Create Elm App is awesome!" and then save:

```
view model =
    div []
        [ img [ src "/logo.svg" ] []
        , h1 [] [ text "Create Elm App is awesome!" ]
        ]
```

Go to your browser and behold the magic. Without refreshing your browser, the displayed text should now read "Create Elm App is awesome!"

Create Elm App uses a feature called *hot module reloading* from Webpack. It detects when a source file changes and swaps it in live without reloading the browser. This provides instantaneous feedback in the browser while you're developing.

You can use this amazing feature with CSS too. Open up src/main.css in your editor. Change the h1 font size to 60px and save:

```
h1 {
  font-size: 60px;
}
```

The font size should immediately increase in the browser. Create Elm App lets you focus on building your application instead of worrying about tooling and manually refreshing the browser to see changes. I cannot overstate how awesome this is for front-end development.

## Port Picshare to Create Elm App

Now that you understand how Create Elm App works, let's use it with the Picshare application. Make sure you're still inside the picshare directory and follow these steps to migrate your Picshare application to Create Elm App:

1. Stop the elm-app development server with Ctrl-c.

2. Install Picshare's package dependencies:

   ```
   elm install elm/json
   elm install elm/http
   elm install NoRedInk/elm-json-decode-pipeline
   ```

3. Copy the Picshare.elm and WebSocket.elm files from your earlier picshare-complete/src directory into the src directory.

   Also inside the src/Picshare.elm file you just created, remove the Html.node "link" tags you added in the previous section for loading CSS.

4. Copy the main.css file from your earlier picshare-complete directory into the src directory, overriding the main.css autogenerated by Create Elm App.

5. Add a link tag to the Font Awesome library inside public/index.html.

   ```
   <link href="https://programming-elm.com/font-awesome-4.7.0/css/font-awesome.min.css" rel="stylesheet">
   ```

6. Change the <title> tag text to Picshare inside public/index.html.

   ```
   <title>Picshare</title>
   ```

7. Copy the contents of the IIFE inside the <script> tag (the code that previously initialized the application) from picshare-complete/index.html and merge them into src/index.js.

   Also inside src/index.js, import the Elm application from ./Picshare.elm instead of ./Main.elm:

   ```
   import './main.css';
   import { Elm } from './Picshare.elm';
   import * as serviceWorker from './serviceWorker';

   var app = Elm.Picshare.init({
     node: document.getElementById('root')
   });

   app.ports.listen.subscribe(listen);

   function listen(url) {
     var socket = new WebSocket(url);

     socket.onmessage = function(event) {
   ```

```
    app.ports.receive.send(event.data);
  };
}
```

```
// If you want your app to work offline and load faster, you can change
// unregister() to register() below. Note this comes with some pitfalls.
// Learn more about service workers: https://bit.ly/CRA-PWA
serviceWorker.unregister();
```

Essentially, you change the Elm.Main.init call to Elm.Picshare.init, accept the app return value like you did before, and wire up the ports for WebSocket communication.

8.  Restart the development server.

```
elm-app start
```

The browser tab that the development server opened earlier should refresh with your Picshare application running inside of it. With Picshare under the control of Create Elm App, you gain the benefits of the development server's hot reloading.

Let's tweak the order of new comments to see the development server in action. Add a new comment to the surfing photo. As expected, the new comment should appear below the previous comment. Open up src/Picshare.elm in your editor, and temporarily change the code to place new comments first with the :: operator in the saveNewComment function and save:

```
| comments = comment :: photo.comments
```

Add another comment. It will magically appear above the other comments. The development server swapped out the Picshare module without refreshing the browser tab, using the new code that prepends instead of appends comments. Revert your changes to the saveNewComment function and save:

```
| comments = photo.comments ++ [ comment ]
```

Now when Create Elm App swaps out the Picshare module, the new comment should remain above the previous comment because the previous one is already part of the existing state. Add another comment, though, and it should appear *below* the first comment as it did before the change. Again, the change took hold without needing to refresh the browser manually.

Hot reloading with Create Elm App is immensely useful. But there is one caveat you should know about: if you change anything about your Model or initial model, those changes won't always show up in your hot reloaded application correctly. If you see any weird issues from model changes after hot reloading, you'll need to manually refresh your browser.

## Deploy Picshare

So far you've focused on speeding up the development cycle of Elm applications. At the end of the day, you'll need to ship your application. Earlier, I presented a couple of concerns with the way we've built applications: the compiled code isn't optimized and minified.

You can optimize code by providing the --optimize flag to elm make. Try it with this command inside your picshare-elm-app/picshare directory:

```
elm make --output optimized.html --optimize src/Picshare.elm
```

You should have an optimized.html file in your current directory now. Open it in your browser. The application should load the feed of photos with no problem. Don't worry about the lack of styling. Since you generated the HTML file from Elm, it doesn't reference the Picshare CSS.

More importantly, the command that was generated optimized JavaScript. Some optimizations include shortening record field names and reducing the need to generate objects for custom type constructors where possible, which reduces memory allocation. The optimized code also removes any debugging features, meaning you can't use the Debug module.

Unfortunately, the Elm compiler doesn't minify code, meaning your users must wait longer to download and use your application. Create Elm App solves that problem with one simple trick (sorry, I'm a millennial and need at least one click-bait sentence).

Create Elm App offers a build command that not only minifies the code but also optimizes with Elm's --optimize flag. Let's build a production version of the Picshare application with Create Elm App. Delete optimized.html and run the following command:

```
elm-app build
```

Eventually, you should see this message along with a listing of the compiled JavaScript and CSS files. Note that your JavaScript and CSS filenames and sizes don't have to exactly match below.

```
Creating an optimized production build...
Compiled successfully.

File sizes after gzip:

  11.63 KB   build/static/js/main.8a4d6a26.chunk.js
  4.68 KB    build/static/js/vendors~main.3ca81432.chunk.js
  1.47 KB    build/static/css/main.2e2b4d3a.chunk.css
  759 B      build/static/js/runtime~main.d53d57e4.js
```

You should now have a new build directory that contains your index.html file and compiled and minified JavaScript and CSS files like the following.

```
build
├── asset-manifest.json
├── favicon.ico
├── index.html
├── logo.svg
├── manifest.json
├── precache-manifest.9888300037ad86fa6e32a78fc79e3559.js
├── service-worker.js
└── static
    ├── css
    │   └── main.3fecdfa5.chunk.css
    └── js
        ├── main.b43999a5.chunk.js
        ├── main.b43999a5.chunk.js.map
        ├── runtime~main.1b922744.js
        ├── runtime~main.1b922744.js.map
        ├── vendors~main.604c6712.chunk.js
        └── vendors~main.604c6712.chunk.js.map
```

If you open up your JavaScript and CSS files, they should be difficult to read because they are minified and obfuscated. Recmember that you want minification to make your application download and boot up faster for your users.

Test out the built application. You'll need to use a static web server to serve the build directory. If you're unsure what to use, the npm serve[5] package is perfect. Run these commands to start your built application with serve:

```
npm install -g serve
serve build
```

When serve boots up, it should copy a URL to your clipboard. It will also display the URL in the terminal. Visit serve's provided URL in the browser, and your Picshare application should load.

Awesome, you're almost there! The only missing piece is to actually deploy your built application somewhere. I recommend hosting your application with a free static file hosting platform such as Surge[6] or GitHub Pages.[7] I personally prefer Surge, and it will be easier to set up, so let's use it.

Install Surge's npm package like so:

```
npm install -g surge
```

---

5.    https://github.com/zeit/serve

6.    http://surge.sh/

7.    https://pages.github.com/

Then, simply deploy the build directory by running surge with the project path -p option:

```
surge -p build
```

Surge will prompt you to login or create an account. Next, it will prompt you for a domain name. You can accept whatever default it generates by hitting the Return key. Finally, Surge will upload the build directory and display a success message. Through the whole process, you should see something similar to this in your terminal.

```
Welcome to Surge! (surge.sh)
Login (or create surge account) by entering email & password.

      email: myemail@example.com
   password:

Running as myemail@example.com

    project: build
     domain: utopian-thunder.surge.sh
     upload: [====================] 100% eta: 0.0s (14 files, 470215 bytes)
        CDN: [====================] 100%
         IP: 1.1.1.1

Success! - Published to utopian-thunder.surge.sh
```

Visit your surge URL, and lo and behold, you will see your Picshare application. Congratulations, you just deployed your first Elm application!

## What You Learned

You accomplished a lot in this chapter. You learned how debugging works in Elm and gained experience with the useful Debug module. Then, you accelerated your development feedback loop with powerful tools: Elm Reactor and Create Elm App. Finally, you deployed your first production-worthy Elm application with the help of Create Elm App and Surge.

You are well-equipped to rapidly create and develop Elm applications and then deploy them to share with the rest of the world. Now that you know how to build and ship new applications, let's turn our attention to the real world via existing applications. In the next chapter, you will explore interacting with JavaScript code, migrating existing JavaScript applications to Elm.

# CHAPTER 8

# Integrate with JavaScript

In the previous chapter, you used versatile tools to debug Elm code, receive immediate development feedback, and deploy an Elm application. These tools make building brand new Elm applications a delight. Unfortunately, not all applications are "greenfield" projects with no existing code or constraints to work around.

As a front-end developer, you deal with a lot of JavaScript. But of course, now you love Elm and its safety, so you can hardly wait to adopt it at work. One problem: your manager will likely question if rewriting your application in Elm is cost-effective. Rewrites steal time from developing new customer features.

Thankfully, Elm has your back. You can use Elm inside existing JavaScript applications and build new features with Elm.

In this chapter, you will enhance a JavaScript application with Elm. You will use ports and flags to let Elm and JavaScript transmit data. You will also use ports to access the DOM and upload files with JavaScript. By the end of this chapter, you will be ready to add new features to JavaScript applications with Elm. Ultimately, this empowers you to slowly migrate JavaScript applications to Elm.

## Embed an Elm Application

Let's set the scene. At work, you're maintaining a productivity application that includes a calendar, contact management, note-taking tool, and more. The application is built with JavaScript and React.[1]

---

1. https://reactjs.org/

Your product manager creates a new ticket to let users upload images to notes. You like React, but you miss Elm's benefits such as type safety and no runtime exceptions. You can't rewrite the entire application in Elm, but you convince your boss to let you add the new feature with Elm.

In this section, you will display an initial image upload button with Elm. You will start small by embedding an Elm application inside a React application. In later sections, you will build upon your work to upload images. Don't worry if you don't know React. I'll explain the React bits as we progress. Nothing about the Elm and JavaScript interaction will actually depend on React, so you can apply this knowledge elsewhere.

## Create an Image Upload App

Before you begin, grab the existing application from this book's code downloads. Copy the contents of code/javascript/migrate-js-to-elm into your own directory called migrate-js-to-elm. Run this command to download dependencies from npm.

```
npm install
```

Give the install command time while it downloads the kitchen sink. When it finishes, run this command to start the application.

```
npm start
```

A development server should start at http://localhost:3000. If another program is using port 3000, the start command should prompt you to run the application on a different port. Once the application starts, it will open a new tab in your browser. You should see an "Info" header with fields for the note's title and contents as shown in the following figure.

# Info

Title:

Contents:

Type some text in the fields and refresh the page. Everything you typed should still be there. This application persists information in the browser with the localStorage[2] API.

Now that you've played a bit with the existing application, let's add the new image upload feature. Remember that, for now, we're going to display an upload button. That may sound like you only need an Elm view function. But, JavaScript can't directly call an Elm function. It could end up passing in any type of argument and break Elm's type guarantees.

Elm closely guards its communication with JavaScript to prevent runtime exceptions. You'll need to create a full-fledged Elm application with the Elm Architecture. Then you can embed the Elm application inside the React Application.

In your migrate-js-to-elm directory, initialize an Elm project:

```
elm init
```

Inside the src directory, create an ImageUpload.elm file. Name the module ImageUpload and expose main:

```
javascript/samples/ImageUpload01.elm
module ImageUpload exposing (main)
```

Next, import Browser and several functions from Html and Html.Attributes like so:

```
import Browser
import Html exposing (Html, div, input, label, text)
import Html.Attributes exposing (class, for, id, multiple, type_)
```

Because you're using the Elm Architecture, you will need a model. Create a type alias for Model to the unit type:

```
type alias Model =
    ()
```

You'll eventually add a record model, but for now the unit type is a perfect placeholder. Create an init function that returns a tuple with a unit value for the initial model and an initial command from Cmd.none:

```
init : () -> ( Model, Cmd Msg )
init () =
    ( (), Cmd.none )
```

---

2.    https://developer.mozilla.org/en-US/docs/Web/API/Window/localStorage

Next, create a view function below init:

```
view : Model -> Html Msg
view model =
    div [ class "image-upload" ]
        [ label [ for "file-upload" ]
            [ text "+ Add Images" ]
        , input
            [ id "file-upload"
            , type_ "file"
            , multiple True
            ]
            []
        ]
```

You use an input element with the *file* type to upload files. The multiple attribute lets you select more than one file at a time.

Browsers limit styling file inputs with CSS. We will use some custom CSS to hide the input element and style the label above it like a button. The label's for attribute and input's id attribute match, so users can instead click on the styled label element to upload images.

Add the Msg type and update function underneath view:

```
type Msg
    = NoOp

update : Msg -> Model -> ( Model, Cmd Msg )
update msg model =
    ( model, Cmd.none )
```

There's no model to modify yet, so you have a placeholder NoOp message value, and return the existing model with no command inside update.

Below update, add a subscriptions function that returns Sub.none:

```
subscriptions : Model -> Sub Msg
subscriptions model =
    Sub.none
```

Finally, create main with Browser.element:

```
main : Program () Model Msg
main =
    Browser.element
        { init = init
        , view = view
        , update = update
        , subscriptions = subscriptions
        }
```

That's a lot of code to only display a label for a file input. However, this Elm file will eventually let us upload images, so Model, Msg, view, update, and subscriptions will all become important in later sections.

## Embed Elm in React

You need to embed the Elm application inside a React *component* to embed it in the React application. A React component is like an Elm view function that can also have its own state and additional helper methods.

Create an ImageUpload.js file inside src and add this code at the top:

```
javascript/samples/ImageUpload01.js
import React, { Component } from 'react';
import { Elm } from './ImageUpload.elm';
import './ImageUpload.css';
```

This is ES2015 import syntax,[3] something you briefly saw in the previous chapter. It lets you import other JavaScript files. Notice that you import React and Component from the react package.

This application uses Webpack with a configuration allowing you to import other files, so you can import ImageUpload.elm. When you import an Elm application, you receive an Elm namespace object that contains your compiled application.

You also import ImageUpload.css, which is already written for you. Recall from the previous chapter that when you import CSS, Webpack will load it in the browser with a <style> tag or <link> tag.

Use the imported Component class to create an ImageUpload component. Extend the Component class with ES2015 class syntax:[4]

```
class ImageUpload extends Component {
  constructor(props) {
    super(props);
    this.elmRef = React.createRef();
  }
  componentDidMount() {
    this.elm = Elm.ImageUpload.init({
      node: this.elmRef.current,
    });
  }
```

---

3.  https://developer.mozilla.org/en-US/docs/Web/JavaScript/Reference/Statements/import
4.  https://developer.mozilla.org/en-US/docs/Web/JavaScript/Reference/Classes

```
  render() {
    return <div ref={this.elmRef} />;
  }
}
```

**export default** ImageUpload;

The render() method displays the ImageUpload component. It returns JSX,[5] which looks like regular HTML. JSX is a special XML-like syntax for creating JavaScript objects. These objects are like Elm's virtual DOM for representing the real DOM. Similar to Elm, React generates the real DOM from virtual DOM.

Inside render(), you create a <div> tag with a ref attribute. Since render() returns virtual DOM, you need to embed the Elm application in the real DOM somehow. The ref attribute lets you eventually access the real <div> tag in the DOM. You provide the instance variable this.elmRef to ref with special JSX brace syntax ref={this.elmRef}.

You create the this.elmRef inside the constructor() method with React's createRef() method. If you're unfamiliar with ES2015 classes, the constructor method() lets you configure the class instance whenever it's instantiated with the new keyword. A ref in React is an object that will have a reference to a real DOM node. The ref receives the DOM node when you assign it in render() and when React has processed the virtual DOM output from render().

Finally, you have a special method called componentDidMount(). When React mounts a component into the real DOM, it will call this method. At that point, the elmRef DOM node is available inside the this.elmRef.current property. You pass that in as the node property to Elm.ImageUpload.init to mount your Elm application inside the React component. Note that you access the ImageUpload module from the imported Elm namespace object. After embedding, you receive an application object that you assign to an elm property. You will need the application object later.

You now have a simple React component to display the ImageUpload Elm application. You expose the component for other files by exporting[6] it with export default ImageUpload.

Now, you must incorporate the component in the overall application. Open src/App.js in your editor. At the top, import the ImageUpload component:

javascript/samples/App01.js
**import** ImageUpload **from** './ImageUpload';

---

5.   https://facebook.github.io/jsx/
6.   https://developer.mozilla.org/en-US/docs/Web/JavaScript/Reference/Statements/export

Then, in the render() method of App, show the ImageUpload component:

```
return (
  <div className="note">
    {/* previous content, don't replace */}

    <div className="note__images">
      <h2>Images</h2>
      <ImageUpload />
    </div>
  </div>
);
```

You display the ImageUpload component inside a <div className="note__images"> tag for styling purposes. Notice that the new JSX still needs to live inside the top level <div className="note"> tag.

Start the local development server with npm start. In your browser, you should now see an "Images" header and a big blue button with the text "+ Add Images" as shown in the following figure.

Click on the button, and a file prompt should appear. You can select files to upload, but the application can't receive them yet. Let's fix that next.

## Upload Images with Ports

Currently, the new image upload feature only opens a file prompt. You need to access the selected files to actually upload them. This presents an interesting problem for Elm. Elm is a pure language, so it can't directly access the DOM to retrieve the selected files.

But, JavaScript easily interacts with the DOM. You just need Elm and JavaScript to talk with each other. They haven't been on speaking terms up to this point. Maybe JavaScript is a little jealous of Elm. Let's help them reconcile with *ports*.

In this section, you will use ports to notify JavaScript that a user has uploaded images from Elm. Then, you will use JavaScript to read the images' file data and update the note with images.

### Notify JavaScript with a Port

You briefly learned about ports in Chapter 5, Go Real-Time with WebSockets, on page 85, but we'll cover them in more depth here. Ports are the magic sauce that let Elm safely communicate with the impure world of JavaScript. Elm and JavaScript can subscribe to and send messages to each other over ports. Ports are like real-life shipping ports. Ships can only dock at designated ports to drop off or pick up cargo. Similarly, Elm ports are designated points for Elm and JavaScript to trade messages and data. The following diagram depicts port communication between JavaScript and Elm.

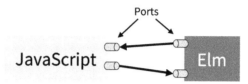

You will use ports to upload images. Elm will notify JavaScript after a user selects images from the prompt. Then, JavaScript will retrieve the images and convert them to Base64-encoded URLs. Finally, JavaScript will update the note and send the image URLs back to Elm to display them.

Open src/ImageUpload.elm in your editor. You'll need to change the ImageUpload module to a *port module* to use ports. Add the port keyword at the beginning of the module declaration:

```
javascript/samples/ImageUpload02.elm
port module ImageUpload exposing (main)
```

Next, create a port called uploadImages above the Model type alias like so:

```
port uploadImages : () -> Cmd msg
```

You create a port with the port keyword, a port name, and a type annotation. Every port is a function that either returns a command or a subscription. A port that returns a command is an *outgoing* port like the uploadImages port. Outgoing ports send messages to JavaScript.

An outgoing port must accept an argument even if you don't need to send data to JavaScript. In this case, uploadImages accepts the unit type as an argument. The port only needs to notify JavaScript that a user has selected images from the prompt.

You need to make the upload button call the port somehow. The port returns a command, so you must call it inside the update function. Thus, the upload button needs to produce a message that update can handle.

Let's create a Msg value for uploading images. Replace the NoOp value with one called UploadImages:

```
type Msg
    = UploadImages
```

To send UploadImages from the button, you actually don't want onClick. Remember the "button" is really a label. The file input produces the true event. If you add onClick to it, the event will fire when you click, *not* when you select images from the prompt.

Instead, you need the DOM change event. The change event fires when a user changes the value of an input element. The Html.Events module lacks an onChange function, but you can make your own with the on function. Import it from Html.Events:

```
import Html.Events exposing (on)
```

The on function lets you build event handlers for any event. In fact, Html.Events uses on to build other event handlers such as onClick.

The on function accepts two arguments, a string event name and a JSON decoder. Elm uses the decoder to decode properties from the DOM event object. For example, the onInput event decodes the event.target.value property to fetch the value typed in a text input.

The onChange event handler doesn't need to decode anything, so you can create an automatically succeeding decoder with the succeed function.

Install the elm/json package:

```
elm install elm/json
```

Then, import succeed from Json.Decode:

```
import Json.Decode exposing (succeed)
```

Event handlers typically accept a message value so Elm can provide it to update later. For the onChange function, you can accept a message and wrap it with succeed. Add onChange above the uploadImages port like so:

```
onChange : msg -> Html.Attribute msg
onChange msg =
    on "change" (succeed msg)
```

Use the onChange event on the file input inside view. Make sure you call it with UploadImages:

```
, input
    [ id "file-upload"
    , type_ "file"
    , multiple True
    , onChange UploadImages
    ]
    []
```

Now when you select images from the file prompt, the change event will fire and cause Elm to call update with UploadImages. Modify update to handle UploadImages:

```
update msg model =
    case msg of
        UploadImages ->
            ( model, uploadImages () )
```

When update receives UploadImages, it calls the uploadImages port with a unit value. Elm will receive the command from uploadImages and notify any JavaScript listeners on the uploadImages port. Look at the following diagram which visualizes the interaction.

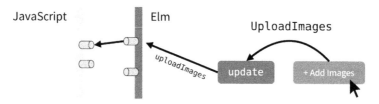

## Read Image Data with JavaScript

Now that Elm can notify listeners through the uploadImages port, you need JavaScript to pay attention. Once JavaScript receives a notification, it needs to retrieve the files, read the image data, add the images to the note, and send the images back to Elm to display. Let's focus on adding the images to the note first.

### Update the Note in App.js

Open src/App.js in your editor. Underneath updateField(), add an addImages() method, like this:

```
javascript/samples/App02.js
addImages(images) {
  this.update('images', this.state.note.images.concat(images));
}
```

The addImages() method accepts an array of new images. It concatenates the new images with any existing note images. Then, it updates the note with the concatenated array of images. The update() method also saves the updated note in localStorage.

Currently when App fetches the note from localStorage, it provides default property values if the note doesn't exist. You need to supply a default value for the new images property. Use an empty array for the images property inside the returned object in fetchSavedNote():

```
return {
  title: '',
  contents: '',
  images: [],
  ...note,
};
```

Notice the ...note code underneath the default values. This is the *spread operator*. The spread operator is a relatively new JavaScript feature. It essentially "spreads" out any existing properties in note into the returned object. Any note properties that exist will override the default values.

Finally, update render() to pass the note images and addImages() method into the ImageUpload component:

```
<ImageUpload
  images={note.images}
  onUpload={this.addImages}
/>
```

In the React world, these are *props*. They let you supply values to another component. When you enclose the value in {}, you pass in the literal value. So, you supply the note.images array and addImages() method. The ImageUpload component can retrieve the props from the names you give them. Here, images and onUpload are the prop names.

ImageUpload can use the images prop to pass the images to Elm to display them. It can also call the onUpload prop to notify App when it reads image data into a new images array. Since you're passing addImages() as a prop, you'll need to avoid JavaScript this binding issues. Bind the method to the App instance inside the constructor() method like so:

```
this.addImages = this.addImages.bind(this);
```

### Read the Images in ImageUpload.js

Let's switch gears to the ImageUpload component to read the image data and use the onUpload prop. Open src/ImageUpload.js in your editor.

You first need to listen to the uploadImages port. Add this code at the bottom of componentDidMount():

```
this.elm.ports.uploadImages.subscribe(this.readImages);
```

You use the application object that you received earlier while embedding your Elm module. If the module is a port module, then the application object will have a ports property. The ports property references every port defined by your Elm module.

You call a port's subscribe function with a callback to listen to it. Here, you call the uploadImages subscribe function with the readImages() method. You will create the readImages() method in a moment. Whenever Elm sends a message on the uploadImages port, JavaScript will call the readImages() method.

You can also unsubscribe from ports to perform any cleanup and prevent memory leaks. For example, if React unmounted the ImageUpload component to display something else, it doesn't need to listen to the uploadImages port anymore. You can use another special method called componentWillUnmount() to perform component cleanup. Add this code underneath componentDidMount():

```
componentWillUnmount() {
  this.elm.ports.uploadImages.unsubscribe(this.readImages);
}
```

Every port has an unsubscribe function too. You call it with the readImages() method again to remove it from the listeners.

The readImages() method must retrieve the files from the input element and read in their image data. Add readImages() above the render() method:

```
readImages() {
  const element = document.getElementById('file-upload');
  const files = Array.from(element.files);

  Promise.all(files.map(this.readImage))
    .then(this.props.onUpload);
}
```

When you upload files with a file input, the DOM adds every selected file to the input's files property. Recall that Elm can't directly access the DOM. That's an unsafe action that could cause runtime exceptions. So, Elm can't touch the files property, but JavaScript can.

In readImages, you grab the input element with document.getElementById and the input's id attribute, file-upload. Then, you access the files via element.files. Notice that you pass the files into Array.from. The files property is array-like but not a real array. You convert it into a real array with Array.from.

You need this real array so you can map over it with files.map. The array map() method is similar to the List.map function in Elm. It creates a new array by applying a function to each item in the original array.

In this case, you map a readImage() method over each file. You'll add readImage() in a moment; it will return a promise.[7] The promise fulfills when the file's image data becomes available.

---

7. https://developer.mozilla.org/en-US/docs/Web/JavaScript/Guide/Using_promises

You wait for all the image promises to complete by wrapping them inside Promise.all. The Promise.all function creates a promise that fulfills when the inner promises fulfill their values. Finally, when the promise from Promise.all completes, it will contain all the files' image data in an array. Then, you pass the images into the onUpload prop with a then callback.

The real magic occurs in the readImage() method. Add it above readImages():

```
readImage(file) {
  const reader = new FileReader();
  const promise = new Promise((resolve) => {
    reader.onload = (e) => {
      resolve({
        url: e.target.result,
      });
    };
  });
  reader.readAsDataURL(file);
  return promise;
}
```

First, you create a new FileReader[8] object for reading the image data. FileReader fires a load event whenever it finishes reading file data. You handle the load event by giving the file reader an onload handler.

The onload handler receives an event object called e. The image data resides at the e.target.result property. Remember that you need to return a promise from readImage() that is fulfilled with the image data. You create a new Promise that wraps over the onload handler. Then, you use the promise's resolve function to fulfill with a new image object. The image object stores the image data inside a url property.

Outside of the promise, you read the image data by calling the readAsDataURL() method with file. The readAsDataURL() method encodes the file's contents into a Base64 string URL. When it finishes, it triggers the load event, which your onload function handles.

Finally, you return the promise variable from readImage().

You need to make one more tweak inside the ImageUpload component. At the bottom of constructor(), bind readImages() to the instance. You pass it as a callback to elm.ports.uploadImages.subscribe so you don't lose your this reference:

```
this.readImages = this.readImages.bind(this);
```

---

8.   https://developer.mozilla.org/en-US/docs/Web/API/FileReader

Awesome! You can now partially upload images. You still have to display them, but you'll handle that in the next section.

Let's recap what you have so far. When a user clicks on the upload button and selects some images, the file input triggers a change event. Elm dispatches the UploadImages message to the update function, which then calls the uploadImages port.

The ImageUpload component receives a port notification, retrieves the files from the input element, and reads in the image data as in the following diagram.

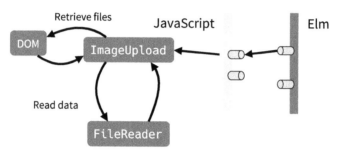

Finally, the ImageUpload component sends the image data to the App component, which updates the note and saves it to localStorage.

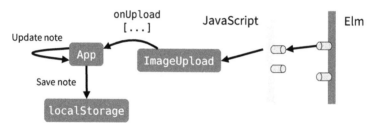

Start the development server with npm start and go to the application browser tab. Click on the upload button and select an image. Choose an image that is relatively small. Browsers limit localStorage to 5 MB.

After selecting an image, open your browser's dev tools console and run this code:

```
JSON.parse(localStorage.getItem('note')).images[0]
```

You should see an object with a long Base64 string url like this. (I've purposely truncated the example URL below for spacing.)

```
{ url: "data:image/png;base64,iVBORw0KGgoAAAANSUhEUgAAB9AA..." }
```

If you don't see an object or you get an error, make sure your App.js, ImageUpload.js, and ImageUpload.elm files match the App02.js, ImageUpload02.js, and ImageUpload02.elm files from the code/javascript directory in this book's code downloads.

# Display Uploaded Images

Now that you can upload images, let's display them. In this section, you will use a port to send the new array of images back to Elm. You will also use flags to send Elm the note's images when embedding the application.

## Receive New Images with a Port

When the App component updates its note, it re-renders. It also re-renders the ImageUpload component. Because you pass the note's images into the images prop, ImageUpload can react to send the new images to Elm.

React has another special method called componentDidUpdate() that it calls any-time a component updates after receiving new props from its parent component. You can leverage that inside ImageUpload to grab the new images and send them to Elm. Inside src/ImageUpload.js, add componentDidUpdate() below componentWillUnmount() like so:

```
javascript/samples/ImageUpload03.js
componentDidUpdate() {
  this.elm.ports.receiveImages.send(this.props.images);
}
```

When React calls componentDidUpdate(), the component's props already contain the new images in this.props.images. You use a new port named receiveImages to send the images to Elm via a send function.

The receiveImages port doesn't exist, so let's add it. Inside src/ImageUpload.elm add the new port underneath uploadImages:

```
javascript/samples/ImageUpload03.elm
port receiveImages : (List Image -> msg) -> Sub msg
```

The receiveImages port accepts a function as an argument. The function argument receives List Image and returns a msg. You'll define the Image type in a moment.

Because the function must return a message, you need to create a Msg value that accepts a List Image argument. Add a ReceiveImages message value to the Msg type:

```
| ReceiveImages (List Image)
```

Look back at the receiveImages port. Notice that it returns Sub msg. A port that returns a subscription is an *incoming* port. JavaScript uses incoming ports to send data to Elm through a subscription. This mimics how you received photos from a WebSocket subscription in Chapter 5, Go Real-Time with WebSockets, on page 85.

But wait…JavaScript sending arbitrary data to Elm sounds like a safety red flag. Surprisingly, you don't need to build a decoder for incoming port data. Elm reads the incoming port's type annotation to create a decoder for you. It uses the decoder to decode incoming data. If decoding fails because JavaScript sends wrong data, then Elm will throw an error.

Yes, that's right. Elm's incoming ports can have runtime exceptions. Technically, the send function throws the error so JavaScript encounters the runtime exception.

Regardless, you should remember that this is the unsafe world of JavaScript. Ports minimize the possibility of exceptions during JavaScript communication. If JavaScript could call regular Elm functions, it would open the door to more exceptions. Just be careful about sending the right data through incoming ports. Honestly, this is safer than a full-blown JavaScript application. At least you know where exceptions could occur, and they will be minimal.

If you want to avoid possible exceptions, your incoming port can accept Json.Decode.Value[9] instead. Json.Decode.Value comes from the Json.Decode module, and it can represent any JavaScript value. You could write a decoder and decode the value yourself with Json.Decode.decodeValue[10] in your subscriptions function before passing the result into your message constructor. You would also have to update your message constructor to wrap a Result instead. If decoding fails, you'll receive an Err value instead of an exception, so you can add some fallback behavior.

You can see an example of decoding Json.Decode.Value in the code/javascript/complete-migration directory from this book's code downloads. This is the finished code for the challenge at the end of the chapter. Don't peek if you want to attempt the challenge yourself first.

Since the port returns a subscription, you can use it like any other subscription in Elm. Update subscriptions at the bottom of the file like this:

```
subscriptions model =
    receiveImages ReceiveImages
```

9.   https://package.elm-lang.org/packages/elm/json/latest/Json-Decode#Value
10.  https://package.elm-lang.org/packages/elm/json/latest/Json-Decode#decodeValue

You call the receiveImages port with the ReceiveImages constructor function. When JavaScript sends an array of images, Elm will decode them to List Image and wrap the list with ReceiveImages.

Before you handle ReceiveImages in update, let's create the Image type. Add this code below the onChange function:

```
type alias Image =
    { url : String }
```

The Image type is a record with a url field, similar to the image object you created in the ImageUpload component.

Next, update the model to hold the list of images. Change the Model type's definition like so:

```
type alias Model =
    { images : List Image }
```

Also, update init to create an initial model with an empty list of images:

```
init () =
    ( Model [], Cmd.none )
```

Now that you've created the Image type and updated the Model type, you can handle ReceiveImages in update. Add this branch to update:

```
ReceiveImages images ->
    ( { model | images = images }
    , Cmd.none
    )
```

The App component is the source of truth for the note's images. The Elm model only holds a copy of the images. So, you overwrite the current images with a new copy from ReceiveImages.

Now, let's display those images. Start by creating a function for displaying an individual image. Add a viewImage function above the view function like so:

```
viewImage : Image -> Html Msg
viewImage image =
    li [ class "image-upload__image" ]
        [ img
            [ src image.url
            , width 400
            ]
            []
        ]
```

The viewImage function displays the img inside an li element. You supply the Base64-encoded image.url field to the src attribute. To enforce one size for styling, you also set the image width to 400 with the width attribute.

You need to import img, li, ul, src, and width by updating the Html and Html.Attributes imports at the top of the file:

```
import Html exposing (Html, div, img, input, label, li, text, ul)
import Html.Attributes exposing (class, for, id, multiple, src, type_, width)
```

Finally, update the view function to display the full list of images. Add the following code under the input element inside view:

```
, ul [ class "image-upload__images" ]
    (List.map viewImage model.images)
```

You use List.map to call viewImage on each image and create a list of children for the ul element.

Make sure that ImageUpload.js and ImageUpload.elm match ImageUpload03.js and ImageUpload03.elm from the code/javascript directory in this book's code downloads. Start the development server and upload some images. After selecting images from the prompt, you should see them appear underneath the upload button. The example screenshot shows an uploaded Elm logo image.

**Images**

Let's recap how JavaScript sends images to Elm. You can visualize it in the following diagram. When ImageUpload receives a new note from App, it uses the receiveImages port to send the array of images to Elm. Elm receives the images via subscriptions inside a ReceiveImages message. It sends the ReceiveImages message to update, which updates the model with the list of images. Finally, it calls view with the new model to display the images, as shown in the figure on page 171.

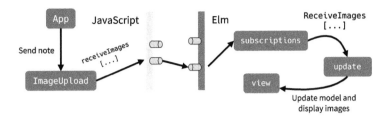

## Receive Initial Images with Flags

You only have one more change to complete the image upload feature. Refresh your browser with the application still open. You should see the note's title and contents reappear but the uploaded images vanish.

The images still live in localStorage. Run this code from the dev tools console to confirm that:

```
JSON.parse(localStorage.getItem('note')).images.length
```

The number of images should be greater than zero. The problem is that the ImageUpload component doesn't send the saved images to the Elm application when embedding it.

React only calls the componentDidUpdate() method inside ImageUpload when the component receives one or more new prop values (or when the component updates its state), not when the component first mounts. That means you don't call the receiveImages port until something about the note changes. Update the note's title and the images will magically appear.

You can fix this problem with flags. Flags are initial data that you pass into an Elm application when embedding it. In this case, you need to pass in the saved images as flags to the Elm image uploader. You can also use flags to eliminate duplicating the "file-upload" string id for the file upload element.

Back inside src/ImageUpload.js in the componentDidMount() method, update embedding the image uploader like so:

```
javascript/samples/ImageUpload04.js
this.elm = Elm.ImageUpload.init({
  node: this.elmRef.current,
  flags: {
    imageUploaderId: IMAGE_UPLOADER_ID,
    images: this.props.images,
  },
});
```

You add a flags property to the object you pass into Elm.ImageUpload.init. Flags can be any data type. Here, you use an object with two properties.

The imageUploaderId property holds the id for the file input. Instead of hard-coding the id, you can provide it whenever you embed an image uploader. This makes the image uploader reusable by preventing id collisions. You'll create the IMAGE_UPLOADER_ID constant next. The images property holds the images. Notice that you retrieve the images from ImageUpload's props.

Add the IMAGE_UPLOADER_ID constant above the ImageUpload component:

```
const IMAGE_UPLOADER_ID = 'file-upload';
```

Also, access the file input in readImages() with IMAGE_UPLOADER_ID instead of the hardcoded string:

```
const element = document.getElementById(IMAGE_UPLOADER_ID);
```

That's all you need for the ImageUpload component. Next, let's update the Elm side to receive and use the flags. Add a Flags type alias underneath the onChange function like this:

javascript/samples/ImageUpload04.elm
```
type alias Flags =
    { imageUploaderId : String
    , images : List Image
    }
```

The Flags type mimics the object you pass from the JavaScript side. It's a record with imageUploaderId and images fields.

You need to inject these fields into the model to use them. First, update the Model type alias to have an imageUploaderId field:

```
type alias Model =
    { imageUploaderId : String
    , images : List Image
    }
```

Recall that Elm applications require an init function that returns a tuple with initial state and an initial command. The init function receives the flags as an argument in case you need to initialize based on the flags. Up to this point, you've ignored flags by accepting a unit value (). Now, you must accept your new Flags type as an argument. Update init like so:

```
init : Flags -> ( Model, Cmd Msg )
init flags =
    ( Model flags.imageUploaderId flags.images, Cmd.none )
```

Elm will automatically decode flags, similar to how it works with incoming ports. The init function uses the imageUploaderId and images fields from the decoded flags to construct an initial model. However, leaving decoding to Elm poses another exception risk which you can again avoid by accepting Json.Decode.Value instead and decoding the flags yourself.

You might notice that Flags and Model have the same structure, so you could use flags as the initial state. Although that works, I like distinguishing between Flags and Model since they are different concepts. Flags are for configuration and the model is for state. It just so happens that you use the flags configuration to create the initial state. Also, sometimes flags might only contain part of the initial state, so you'll need a separate Flags and Model anyway.

At this point, you should have a type error with your main constant at the bottom. Recall that the first type variable to Program is flags.

```
type Program flags model msg = Program
```

Your main constant type annotation set that to (), but Elm detects that it should be Flags. Update the type annotation:

```
main : Program Flags Model Msg
```

Finally, remove the hardcoded file-upload id and use the imageUploaderId field from the model. Update the label and input elements inside view, like this:

```
➤ [ label [ for model.imageUploaderId ]
      [ text "+ Add Images" ]
  , input
➤     [ id model.imageUploaderId
      , type_ "file"
      , multiple True
      , onChange UploadImages
      ]
      []
```

Perfect. Now you've eliminated the id duplication to make the image uploader reusable. More importantly, you should now receive any saved images from localStorage when embedding.

Be sure ImageUpload.js and ImageUpload.elm match ImageUpload04.js and ImageUpload04.elm from the code/javascript directory in this book's code downloads. Refresh your application, and you should see any previously uploaded images under the upload button.

## What You Learned

Great job in this chapter. You added a complex feature to an existing JavaScript application with Elm. You embedded an Elm application inside an existing React application. Then, you created your own onChange event handler and used a port to notify JavaScript when a user selected images. You used a FileReader and promises to encode images into Base64 URLs and sent the URLs back to Elm through another port. Finally, you used flags to display previously uploaded images when embedding the Elm application.

You're now ready to introduce Elm into your JavaScript applications. You can add new features with Elm and convert existing parts of your application to Elm. Over time, you can migrate an entire application to Elm.

In fact, try doing that with the note application from this chapter. Migrate the remaining parts of the React application to Elm. You will need to combine the React components and ImageUpload.elm into a single Elm file that uploads images, manages the note state in a model, and saves the note to localStorage through a port. You'll also need to use flags to embed the saved note instead of only the uploaded images.

For an additional challenge, update the flags and incoming ports to accept Json.Decode.Value, and create decoders to decode values yourself with Json.Decode.decodeValue. That way, you'll eliminate any possible exceptions.

By the end, you should have no React code, and the only remaining JavaScript code should read image data and interact with the localStorage API. If you need a little help along the way, peek inside the code/javascript/complete-migration directory from this book's code downloads.

Elm actually offers a native package for handling file uploads called elm/file.[11] We skipped using it here in order to focus on ports and integrating Elm with existing JavaScript projects. If you want to go a step further, though, feel free to remove the JavaScript code and port handling for files, and use the native elm/file package as a final challenge.

Now that you can ship Elm applications and add Elm to JavaScript applications, we can look at testing Elm code. In the next chapter, you will learn how to test Elm functions and Elm applications.

---

11. https://package.elm-lang.org/packages/elm/file/latest/

# CHAPTER 9

# Test Elm Applications

Until now, you have focused on building Elm applications. You can create your own applications with the Elm Architecture, scale applications with powerful patterns, debug and deploy applications rapidly, and integrate Elm with existing JavaScript projects. Elm's type safety makes most of this possible with no bugs. But, bugs in your application's business logic can still appear.

In this chapter, you will address this dilemma by testing Elm code. Testing ensures your code behaves as expected and keeps bugs from creeping in. You will use test-driven development and the elm-test package to create and test a date library. Next, you will test certain properties of the library without worrying about specific test cases via fuzz testing. Finally, you will test an Elm application that depends on the date library. Once you finish this chapter, you will be ready to test drive your own Elm code and applications to prevent bugs.

## Test-Driven Development in Elm

You learned in Chapter 7, Develop, Debug, and Deploy with Powerful Tooling, on page 131 that the use of static types won't prevent all bugs. Recall the Picshare bug that added new photos to the end of the feed instead of the beginning.

```
feed ++ model.streamQueue
```

Elm's type system doesn't notice the bug because feed and model.streamQueue have the same type. A test could have prevented this bug.

Testing also helps you to better design your code modules' APIs. Developers call this *test-driven development* (TDD), or test-driven design. Some developers claim that test-driven development and design are different while others say they're the same. We won't wade into that debate; it's almost as bad as whether or not you should use semicolons in JavaScript.

Ignoring semantics, we'll focus on TDD's practicality. Essentially, you write your tests before you write code. This lets you define your code's requirements and gather feedback on your proposed API. If you find the API cumbersome to use or hard to test, then you can change it without refactoring the code.

In this section, you will begin building a small date library with TDD. You will use the elm-test package to write tests that clearly describe what you're testing. Then, you will implement the date library's functionality based on testing feedback.

## Use elm-test

Before we begin, let's touch on what you should test in Elm. Most Elm code comes from functions. Because Elm's functions are pure, you can easily *unit test* functions to test almost all of your code. Unit tests isolate and verify the behavior of one small piece of software. A function unit test verifies that a function returns a specific value given a particular set of arguments. For example, take this sayHello function.

```
sayHello : String -> String
sayHello name = "Hello, " ++ name
```

A unit test verifies that passing in the string "Tucker" returns "Hello, Tucker".

When you build helper modules for your applications, you should unit test their exposed functions. As you'll see later in this chapter, you will use *integration testing* to test the applications that use your modules. Integration testing verifies that your units work together correctly.

Let's focus on unit testing with TDD for now. In order to TDD a date library, you will need elm-test. The elm-test library has two parts, an Elm package for writing tests and an npm package for running tests. Install the npm package with this command:

```
npm install -g elm-test
```

You should now have an elm-test binary on your path. You can use the elm and elm-test binaries to bootstrap testing a project. Create a new directory called awesome-date and initialize an Elm project inside it:

```
elm init
```

Next, inside the awesome-date directory, run this command to enable testing:

```
elm-test init
```

The previous command added the elm-explorations/test[1] package to your elm.json's test-dependencies. It also created a tests directory. Inside tests, it made an example test file called Example.elm. Delete the example file and create a fresh AwesomeDateTest.elm file. A test's module name must match its filename, so name the module AwesomeDateTest. Expose suite from the module. You'll define it in a moment:

test-applications/AwesomeDateTest01.elm
```
module AwesomeDateTest exposing (suite)
```

You can use a different suffix or prefix in the filename and module name such as "Spec". The key point is that your test module and source module can't have the same name, so adding "Test" to the test module name prevents that. Next, import the Expect and Test modules from elm-test:

```
import Expect
import Test exposing (..)
```

The Expect module contains assertion or expectation functions. The Test module contains functions to define and organize your tests. You expose everything from Test but not Expect. Let's write our first test to understand why. Create a new test suite like this:

```
suite : Test
suite =
    describe "AwesomeDate" []
```

You have a constant called suite with type Test. The Test type comes from the Test module. Many Elm developers name this constant suite, but you can call it something else such as tests or testSuite. The elm-test runner doesn't care about the name. It runs all exposed Test constants.

You construct a test with the describe function, which comes from the Test module. It accepts a String description and a list of other tests. Basically, describe lets you group together related tests.

Inside the awesome-date directory, run an initial test suite with this command:

```
elm-test
```

After compiling, the test should fail with a message like this.

```
× AwesomeDateTest
    This `describe "AwesomeDate"` has no tests in it. Let's give it some!
```

The output tells you there are no real tests, so let's fix that.

---

1. https://package.elm-lang.org/packages/elm-explorations/test/latest/

## Write a Failing Test

The AwesomeDate module must let you create a date and extract a date's information such as the year, so let's test that first. Start by importing the Awesome-Date module, which doesn't exist yet:

test-applications/AwesomeDateTest02.elm
```
import AwesomeDate as Date exposing (Date)
```

Recall from Chapter 7, Develop, Debug, and Deploy with Powerful Tooling, on page 131 that the import..as syntax lets you shorten long module names. Here, you import AwesomeDate and alias it to Date. Then, you expose a Date type.

You need a sample date to test. This gives you the opportunity to define the AwesomeDate API before writing its implementation. A date has a year, month, and day. So, you could have a create function that accepts those values. Before the suite constant, make an exampleDate constant with the hypothetical create function:

```
exampleDate : Date
exampleDate =
    Date.create 2012 6 2
```

You call create with 2012, 6, and 2 to define exampleDate. This translates to June 2, 2012. Now, let's test extracting the year from exampleDate. Add a new test to the list in describe like so:

```
describe "AwesomeDate"
    [ test "retrieves the year from a date"
        (\() -> Expect.equal (Date.year exampleDate) 2012)
    ]
```

You write tests with the test function, which comes from the Test module. It takes two arguments, a String description and a function with the actual test. Inside the function argument, you accept a unit type () and return an Expectation. Expectations come from the Expect module's assertion functions.

You use an anonymous function that starts with \() ->. Recall from Chapter 2, Create Stateful Elm Applications, on page 27 that () is an empty value. The type system will infer that this anonymous function will receive a () argument, so you can pattern match it in the function definition. The () serves as an unused argument, allowing you to write a function that *delays* running the test code until needed.

The Expect.equal function checks that its two arguments are equal. The first argument is the *actual* output of the code under test. The second argument is what you *expect* the output of the code to be. In this case, you expect the output to be 2012.

Let's slightly reformat this test. Typically, you use the pipe operator to help distinguish the actual output from the expected output. Rewrite the anonymous function like so:

```
(\() ->
    Date.year exampleDate
        |> Expect.equal 2012
)
```

Ideally, a test's first line should be the test subject. Here, that's the Date.year function. You pipe its result into Expect.equal. This structure places the actual output at the start of the pipe chain and the expected output at the end, which makes tests easier to read.

One downside to using anonymous functions here is that you must wrap them in parentheses to avoid syntax errors. You can avoid doing that with this one cool trick. Rewrite the test like so:

```
describe "AwesomeDate"
    [ test "retrieves the year from a date" <|
        \_ ->
            Date.year exampleDate
                |> Expect.equal 2012
    ]
```

You remove the parentheses and add a <| operator between the test description and the anonymous function. This is the reverse pipe operator that you saw in Chapter 7, Develop, Debug, and Deploy with Powerful Tooling, on page 131. It passes in its right operand as the last argument to its left operand function. This prevents needing parentheses.

You also replace the () argument with the wildcard _. This may only be my personal preference, but I use the _ to signal that I don't care about the argument.

Now that you have added a test, run elm-test again. This time you should see a compiler error.

```
The AwesomeDateTest module has a bad import:

    import AwesomeDate

I cannot find that module! Is there a typo in the module name?
```

## Fix the Test

Fix the failing test by adding the AwesomeDate module. Create src/AwesomeDate.elm and name it AwesomeDate. Expose a Date type, create function, and year function:

test-applications/AwesomeDate01.elm
```
module AwesomeDate exposing (Date, create, year)
```

Next, add the Date type:

```
type Date
    = Date { year : Int, month : Int, day : Int }
```

The Date type is a custom type with one value called Date. Yes, you can give a custom type and one of its values the same name. The Date value accepts a record argument with three Int fields: year, month, and day.

You might wonder why we didn't create a type alias to the record instead. If you did, users could directly access the year field. If you shared the AwesomeDate module with the rest of the world, you wouldn't want to expose the Date type's implementation details. Why? Because changing the name of a field would introduce a breaking change to your users. They would have to update their codebases to use the new field before they could use your library's newest version.

You should instead expose an *opaque type*. An opaque type lets you offer a type for developers to use in type annotations without exposing implementation details. You can provide functions to use with the opaque type. For example, the year function would accept the opaque type and return the date's year. Later, you could change the internal year *field name* without causing a breaking change as long as you don't change the year *function's* type annotation.

Since Date is an opaque type, you need to implement the create function to build a date. Add create after the Date type:

```
create : Int -> Int -> Int -> Date
create year_ month_ day_ =
    Date { year = year_, month = month_, day = day_ }
```

You accept year_, month_, and day_ as Ints. Then, you build the record and pass it into the Date constructor function. You include underscores in each argument name to avoid *shadowing* the year function you will add next. What I mean here is if you were to use year inside the create function, it would refer to the argument and not the function with the same name. The argument year would shadow the function year. The Elm compiler disallows this ambiguity to make your code more readable. Adding the underscore fixes the ambiguity. (You don't have to use an underscore. You could have named the argument something else such as yr.)

Finally, let's implement the year function to make the test pass. Add the function after create:

```
year : Date -> Int
year (Date date) =
    date.year
```

In the type annotation, you accept a Date and return an Int. The function definition looks interesting, though. Instead of a date argument name, you have (Date record). This is *argument destructuring*. You've seen destructuring before in case expressions over custom type values. If a custom type has one value such as Date, then you can destructure it in a function argument. So, you unwrap the record from the Date value and return date.year.

You've now implemented all of AwesomeDate's missing pieces. Run elm-test, and you should have a passing test.

```
TEST RUN PASSED
Duration: 147 ms
Passed:   1
Failed:   0
```

Let's temporarily break the test to see a failing test case. In your AwesomeDate module, make the year function return -1. Run the tests, and you should see a failure like this.

```
✗ retrieves the year from a date
    -1

    │ Expect.equal

    2012
TEST RUN FAILED
Duration: 145 ms
Passed:   0
Failed:   1
```

The error message shows the actual output -1 and the expected output 2012. It mimics the test formatting from the pipe operator so you can see if the actual or expected output is wrong.

Great work. You just test-drove your first Elm library. Revert the temporary failure in the year function. Before proceeding to the next section, use TDD to implement similar month and day functions. Then, verify that your library and test files look similar to code/test-applications/AwesomeDate02.elm and code/test-applications/AwesomeDateTest02.elm from this book's code downloads.

# What to Expect When You're Expecting

Now that you're familiar with elm-test, let's explore its API further. So far, you've used the simple Expect.equal expectation. The Expect module has other expectations such as Expect.notEqual, Expect.lessThan, and Expect.greaterThan when a simple Expect.equal doesn't cut it. As you might imagine, an expectation such as Expect.greaterThan would expect the second argument (value to the left of the pipe operator) to be greater than the first argument. Look at this example to see what I mean.

```
describe "greaterThan"
    [ test "expects second argument to be greater than first" <|
        \_ -> 42 |> Expect.greaterThan 41
    ]
```

You can see more examples on the Expect module's documentation page.[2]

In this section, you will use other expectations such as Expect.true and Expect.false to continue test driving AwesomeDate. You will also create your own custom expectation with Expect.pass and Expect.fail.

## Expect True or False

The Expect.true and Expect.false expectations let you test Bool values. Each function expects a Bool of the same name. Let's use this pair of expectations to create an isLeapYear function for the AwesomeDate library.

Instead of adding new tests to suite, let's reorganize the tests. Duplicate the suite constant and tests. Rename the duplicated constant to testDateParts. Also, change the describe string to "date part getters":

```
test-applications/AwesomeDateTest03.elm
testDateParts : Test
testDateParts =
    describe "date part getters"
```

Modify the list of tests in suite to contain testDateParts. Since describe returns the Test type, you can nest describes inside each other:

```
suite : Test
suite =
    describe "AwesomeDate"
        [ testDateParts ]
```

Run the tests to verify they still pass. After testDateParts add a new testIsLeapYear constant like so:

---

2.   https://package.elm-lang.org/packages/elm-explorations/test/latest/Expect

```
testIsLeapYear : Test
testIsLeapYear =
    describe "isLeapYear"
```

The isLeapYear function must accept a year and return True if it's a leap year, or False otherwise. A leap year in the Gregorian calendar is divisible by 4 but not divisible by 100 unless it's also divisible by 400. For example, 2012 is divisible by 4 but not 100, so it's a leap year. 3000 is divisible by 4 and 100 but not divisible by 400, so it isn't a leap year. 2000 is also divisible by 4 and 100. But, it's divisible by 400, so it's still a leap year. Add an initial test for the year 2012:

```
[ test "returns true if divisible by 4 but not 100" <|
    \_ ->
        Date.isLeapYear 2012
            |> Expect.true "Expected leap year"
]
```

You call the nonexistent Date.isLeapYear function with 2012 and pipe the result into Expect.true. If isLeapYear returns True here, then Expect.true will pass. Because Expect.true only works with Booleans, it can't provide meaningful test runner feedback if the value is false. Thus, it takes a string message argument for the test runner to print when it fails. In this case, if the test fails, then the test runner will print "Expected leap year".

Add testIsLeapYear to the list of tests inside suite and run the tests:

```
suite =
    describe "AwesomeDate"
        [ testDateParts
        , testIsLeapYear
        ]
```

You should receive a compilation error since isLeapYear doesn't exist. Add a minimal isLeapYear implementation in AwesomeDate to make the test pass. Make sure you expose the isLeapYear function too:

```
isLeapYear : Int -> Bool
isLeapYear year_ =
    let
        isDivisibleBy n =
            remainderBy n year_ == 0
    in
    isDivisibleBy 4
```

You create a helper function called isDivisibleBy. It uses the remainderBy function, which returns the remainder of a division operation. You find the remainder of dividing the year by a given value. If the remainder is 0, then the year is divisible by that value. Here, you check if the year is divisible by 4.

Run the test suite again and it should pass. Next, add a test for a year that isn't divisible by 4 such as 2010:

```
, test "returns false if not divisible by 4" <|
    \_ ->
        Date.isLeapYear 2010
            |> Expect.false "Did not expect leap year"
```

You use Expect.false because isLeapYear should return False. Just like Expect.true, you provide a custom message if the test fails. Run the test suite and the new test should pass.

Now, let's add some failing test cases to finish implementing isLeapYear. Add tests for the years 3000 and 2000, like this:

```
, test "returns false if divisible by 4 and 100 but not 400" <|
    \_ ->
        Date.isLeapYear 3000
            |> Expect.false "Did not expect leap year"
, test "returns true if divisible by 4, 100, and 400" <|
    \_ ->
        Date.isLeapYear 2000
            |> Expect.true "Expected leap year"
```

The test case for 3000 ensures that a year divisible by 4 and 100 but not 400 is not a leap year. The test case for 2000 ensures that a year divisible by 4, 100, and 400 is a leap year. Run the test suite, and the test for 3000 should fail. Update the isLeapYear implementation to fix it:

```
isDivisibleBy 4 && not (isDivisibleBy 100)
```

Now you check that the year isn't divisible by 100. Run the test suite. The test for 3000 should pass, but the test for 2000 should fail. Add another check to isLeapYear to fix it:

```
isDivisibleBy 4 && not (isDivisibleBy 100) || isDivisibleBy 400
```

Run the test suite, and all the tests should pass. You again used TDD along with some new expectations to implement the isLeapYear function.

## Write a Custom Expectation

Now that you have an isLeapYear function, you can add functions to modify a date. You will write a simple function called addYears to change a date by a given amount of years. Create a new test constant called testAddYears:

```
testAddYears : Test
testAddYears =
    describe "addYears"
```

Use the exampleDate constant from earlier and the nonexistent Date.addYears function to add a test for changing the year:

```
[ test "changes a date's year" <|
    \_ ->
        Date.addYears 2 exampleDate
            |> Expect.equal (Date.create 2014 6 2)
]
```

You add 2 years to exampleDate and expect to receive the date June 2, 2014. Add testAddYears to suite and run the test, which should fail:

```
suite =
    describe "AwesomeDate"
        [ testDateParts
        , testIsLeapYear
        , testAddYears
        ]
```

Implement the addYears function:

```
addYears : Int -> Date -> Date
addYears years (Date date) =
    Date { date | year = date.year + years }
```

You unwrap the inner date record and use record update syntax to make the new year field equal date.year plus years. Then, you pass the new record back into the Date constructor. Run the tests, and they should all pass.

Make the test fail by changing the expected year in the test to 2016. Run the tests, and you should see a failure like this.

```
✘ changes a date's year
    Date { day = 2, month = 6, year = 2014 }

    │ Expect.equal
    │
    Date { day = 2, month = 6, year = 2016 }
```

This output works fine. It lets you know how the dates don't match. But, what if you wanted a custom failure message with formatted dates? Also, you may grow tired of writing Expect.equal (Date.create ...) for each test. You can make your own custom date expectation to solve both issues. Before you create it, you need to format dates. Add and expose a toDateString function inside AwesomeDate:

```
toDateString : Date -> String
toDateString (Date date) =
    [ date.month, date.day, date.year ]
        |> List.map String.fromInt
        |> String.join "/"
```

The toDateString function formats dates in the "month/day/year" convention used in the United States. You unwrap the record and create a list with date.month, date.day, and date.year in that order. Then, you convert each value to a string with List.map and String.fromInt. Finally, you combine the values into one string with a "/" separator via the String.join[3] function. For example, June 2, 2012, would become "6/2/2012".

Now you can format dates. Back in the test file, add a custom expectation function called expectDate:

```
expectDate : Int -> Int -> Int -> Date -> Expect.Expectation
expectDate year month day actualDate =
    let
        expectedDate =
            Date.create year month day
    in
    if actualDate == expectedDate then
        Expect.pass

    else
        Expect.fail <|
            Date.toDateString actualDate
                ++ "\n╷\n│ expectDate\n╵\n"
                ++ Date.toDateString expectedDate
```

The expectDate function accepts year, month, and day as Int arguments. It also accepts an actualDate argument. It creates an expectedDate with Date.create and checks if actualDate and expectedDate are equal. If so, then it returns Expect.pass which automatically passes a test.

If the dates aren't equal, it returns Expect.fail. Expect.fail accepts a String failure message and fails a test. You build a failure message with the new Date.toDateString function. You display the actual value above the expected value to mimic the test failure pipe formatting from other Expect functions. Between the two values, you use newlines and the Unicode characters U+2577, U+2502, and U+2575 to build the pipe. You can copy the Unicode characters from Wikipedia.[4] If you have trouble, you can use the ASCII | character.

---

3.   https://package.elm-lang.org/packages/elm/core/latest/String#join
4.   https://en.wikipedia.org/wiki/Box_Drawing

In your previous test, replace Expect.equal with expectDate. Keep the incorrect year so you can test your custom failure message:

```
Date.addYears 2 exampleDate
    |> expectDate 2016 6 2
```

Run the test suite again. You should now see a failure like this.

```
✗ changes a date's year
    6/2/2014

    │
    │  expectDate
    │

    6/2/2016
```

Looking good. Put the correct year of 2014 back in and run the tests. They should pass again.

Let's finish implementing addYears to conclude this section. Add a test leapDate after the exampleDate constant:

```
leapDate : Date
leapDate =
    Date.create 2012 2 29
```

Then, add a test for changing the year of leapDate:

```
, test "prevents leap days on non-leap years" <|
    \_ ->
        Date.addYears 1 leapDate
            |> expectDate 2013 2 28
```

Run the tests. The leap date test should fail. The addYears function doesn't account for leap years when changing the date. If you change the year on February 29 to a non-leap year, then you must roll back to February 28. Add a preventInvalidLeapDates function after addYears in AwesomeDate.elm:

```
preventInvalidLeapDates : Date -> Date
preventInvalidLeapDates (Date date) =
    if not (isLeapYear date.year) && date.month == 2 && date.day >= 29 then
        Date { date | day = 28 }

    else
        Date date
```

You accept a Date and return a Date. You check if the year is not a leap year and if the date is February 29. If so, then you change the date to February 28 with record update syntax. In the else branch, you reuse the date record and pass it back into the Date constructor because nothing should change.

Inside addYears, pipe the new date into preventInvalidLeapDates:

```
addYears : Int -> Date -> Date
addYears years (Date date) =
    Date { date | year = date.year + years }
        |> preventInvalidLeapDates
```

Run your test suite, and all addYears' tests should pass. Now you can build and use your own custom expectations for richer tests. Before you proceed, verify that your library and test files look similar to code/test-applications/Awesome-Date03.elm and code/test-applications/AwesomeDateTest03.elm from this book's code downloads.

# Fuzz Your Tests

Selecting test inputs and considering edge cases can consume a lot of testing time. You mainly care that a certain property of a function holds true regardless of the input. For example, after you call addYears, you expect the difference between the old and new dates' years to equal the argument to addYears.

In this section, you will use fuzz testing to test properties of your date library. You will generate random test input with fuzzers and use the input inside test code. You will discover the pros and cons of fuzz testing and learn when you should use it. You will also create your own fuzzer to randomly generate dates.

## Create Your First Fuzz Test

Historically, developers in languages such as C++ and Java use fuzz testing to generate random inputs and random orderings of method calls to cause crashes. Thanks to these crashes, they can find buggy edge cases. Elm doesn't have this concern because of its richer types and no runtime exceptions. Elm's fuzz testing resembles *property-based testing*. As I mentioned earlier, this fuzz testing style tests certain properties of functions. You can test a function without worrying about the specific test inputs.

Let's write our first fuzz test to see what all the fuzz is about. Let's use the example I suggested earlier to ensure that addYears always changes the year by a given amount. In your test file, import the Fuzz module from elm-test. Expose Fuzzer, int, and intRange:

test-applications/AwesomeDateTest04.elm
```
import Fuzz exposing (Fuzzer, int, intRange)
```

The int fuzzer generates a random integer and the intRange fuzzer generates a random integer between two values. Fuzzer is the type for fuzzers. Next, add a fuzz test to testAddYears like so:

```
, fuzz int "changes the year by the amount given" <|
    \years ->
        let
            newDate =
                Date.addYears years exampleDate
        in
        (Date.year newDate - Date.year exampleDate)
            |> Expect.equal years
```

The fuzz function comes from the Test module. It accepts a fuzzer, test description, and test function. Here, you give it the int fuzzer. Inside the test function, instead of (), you receive the random integer as an argument called years. Then, you compute a newDate by calling Date.addYears with the randomly generated years and exampleDate. You calculate the difference between newDate's and exampleDate's years and verify it equals the years argument.

The fuzz function will run the test multiple times and use the int fuzzer to generate a random integer each time. By default, elm-test will run a fuzz test 100 times. You can specify a different number of runs with the --fuzz flag. For example, elm-test --fuzz 200 would run fuzz tests 200 times. Multiple runs ensure that no matter what input, addYears will create a date with the correct new year. Run the tests, and the new fuzz test should pass.

Let's break the addYears function to see how fuzz testing discovers bugs. Let's say we originally called the function increaseYears and only supported positive arguments. Later, we renamed it to addYears but forgot to allow negative arguments. Inside AwesomeDate.elm, temporarily change the addYears implementation to this:

```
if years < 0 then
    Date date

else
    Date { date | year = date.year + years }
        |> preventInvalidLeapDates
```

Rerun the test suite. You should see a failure similar to this.

```
✗ changes the year by the amount given
Given -1
    0

    |
    |  Expect.equal
    |
    -1
```

The fuzz test prints the failing input along with the actual and expected output. In my example, the test received -1. Your test might receive a different value.

If this were a real failure, you would quickly realize you forgot to fix the implementation. Revert the "bug" and run the test suite. All tests should pass again.

## Build Fuzz Ranges

Now that you're familiar with the int fuzzer, let's try out the intRange fuzzer. You will use it to reduce the number of isLeapYear tests to one. Before you begin, you'll need a list of valid leap years. From this book's code downloads, copy the contents of the code/test-applications/leap-years.txt into your test file. The copied code contains a validLeapYears list.

Next, replace all the tests in testIsLeapYear with the following code:

```
describe "isLeapYear"
    [ fuzz (intRange -400 3000) "determines leap years correctly" <|
        \year ->
            if List.member year validLeapYears then
                Date.isLeapYear year
                    |> Expect.true "Expected leap year"

            else
                Date.isLeapYear year
                    |> Expect.false "Did not expect leap year"
    ]
```

You call the intRange fuzzer with a starting year of -400 and an ending year of 3000 and pass it into fuzz. Inside the test code, the fuzzer will only generate years between -400 and 3000. You check if validLeapYears contains the year via List.member. If so, then you expect Date.isLeapYear to return True. Otherwise, you expect Date.isLeapYear to return False.

Run the test suite and it should pass. Then, break the code to see an example failure. Temporarily change isLeapYear to only check divisibility by 4:

```
isDivisibleBy 4
```

Run the tests and you should see a failure like this.

```
× determines leap years correctly
Given 1500
    Did not expect leap year
```

I had one failing year. You might have more and they might be different years. Regardless, the fuzzer found a bug in the implementation thanks to the hardcoded validLeapYears list. Of course, validLeapYears could contain years beyond 2996, but its current range provides a good sample size. If isLeapYear passes for them, then the implementation should be sound. Revert isLeapYear and run the tests to verify they pass.

Before you celebrate reducing the number of isLeapYear tests, realize that it cost something. Although you can test multiple inputs with little code, you lost some debuggability. When the test failed, you didn't immediately know *why* it failed. The previous tests at least described which leap year property the code violated. For example, the description "returns false if divisible by 4 and 100 but not 400" clearly indicates why the test failed.

Some developers might say that those tests couple the descriptions to the function's implementation and that the fuzz test offers a better "black box" approach. I believe that describing specific test cases makes it easy to know what to fix when tests fail. Specific test cases also document specific behavior and help new developers learn the codebase quicker.

You could use a hybrid approach. Build a catch-all fuzz test to find unexpected edge cases and specific tests for documenting behavior and covering known edge cases. If your fuzz test discovers a bug in the future, then you can write a specific test case for the bug fix. Ultimately, find a balance that helps you test and document code without sacrificing debuggability.

## Create a Fuzzer

Before you finish this section, let's explore advanced fuzz testing by building a custom fuzzer. Earlier, you added an untested toDateString function. Let's test it now. You'll need another function called daysInMonth. To avoid going down a rabbit hole, you will copy daysInMonth and several other functions instead of writing and testing them yourself. Copy them from code/test-applications/extra-date-functions.txt in this book's code downloads and paste them at the bottom of AwesomeDate.elm. Expose Weekday(..), addDays, addMonths, daysInMonth, fromISO8601, toISO8601, weekday, and weekdayToString from AwesomeDate.elm.

I've based these functions and the AwesomeDate library on the defunct elm-community/elm-time package. I copied some functions from it and adapted others. I have minimally tested my adaptations, so they will work fine for you here and in the next section. But, I encourage you to examine them and test them yourself. You might improve them through testing.

In order to fuzz test toDateString, you need to generate a random date. Essentially, you must generate a random year, month, and day together. You can almost do that with the fuzz3 function.[5] It accepts three fuzzer arguments and provides each random value to your test. You can pick a random year with int, a random month with intRange between 1 and 12, and a random day with

---

5. https://package.elm-lang.org/packages/elm-explorations/test/latest/Test#fuzz3

intRange. But, if you want a valid date, you can't hardcode the random day range. It depends on the month and year.

Instead, let's create our own date fuzzer to solve this dilemma. You'll need to use the elm/random package. The elm-test init already added elm/random to the indirect test-dependencies inside elm.json, but you should be explicit and move it to the direct test-dependencies. Run this command inside your awesome-date directory:

```
elm-test install elm/random
```

Back inside your test file, import the Random module as well as the Shrink module, which comes from elm-test. I'll explain Shrink in a second:

```
import Random
import Shrink
```

Add a dateFuzzer after the leapDate constant:

```
dateFuzzer : Fuzzer ( Int, Int, Int )
dateFuzzer =
    let
        randomYear = Random.int Random.minInt Random.maxInt
        randomMonth = Random.int 1 12
        generator =
            Random.pair randomYear randomMonth
                |> Random.andThen
                    (\( year, month ) ->
                        Random.int 1 (Date.daysInMonth year month)
                            |> Random.map (\day -> ( year, month, day ))
                    )
        shrinker dateTuple =
            Shrink.tuple3 ( Shrink.int, Shrink.int, Shrink.int ) dateTuple
    in
    Fuzz.custom generator shrinker
```

You give dateFuzzer a Fuzzer type. The Fuzzer type has a type variable that you fill in with a 3-tuple of Ints. You create the custom fuzzer with Fuzz.custom at the bottom. It accepts two arguments, a *generator* and a *shrinker*.

Generators produce random values for fuzz tests. Here, you use the Random module to create a generator. Inside the let expression, you make two local constants with Random.int, randomYear and randomMonth. Random.int produces a random integer between starting and ending values.

For randomYear, you pass in Random.minInt and Random.maxInt, the smallest and largest integers that work well for generating random integers. Like most of Random's functions, Random.int returns a Generator type. Generating a random value is a side effect like fetching from a REST API. Elm uses the Generator to generate the random value on your behalf when you run the test suite.

For randomMonth, you pass in 1 and 12 to produce a random month. Then, you create a local generator constant. You pass randomYear and randomMonth into Random.pair, which generates a tuple pair. The first item in the pair will be the randomly generated year and the second item will be the randomly generated month.

You pipe the pair generator into Random.andThen. Random.andThen resembles the Json.Decode.andThen function from Chapter 7, Develop, Debug, and Deploy with Powerful Tooling, on page 131. Random.andThen lets you create a Generator from the randomly generated value of another Generator. The anonymous function you provide to andThen receives the tuple with the random year and month.

You generate a random valid day based on the year and month. You again use Random.int with 1 and the result of calling Date.daysInMonth with the randomly generated year and month. You pipe this day generator into Random.map. Random.map mimics List.map and Maybe.map, letting you transform the generated value. In this case, you convert the randomly generated day into a 3-tuple that holds the randomly generated year, month, and day.

Whew! That handles the generator, but let's decipher the shrinker. You create a local shrinker constant and pass it into Fuzz.custom. The Shrink module comes from elm-test. The test runner uses shrinkers to reduce inputs down to the smallest inputs needed to produce fuzz-test failures. With no shrinker, a fuzz test could return many redundant failing test cases that would make reading the test output difficult.

The shrinker is a function that accepts the current input and returns a LazyList of "shrunk" inputs (i.e., smaller values). (LazyList is an internal type inside elm-test.) You create a shrinker with Shrink.tuple3 and Shrink.int. Shrink.tuple3 takes a tuple of three shrinkers to apply to each respective input inside the 3-tuple. Since all three inputs are Int, you place Shrink.int inside each tuple slot.

Now you can generate random dates as a tuple of year, month, and day to use in fuzz tests. Create a new testToDateString constant that uses your dateFuzzer:

```
testToDateString : Test
testToDateString =
    describe "toDateString"
        [ fuzz dateFuzzer "creates a valid date string" <|
            \( year, month, day ) ->
                Date.create year month day
                    |> Date.toDateString
```

```
                        |> Expect.equal
                           (String.fromInt month
                               ++ "/"
                               ++ String.fromInt day
                               ++ "/"
                               ++ String.fromInt year
                           )
         ]
```

You provide dateFuzzer to the fuzz function. Inside your test function, you destructure the tuple to access the random year, month, and day. Then, you use year, month, and day to construct a Date. You convert it to a string with toDateString and use Expect.equal to compare the output with the expected output.

Add testToDateString to suite:

```
suite =
    describe "AwesomeDate"
        [ testDateParts
        , testIsLeapYear
        , testAddYears
        , testToDateString
        ]
```

Run the tests and they should pass. Verify the test truly works by breaking the implementation. Temporarily change the delimiter in toDateString to "-" instead of "/". You likely will see one failing test case when year, month, and day are all 0.

```
✗ creates a valid date string
Given (0,0,0)
    "0-0-0"

    │ Expect.equal
    │
    "0/0/0"
```

If you want to see more failing test cases, modify the shrinker in dateFuzzer to call Shrink.noShrink with the dateTuple. Shrink.noShrink does not shrink down test inputs:

```
shrinker dateTuple =
    Shrink.noShrink dateTuple
```

Revert the change of "/" to "-" inside toDateString and verify your tests pass again.

Now that you have a dateFuzzer, you can improve the fuzz test for addYears. You generate a random number of years, but use the same exampleDate. As an exercise use dateFuzzer and the fuzz2 function to provide a random date to the test. Construct a date from the random year, month, and day and then add the random years to it with addYears. Check fuzz2's documentation[6] for guidance.

Before proceeding, verify your library and test files look similar to code/test-applications/AwesomeDate04.elm and code/test-applications/AwesomeDateTest04.elm from this book's code downloads.

## Test an Application

Earlier in this chapter, you learned about unit and integration testing. Fully testing Elm projects requires both types of testing. Unit tests ensure that functions behave correctly in isolation. Integration tests ensure that those functions work together as expected.

So far, you've focused on unit testing the AwesomeDate module. In this section, you will test an Elm application that uses it. You will use a combination of unit and integration tests to test the update and view functions. Let's get started.

First, you need the application. Outside of your awesome-date directory, create a new directory called awesome-date-app. Copy the contents of the code/test-applications/awesome-date-app directory from this book's code downloads into your new awesome-date-app directory.

The application needs the AwesomeDate library, so copy it from your awesome-date/src directory into your awesome-date-app/src directory. Then, install dependencies with npminside awesome-date-app:

```
npm install
```

Once installation finishes, start the application:

```
npm start
```

The application will listen on port 3000 or prompt you to run on a different port. Once it boots, it will open a new browser tab. You should see something similar to the following screenshot.

<table>
<tr><td>**1. Pick a Date**</td><td>**2. Find a Future Date**</td></tr>
</table>

| | | |
|---|---|---|
| 02/01/2018 | Years: 0   Months: 0   Days: 0 | |

**Weekday** Thursday
**Days in Month** 28
**Leap Year?** No

**Future Date:** 2/1/2018

---

6.   https://package.elm-lang.org/packages/elm-explorations/test/latest/Test#fuzz2

Try out the application. Click the date input on the left to select a date. The application uses a native HTML date picker. If a date picker doesn't pop up, make sure you're using a modern version of Chrome or Firefox. The application displays information about the selected date, including the weekday, days in the month, and whether it falls on a leap year. On the right, you can add years, months, and days to the selected date to display a future date.

## Test the Update Function

Elm applications depend on the update function to be interactive. Without an update function, an application can't change state. Critical logic lives in update so you should test it. The update function may appear magical in the Elm Architecture, but it's just a function—you can test it like any other function. If you pass in certain message and model arguments, you should expect back a particular change in the new model.

Open src/App.elm to examine the application's source code. The Model contains fields for the selected date and the amount of years, months, and days to calculate the future date.

test-applications/awesome-date-app/src/App.elm
```
type alias Model =
    { selectedDate : Date
    , years : Maybe Int
    , months : Maybe Int
    , days : Maybe Int
    }
```

The application only has two Msg values, SelectDate and ChangeDateOffset. SelectDate accepts a Maybe Date argument because parsing the selected string date from an input could fail. ChangeDateOffset accepts DateOffsetField and Maybe Int arguments. DateOffsetField is a custom type with values to represent the years, months, and days fields.

```
type DateOffsetField
    = Years
    | Months
    | Days


type Msg
    = SelectDate (Maybe Date)
    | ChangeDateOffset DateOffsetField (Maybe Int)
```

The update function actually does very little. It calls an updateModel function with the msg and model arguments to compute a new model.

```
updateModel : Msg -> Model -> Model
updateModel msg model =
```

```
case msg of
    SelectDate (Just date) ->
        { model | selectedDate = date }
    ChangeDateOffset Years years ->
        { model | years = years }
    ChangeDateOffset Months months ->
        { model | months = months }
    ChangeDateOffset Days days ->
        { model | days = days }
    _ ->
        model
```

The updateModel function changes the selectedDate if SelectDate contains Just date. ChangeDateOffset holds Maybe of years, months, or days. updateModel sets those values directly to their respective fields in the model based on the inner Date-OffsetField argument value. Otherwise, updateModel ignores the Msg and returns the current model.

Although updateModel contains the critical update logic, you will unit test it indirectly by testing the public update function. You should try to test through your public API as much as possible before reaching to test "private" functions. Testing something private requires exposing it.

Let's run the initial test suite. First, to have a complete test suite, copy your AwesomeDateTest.elm file from your awesome-date/tests directory into your awesome-date-app/tests directory. Then, inside awesome-date-app, run the tests with npm:

```
npm test
```

The test script will run elm-test for you. You should see a passing test suite with some TODOS.

```
TEST RUN INCOMPLETE because there are 3 TODOs remaining
Duration: 180 ms
Passed:   8
Failed:   0
Todo:     3
◦ TODO: implement event tests
◦ TODO: implement view tests
◦ TODO: implement update tests
```

These TODOS come from the tests/AppTest.elm file. Open the file in your editor. It already imports App, AwesomeDate, Expect, and Test. It also contains test dates, helper functions, and test placeholders. For example, the testUpdate placeholder is a Test type that uses the todo function from the Test module. The todo function lets you describe a test without writing it. Running the test suite reminds you about it.

Let's add real tests to testUpdate. Start by testing changing the selected date. Replace testUpdate's todo with a describe that contains one test:

```
describe "update"
    [ test "selects a date" <|
        \_ ->
            App.update (selectDate futureDate) initialModel
                |> Tuple.first
                |> Expect.equal { initialModel | selectedDate = futureDate }
    ]
```

You call App.update with the SelectDate message and a test initialModel provided in the file. You use the selectDate function helper to simplify creating a SelectDate message. You then use a test futureDate created earlier in the file as the date to select:

```
selectDate : Date -> App.Msg
selectDate date =
    App.SelectDate (Just date)
```

After you call App.update, you receive the new model and a Cmd inside a tuple. You only need the model, so you pipe the tuple into Tuple.first, which returns the first item from a tuple pair. Then, you compare the returned model with an expected model. You build the expected model with record update syntax to change the initialModel's selectedDate to futureDate.

Run the tests. The TODO for testUpdate should disappear, and you should have a new passing test.

Let's test the ChangeDateOffset message next. Add a test for changing the years field like so:

```
, test "changes years" <|
    \_ ->
        App.update (changeDateOffset App.Years 3) initialModel
            |> Tuple.first
            |> Expect.equal { initialModel | years = Just 3 }
```

This resembles the previous test. Here, you use the provided changeDateOffset helper function to easily build a ChangeDateOffset message:

```
changeDateOffset : App.DateOffsetField -> Int -> App.Msg
changeDateOffset field amount =
    App.ChangeDateOffset field (Just amount)
```

Since you're changing the years field, you provide the Years DateOffsetField value. You also provide 3 as the amount of years. After updating, you extract the new model with Tuple.first and compare it to the expected model. You use record update syntax to create an expected model with years equal to Just 3.

Run the tests, and you should have another passing test. Add similar tests for changing the months and days fields as an exercise. Once you're done, check that your AppTest.elm file matches code/test-applications/AppTest01.elm from this book's code downloads.

## Test the View

After the update function, an Elm application heavily depends on the view function, so you need to test it. Deciding how to test the view function poses a challenge. You don't want to test the literal output because that highly couples your test to the implementation. If you slightly altered the markup for styling purposes, you would break the test.

Instead, you should write tests that focus on important logic. If a view function conditionally displays certain text based on a model field, you want to test that. Also, you must guard these tests from breaking due to inconsequential markup changes.

Thankfully, elm-test offers modules for testing view functions. Add these imports to AppTest.elm:

```
test-applications/AppTest02.elm
import Test.Html.Query as Query
import Test.Html.Selector exposing (attribute, id, tag, text)
```

You import Test.Html.Query and alias it to a shorter Query name with the as keyword. Then, you import Test.Html.Selector, exposing attribute, id, tag, and text functions. You will use Query's and Selector's functions to query and make expectations against the virtual DOM returned from view.

You'll also need the Html.Attributes module. Import it and expose type_ and value:

```
import Html.Attributes exposing (type_, value)
```

Great. Let's first test that the date input holds the selected date value. Replace testView's todo with a describe, and the following test:

```
describe "view"
    [ test "displays the selected date" <|
        \_ ->
            App.view initialModel
                |> Query.fromHtml
                |> Query.find [ tag "input", attribute (type_ "date") ]
                |> Query.has [ attribute (value "2012-06-02") ]
    ]
```

You pass the test initialModel into the view function which produces virtual DOM. You can't easily inspect Elm's virtual DOM so you convert it into a queryable version via the Query.fromHtml function.

Then, you pipe the result into the Query.find function. Query.find accepts a list of selectors that specify what element to find. In this case, you use the tag and attribute functions from the Selector module. The tag function accepts a string tag name, and the attribute function accepts an Html.Attribute. Here, you request an input tag with a date type. If Query.find can't locate the element, then it fails the test. Otherwise, it returns the element.

Finally, you pipe the element into Query.has. Query.has checks that an element matches the list of given selectors. It returns an Expectation type. In this case, you verify that the date input has a value attribute of "2012-06-02". That date comes from the test initialModel which uses the test selectedDate as the initially selected date. The "year-month-day" date format comes from native HTML date inputs. You format dates in App.elm with the Date.toISO8601 function which you copied and pasted in the previous section.

Run the tests and the new testView test should pass. Break the test by changing the expected date. The test failure should print the rendered HTML and specify which part of Query failed, in a manner similar to this. (I'm purposely leaving out all the rendered HTML for space.)

```
✗ displays the selected date
    ▼ Query.fromHtml
        <div class="content">
          ...
        </div>

    ▼ Query.find [ tag "input", attribute "type" "date" ]
        1)   <input type="date" value="2012-06-02">

    ▼ Query.has [ attribute "value" "2013-06-02" ]
    ✗ has attribute "value" "2013-06-02"
```

Revert your change, and make sure the tests pass again.

You want to carefully approach how you query the virtual DOM. For example, let's test the displayed weekday next. Inside App.elm, you use a copied-and-pasted Date.weekday function to determine the weekday. You display the weekday inside a table via the viewDateInfo and viewTableRow functions. You would need to query for a specific row in the table to test this. Later, if you moved the weekday to an unordered list, your test would break even though you still display the weekday.

To prevent this problem, you can add a unique id to the row and query it instead. In fact, I've already set the table rows up with ids in App.elm. Notice that you call viewTableRow with the string "info-weekday".

```
viewTableRow
    "info-weekday" "Weekday" (Date.weekdayToString <| Date.weekday date)
```

Inside viewTableRow, you accept the first argument as an identifier that you pass into the id function from Html.Attributes.

```
viewTableRow identifier label value =
    tr [ id identifier ]
        [ th [] [ text label ]
        , td [] [ text value ]
        ]
```

Back in AppTest.elm, add a new test that queries for the id like so:

```
, test "displays the weekday" <|
    \_ ->
        App.view initialModel
            |> Query.fromHtml
            |> Query.find [ id "info-weekday" ]
            |> Query.has [ text "Saturday" ]
```

You convert view's output with Query.fromHtml and locate the element with Query.find and the id Selector function. Then, you check that the element has the text "Saturday" via Query.has and the text Selector function. Run the tests and they should pass.

Peppering your source code with ids may feel hacky, but it's a fair trade-off. You can prevent brittle tests that fail from small markup changes.

Now, practice adding some view tests of your own. Start by testing the other table rows, including the days in the month and if the date falls on a leap year. Then, write some tests for the part of the application that displays a future date. Use initialModel with App.view to test that the inputs display an initial 0. Next, use modelWithDateOffsets at the top of the file to test that the inputs display the correct year, month, and day field values. Finally, use modelWithDate-Offsets to test that view displays the correct future date below the inputs.

Once you finish, check that your AppTest.elm file matches code/test-applications/AppTest02.elm from this book's code downloads.

## Test the Events

Not only can you test what view displays, but also the events, or messages, that it produces. These tests ensure that you've wired up input and click event handlers with the correct Msg value. In the test file, import the Test.Html.Event module and alias it to Event with the as keyword:

test-applications/AppTest03.elm
```
import Test.Html.Event as Event
```

Replace testEvents' todo with a describe and this test:

```
describe "events"
    [ test "receives selected date changes" <|
        \_ ->
            App.view initialModel
                |> Query.fromHtml
                |> Query.find [ tag "input", attribute (type_ "date") ]
                |> Event.simulate (Event.input "2015-09-21")
                |> Event.expect (selectDate futureDate)
    ]
```

You call App.view with initialModel and convert the result with Query.fromHtml. Then, you find the date input. Next, you pipe the element into Event.simulate. The Event.simulate function mimics an event on an element. In this case, you create an input event with the Event.input function. You provide futureDate as a formatted date String to Event.input to simulate the date selection. Recall that Elm's real onInput event handler receives a String input value.

Event.simulate returns an Event type which you then pipe into Event.expect. The Event.expect function takes a message and compares it to the message inside the Event value. In this case, you call the selectDate helper with futureDate to check that the event produces a SelectDate Msg containing futureDate.

Run the test suite and it should pass. Also, the test output shouldn't have any TODOS. Feel free to temporarily break the test to preview a failure message. Try providing a different formatted date to Event.input. Be sure to revert any purposeful failures before moving on.

For more practice, let's test the input for changing the years field. Add this test to testEvents:

```
, test "receives years offset changes" <|
    \_ ->
        App.view initialModel
            |> Query.fromHtml
            |> Query.find [ id "offset-years" ]
            |> Event.simulate (Event.input "3")
            |> Event.expect (changeDateOffset App.Years 3)
```

This test closely resembles the previous one. You convert the virtual DOM and locate the year input with the id selector. Then, you simulate an input event with a String "3" as the value. You expect the message to match Change-DateOffset Years (Just 3) thanks to the changeDateOffset helper.

Run your tests and they should still pass. As an exercise, add similar tests for the months and days inputs.

When you're done, make sure the tests pass and that your AppTest.elm file matches code/test-applications/AppTest03.elm from this book's code downloads.

You've built a well-rounded test suite. You used unit tests and integration tests along with the Test.Html.* modules from elm-test to test important parts of the update and view functions.

## What You Learned

Well done. You achieved a lot in this chapter. You learned about unit tests and integration tests in Elm. You practiced TDD to build a date library. You used elm-test to create tests and expectations. Then, you used fuzz testing to test properties of code with random inputs. You even built your own date fuzzer. Finally, you tested an Elm application. You tested the update function to verify that the application's state changed correctly. You ensured the view function displayed expected information and produced correct event messages without heavily coupling tests to the markup.

You are ready to start test-driving your own Elm code and applications. Now that you can build and test Elm applications, we can focus on more complex types of applications. In the next chapter, you will learn how to build your own single-page applications with Elm.

# CHAPTER 10

# Build Single-Page Applications

In the previous chapter, you tested an Elm library and an entire Elm application. You have progressed through many concepts to become a skilled Elm developer who can build, scale, and test Elm applications. But, in this book, you've only worked on applications with one responsibility.

Over the past several years, front-end applications have grown increasingly complex. In ye olden days, teams managed complexity with back-end frameworks. They generated and served almost all HTML from the framework. Then, they sprinkled in additional functionality with simple JavaScript files.

User experience and performance sometimes suffered under this model. Servers delivered lots of the same content, such as an application's layout, to the browser for each new page request. Nowadays, many teams have adopted *single-page applications* (SPA). In an SPA, the server sends a minimal HTML file and a single JavaScript file. The JavaScript application seamlessly renders new "pages" for a user by responding to URL changes and making API calls to the back end.

In this chapter, you will learn how to build SPAs in Elm. You will access, parse, and store the current URL as a route with the Url module and Browser.application function. Then, you will represent separate pages with Elm components. Finally, you will use the Elm Architecture to store state for each component and display the appropriate component for the current URL. When you complete this chapter, you will be able to create your own Elm SPAs that handle multiple routes and provide rich experiences for your users.

## Build a Skeleton SPA

In this book's beginning chapters, you built a nifty Picshare application that displayed a feed of photos. We're welcoming it back for one last hurrah. You will convert Picshare into a single-page application. By the end of this chapter, your Picshare application will display a public feed of photos, an individual user's feed of photos, and an account page.

You'll slowly work toward the final result. First, you need to connect some SPA plumbing. In this section, you will create an SPA skeleton. You will use the elm/url package to convert the current URL into a route. Then, you will access the current URL with a new function from the Browser module and store page state with the Elm Architecture. Finally, you will display different content based on the current page state. Let's dig in.

## Routing All URLs

Grab a copy of the base application. Create a new directory called picshare-spa and populate it with the contents of the code/single-page-applications/picshare directory from this book's code downloads. Inside your picshare-spa directory, run these commands to install dependencies and start the development server:

```
npm install
npm start
```

The last command should start a development server on port 3000 and open a new tab in your browser. You should see the text "Single Page Applications." The skeleton application resides in src/Main.elm. Review it in your editor.

The application already defines Model, initialModel, init, view, Msg, update, and subscriptions. You'll return to Main.elm in a bit.

Inside the picshare-spa directory, install the elm/url[1] package:

```
elm install elm/url
```

You need to define routes for your Picshare SPA. Create a new file in src called Routes.elm. Make a custom type called Route with two constructors, Home and Account:

single-page-applications/samples/Routes01.elm
```
type Route
    = Home
    | Account
```

A custom type lets the type system enforce which routes are valid. If you used string routes, then the type system would allow any string value. The Home route will eventually display the public feed, and the Account route will eventually display the account page.

---

1. https://package.elm-lang.org/packages/elm/url/latest

Next, you need to convert string URLs into the appropriate Route constructor. Before the Route type, import the Url and Url.Parser modules from elm/url:

```
import Url exposing (Url)
import Url.Parser as Parser exposing (Parser)
```

You expose the Url type from the Url module. You also use import..as syntax to shorten Url.Parser to Parser for brevity's sake and expose the Parser type. Url.Parser provides several functions to build parsers that attempt to parse URLs into Elm types. Make a parser for your routes like so:

```
routes : Parser (Route -> a) a
routes =
    Parser.oneOf
        [ Parser.map Home Parser.top
        , Parser.map Account (Parser.s "account")
        ]
```

You create a parser called routes with a Parser type. The type arguments appear confusing. We won't explore Url.Parser's implementation details, so just focus on the first type variable. Notice that it uses the Route custom type. This essentially signifies that the routes parser will produce routes of type Route.

In the definition of routes, you call Parser.oneOf. It accepts a list of other URL parsers. It tries each parser until one succeeds. Inside the list, you create two path parsers.

The first Parser.top parser captures the root path /. Then, you pass Parser.top into Parser.map along with the Home constructor. In this case, Parser.map will return Home if the current path matches /.

The second Parser.s parser captures a specific path segment. You call it with "account", so it will attempt to match the /account path. You again pass the parser into Parser.map to return a different value. In this case, you return the Account constructor.

Create a match function that uses the routes parser to convert URLs:

```
match : Url -> Maybe Route
match url =
    Parser.parse routes url
```

The match function accepts the Url type from the Url module. Url is a record type with similar properties to the window.location object in JavaScript. You will access the current Url later with a special function from the Browser module and the Elm Architecture.

The match function calls Parser.parse. You pass in the routes parser and the url. Parser.parse tries to parse the url's path field with the provided parser. It returns a Maybe because the parser may not match the current path. In this case, if the parser matches, then Parser.parse will return a Route constructor inside Just. Otherwise, it will return Nothing.

Declare the Routes module at the top of the file and expose all Route constructors and the match function:

```
module Routes exposing (Route(..), match)
```

Let's try out Routes inside the application next.

## Create a Browser.application

Switch back to Main.elm, and import your Routes module and the Url module, exposing the Url type:

single-page-applications/samples/Main01.elm
```
import Routes
import Url exposing (Url)
```

Also, update the Browser import to expose the Document and UrlRequest types, and import the Browser.Navigation module, aliasing it to Navigation:

```
import Browser exposing (Document, UrlRequest)
import Browser.Navigation as Navigation
```

You will use these types and Browser.Navigation in a moment.

You need to display different content based on the current route. So, you need to store some form of route information in the model. Instead of storing a Route constructor, you will build and use a Page type. Add it before the Model type alias:

```
type Page
    = PublicFeed
    | Account
    | NotFound
```

The Page type has three constructors, PublicFeed, Account, and NotFound. You will eventually use PublicFeed to display the public Picshare feed, Account to display the account page, and NotFound to display a "not found" page.

You may claim that the Page type is redundant, but Route and Page have different responsibilities. Page concerns itself with the state of the current page. Later, you will introduce model parameters to the Page constructors to manage an individual page's state.

Add a page field to the Model type alias and initialModel instance. Start off with a NotFound page. Also, add a navigationKey field of type Navigation.Key. Later in the chapter, you will need this key to change the URL in the browser:

```
type alias Model =
    { page : Page
    , navigationKey : Navigation.Key
    }

initialModel : Navigation.Key -> Model
initialModel navigationKey =
    { page = NotFound
    , navigationKey = navigationKey
    }
```

Notice that you convert initialModel into a function that accepts navigationKey because your program will supply navigationKey at runtime.

Next, you need to access the current URL. Directly accessing it would be impure just like directly manipulating the DOM. Instead, Browser provides a pure way. The URL changes when the user navigates, so Browser can generate URL change events similar to DOM events. Recall that you handle events as messages in the update function.

Scroll down to the Msg type and replace NoOp with two new messages, NewRoute and Visit:

```
type Msg
    = NewRoute (Maybe Routes.Route)
    | Visit UrlRequest
```

The NewRoute message wraps Maybe Routes.Route because route parsing could fail. The Visit message wraps UrlRequest from Browser.Navigation. You need a different type of program to receive NewRoute and Visit. Modify the definition of main at the bottom of the file like so:

```
main =
    Browser.application
        { init = init
        , view = view
        , update = update
        , subscriptions = subscriptions
        , onUrlRequest = Visit
        , onUrlChange = Routes.match >> NewRoute
        }
```

You replace Browser.element with Browser.application. It still accepts a record of init, view, update, and subscriptions along with two new fields called onUrlRequest and onUrlChange.

Browser.application captures any link clicks in your application and forwards them to onUrlRequest as a UrlRequest. The UrlRequest type is a custom type with two constructors, Internal and External.

The Internal constructor represents links within your application's domain, i.e., /account. It wraps a Url type.

The External constructor represents links outside your domain, i.e., https://elm-lang.org. It wraps a String type.

You must provide a message constructor to wrap the UrlRequest, which is why you supply Visit for onUrlRequest. You'll decide how to handle the UrlRequest inside your update function in a bit. So let's look at onUrlChange next.

Browser.application uses onUrlChange to wrap the current Url whenever the URL changes in the browser. It then passes the wrapped value to your update function.

Notice that you provide (Routes.match >> NewRoute). The >> operator is the *forward composition operator*. It composes functions similar to << but from left to right.

In this instance, you first transform the incoming Url into Maybe Route with Routes.match. Then, you pass Maybe Route onto the NewRoute constructor.

Now you can handle NewRoute in update. Before you modify update, create a helper function called setNewPage:

```
setNewPage : Maybe Routes.Route -> Model -> ( Model, Cmd Msg )
setNewPage maybeRoute model =
    case maybeRoute of
        Just Routes.Home ->
            ( { model | page = PublicFeed }, Cmd.none )

        Just Routes.Account ->
            ( { model | page = Account }, Cmd.none )

        Nothing ->
            ( { model | page = NotFound }, Cmd.none )
```

The setNewPage function updates the model's page based on the new route. It accepts Maybe Route and the model, and returns a model-command tuple. Inside, you use nested pattern matching to match routes inside Just. You map Routes.Home to the PublicFeed page and Routes.Account to the Account page. If you match Nothing, then you map to the NotFound page.

Now, handle NewRoute in update with setNewPage:

```
update : Msg -> Model -> ( Model, Cmd Msg )
update msg model =
    case msg of
```

```
    NewRoute maybeRoute ->
        setNewPage maybeRoute model

    _ ->
        ( model, Cmd.none )
```

You unwrap the route as maybeRoute and call setNewPage with maybeRoute and the current model. You also ignore Visit for now with a wildcard match that returns the current model and Cmd.none. Be forewarned, though—this catch-all branch comes with a trade-off. If you add new Msg or Page constructors, the compiler won't make you explicitly handle them because _ will match them.

Your new program requires one more adjustment. It will supply the initial Url when the application boots. It expects init to be a function that accepts Url and Browser.Navigation.Key as arguments after flags, and returns a model-command tuple. Modify init like so:

```
init : () -> Url -> Navigation.Key -> ( Model, Cmd Msg )
init () url navigationKey =
    setNewPage (Routes.match url) (initialModel navigationKey)
```

You accept url and convert it into a route with Routes.match. Then, you construct a initial model by passing navigationKey into initialModel. Finally, you pass the route and the initial model into setNewPage to set the initial page.

You are almost finished, but you should display different content depending on the page field. Add a viewContent function:

```
viewContent : Page -> ( String, Html Msg )
viewContent page =
    case page of
        PublicFeed ->
            ( "Picshare"
            , h1 [] [ text "Public Feed" ]
            )

        Account ->
            ( "Account"
            , h1 [] [ text "Account" ]
            )

        NotFound ->
            ( "Not Found"
            , div [ class "not-found" ]
                [ h1 [] [ text "Page Not Found" ] ]
            )
```

You accept a Page argument and return ( String, Html Msg ). Browser.application gives you more control over what you display. It lets you set the contents of the <title> tag and the <body> tag with the Document type. You return a tuple so you can specify the title along with the content of the page. You will assemble the tuple into a Document type in the view function in a moment.

You map each Page constructor to different placeholder content. For PublicFeed, you display a title of "Picshare" and an h1 tag with the text "Public Feed". For Account, you display a title of "Account" and an h1 tag with the text "Account". And for NotFound, you display a title of "Not Found" and an h1 tag with the text "Page Not Found" inside a wrapper div tag. Main.elm already imports the class attribute function for you.

Wire up viewContent inside the view function, like this:

```
view : Model -> Document Msg
view model =
    let
        ( title, content ) =
            viewContent model.page
    in
    { title = title
    , body = [ content ]
    }
```

You change the return type to Document Msg. Then, inside a let expression, you call viewContent on model.page and extract the title and content from the tuple. Finally, you return a Document record with title and body fields. The title field must be a String, and the body field must be a List (Html msg).

Boot up the development server with npm start and check the application in your browser. Visit the root path (/). You should see the text "Public Feed". Your application accepted the root path, converted it into the Home route, mapped the route to the PublicFeed page, and displayed the appropriate text for PublicFeed. Change the path to /account in your browser's address bar. The application should reload and display the text "Account". Try a non-matching path such as /yolo and you should see "Page Not Found".

Great work. You just built your first skeleton SPA with Elm. You have more work ahead such as adding navigation links and displaying the real Picshare application, but this was an important first step. You should reward yourself with a day at the spa. Verify your code matches Main01.elm and Routes01.elm in the code/single-page-applications/samples directory from this book's code downloads.

## Route to a Component Page

So far, your single-page application only displays placeholder content. You need it to display a feed of photos and an account page. Inside your picshare-spa/src directory, you have an Account.elm application so you could port its code and Picshare's code into Main.elm. But then that would create a large, unwieldy application.

Instead, you will build a modular application with *components*. In this section, you will learn what components are and how to wire up an Account component inside the Main module. You will store Account's model inside Main's model, route Account messages from Main to Account, and display Account's content inside Main's view function.

## Build an Account Component

Before you begin, familiarize yourself with the Account application. Boot up the development server and open src/index.js. Temporarily import Account.elm instead of Main.elm like so:

```
import { Elm } from './Account.elm';
```

Then, temporarily call init from Elm.Account instead of Elm.Main:

```
➤ Elm.Account.init({
    node: document.getElementById('root')
});
```

You essentially swap out the Main application for the Account application. Save the changes. The application should refresh and display the following information.

The Account application loads a fake account from an API. You can modify the account and click Save to send changes back to the server. The server doesn't persist the changes; if you refresh, you'll see the old values. Otherwise, you and every other reader would override each other's changes.

 You can run the server locally to fetch from the /account API endpoint. Follow the instructions in Appendix 2, Run the Local Server, on page 267, and change accountUrl to http://localhost:5000/account.

We won't go over the details of Account.elm's code, but glance at it in your editor. It's your typical Elm application with a model, view function, and update function. If you have wondered how to send data to an API, look at the saveAccount function. It builds the opposite of a JSON decoder—a JSON *encoder*. JSON encoders convert Elm types into JavaScript values you can use with POST, PUT, and PATCH API calls. The saveAccount function encodes the Account type into a JSON body for an API PUT request.

You want the Account application to start whenever you visit the Account route. To do that, you need to convert Account into a component. An Elm component is basically an Elm application that doesn't expose a program. It exposes its initial model (or init tuple), view function, and update function for other modules to use. In this case, Main will use Account.init to initialize and store Account's state, Account.update to manage that state, and Account.view to display that state.

With Account.elm open in your editor, remove the main constant at the bottom because Account will no longer mount itself as an application. Also, remove the Browser import. Next, expose Model, Msg, init, update, and view:

single-page-applications/samples/Account01.elm
```
module Account exposing (Model, Msg, init, update, view)
```

You won't need the unit argument inside the init function. Remove it and make init a model-command tuple:

```
init : ( Model, Cmd Msg )
init =
    ( initialModel, fetchAccount )
```

That's it. You converted Account into a full-fledged component. Let's put it to good use. Be sure to revert your changes in index.js before proceeding.

## Store Component State

Back in Main.elm, import Account:

single-page-applications/samples/Main02.elm
```
import Account
```

I mentioned that Main will manage Account's state. You could store an instance of Account's model inside Main's model with an account field. However, the fields in Model would grow with every new page. You already hold the current page in Model, so you can store Account's model inside the Account Page constructor instead. Add an Account.Model parameter like so:

```
type Page
    = PublicFeed
    | Account Account.Model
    | NotFound
```

You wrap Account.Model with the Account constructor. Go back to the setNewPage function and change the Just Routes.Account branch to wrap an instance of Account's model:

```
Just Routes.Account ->
    let
        ( accountModel, accountCmd ) =
            Account.init
    in
    ( { model | page = Account accountModel }
    , Cmd.none
    )
```

You use a let expression to destructure the Account.init tuple and assign the initial Account model to a constant called accountModel. Then, you pass accountModel into the Account Page constructor to set the page field. Now, Main's model will hold an instance of Account's model whenever the current page is Account.

You also assign the initial Account command to accountCmd but do nothing with it. Inside the returned tuple, you return Cmd.none. Account's initial command fetches an account. By ignoring the command, you won't fetch the account. You could replace Cmd.none with accountCmd but you would encounter a type error. The setNewPage function returns ( Model, Cmd Msg ), but you would return ( Model, Cmd Account.Msg ).

You can reuse a trick from Chapter 6, Build Larger Applications, on page 103 to solve this problem. Previously, you wrapped messages with other messages to create modular update functions. You can do that here too. Add an AccountMsg wrapper to Main's Msg type:

```
| AccountMsg Account.Msg
```

The AccountMsg constructor wraps over Account.Msg values. Return back to setNew-Page and replace Cmd.none with this:

```
Cmd.map AccountMsg accountCmd
```

Just as Html.map applies a function to messages that DOM events produce, Cmd.map applies a function to messages that commands produce. In this case, you apply the AccountMsg constructor to wrap Account.Msg values that accountCmd could generate.

## Display and Update Component State

Now that you haved initialized and stored Account's state, you need to display it. Modify the Account branch in viewContent like so:

```
Account accountModel ->
    ( "Account"
    , Account.view accountModel
        |> Html.map AccountMsg
    )
```

You unwrap the accountModel from the Account Page constructor. Then, you call Account.view with accountModel. You'll run into another message type mismatch, so you pipe the result into Html.map with AccountMsg to wrap Account.Msg values.

Next, you need to handle Account's messages to update its state. Whenever Account produces a message, Html.map will wrap it with AccountMsg. AccountMsg is a just regular Msg value to Main, so you need to handle it in the update function. Change update like so:

```
update msg model =
    case ( msg, model.page ) of
        ( NewRoute maybeRoute, _ ) ->
            setNewPage maybeRoute model

        ( AccountMsg accountMsg, Account accountModel ) ->
            let
                ( updatedAccountModel, accountCmd ) =
                    Account.update accountMsg accountModel
            in
            ( { model | page = Account updatedAccountModel }
            , Cmd.map AccountMsg accountCmd
            )

        _ ->
            ( model, Cmd.none )
```

Let's break it down. You pattern match over a tuple of msg and model.page instead of only msg. You deeply destructure the tuple and inner custom type values.

For the first branch, you match NewRoute in the tuple's first position and unwrap maybeRoute. Then, you call setNewPage as before. You ignore the current page in the tuple's second position with _ because it doesn't matter when setting a new page.

In the next branch, you access AccountMsg and the Account Page constructor. This match only succeeds if both inner tuple values match the given patterns. You gain a couple of benefits from tuple pattern matching here.

1. You ensure you only handle AccountMsg if the current page is Account.

2. You can avoid messy nested pattern matching. If you kept the earlier case expression, you would have to nest like this:

```
AccountMsg accountMsg ->
  case model.page of
      Account accountModel ->
          . . .
```

In the final branch, you continue to ignore all remaining possibilities with _ and simply return the current model and Cmd.none. For example, this branch would match if you somehow received AccountMsg while the current page was Home.

Return back to the AccountMsg-Account branch. You unwrap the inner accountMsg and inner accountModel. Then, you mimic the Routes.Account branch from setNewPage. Inside a let expression, you call Account.update with accountMsg and accountModel. Account.update returns a tuple of an updated model and command, which you destructure into updatedAccountModel and accountCmd.

You use updatedAccountModel to update the page field in Main's model. Notice that you call the Account Page constructor with updatedAccountModel. You also call Cmd.map with AccountMsg and accountCmd to ensure you hand off Account commands to the Elm Architecture.

Let's try it all out. Start the development server and go to http://localhost:3000/ account. You should see the Account application boot up and load the account from the API. Change the field values, especially the "Username" field. You should see the username next to the avatar change as well. If you click Save, you should see the network request go out from your browser's devtools with the UI eventually displaying "Saved Successfully". This means that you have properly routed Account's messages and commands.

For a recap: when you type in a field, Elm dispatches the appropriate Account message wrapped inside AccountMsg. Main's update function matches that and calls Account's update function to modify Account's state. Then, the Elm Architecture calls Main's view function, which in turn calls Account's view function to display the changes.

You just built a real SPA with a component, so high-five yourself. Verify your code matches Main02.elm and Account01.elm in the code/single-page-applications/samples directory from this book's code downloads.

## Welcome Back Picshare

You have progressed nicely with this SPA. Next, you need to make your original Picshare application the public feed page. In this section, you will wire up Picshare as a component inside Main.elm. You will also add navigation links to the application.

To start, you need an existing Picshare application. There's one in the files you copied at the start of this chapter. The file is named Feed.elm, and it exposes all you need to use it as a component. Also provided is the WebSocket.elm port module.

However, if you followed the first five chapters of this book and want a little challenge, copy your Picshare.elm and WebSocket.elm files into your picshare-spa/src directory. Rename Picshare.elm to Feed.elm. You might want to back up the existing Feed.elm and WebSocket.elm files just in case. I'll reiterate—only do this if you followed the first five chapters. This chapter assumes Picshare uses WebSockets. If you decide to use your own Feed.elm file, open it in your editor. Then, rename the module to Feed, remove the Browser module import, remove the main constant, and expose Model, Msg, init, subscriptions, update, and view.

Back in Main.elm, import Feed but alias it to PublicFeed. The alias will aid you later:

single-page-applications/samples/Main03.elm
```
import Feed as PublicFeed
```

Convert the PublicFeed Page constructor to accept PublicFeed.Model as an argument. Then, you can store and update PublicFeed's state:

```
= PublicFeed PublicFeed.Model
```

In fact, you will essentially copy everything you did for the Account component with the PublicFeed component. Add a PublicFeedMsg wrapper to Msg:

```
| PublicFeedMsg PublicFeed.Msg
```

Update the PublicFeed branch of viewContent to unwrap the PublicFeed model and display it with PublicFeed.view:

```
PublicFeed publicFeedModel ->
    ( "Picshare"
    , PublicFeed.view publicFeedModel
        |> Html.map PublicFeedMsg
    )
```

Modify the Just Routes.Home branch inside setNewPage to initialize the PublicFeed model and use it to set the page with the PublicFeed Page constructor. Also, pass along the initial PublicFeed command:

```
Just Routes.Home ->
    let
        ( publicFeedModel, publicFeedCmd ) =
            PublicFeed.init ()
    in
    ( { model | page = PublicFeed publicFeedModel }
    , Cmd.map PublicFeedMsg publicFeedCmd
    )
```

Note that you call the PublicFeed.init function with the unit value. Unlike Account, init is kept as a function because you will change the argument later in this chapter anyway.

Then, match a tuple of PublicFeedMsg and the PublicFeed Page inside the update function as in the following. Note how it resembles the Account tuple branch:

```
( PublicFeedMsg publicFeedMsg, PublicFeed publicFeedModel ) ->
    let
        ( updatedPublicFeedModel, publicFeedCmd ) =
            PublicFeed.update publicFeedMsg publicFeedModel
    in
    ( { model | page = PublicFeed updatedPublicFeedModel }
    , Cmd.map PublicFeedMsg publicFeedCmd
    )
```

One more step. You can hand off subscriptions from components just like with commands. The PublicFeed component subscribes to feed updates, so you need to wire up its subscription. Change the subscriptions function inside Main like so:

```
subscriptions model =
    case model.page of
        PublicFeed publicFeedModel ->
            PublicFeed.subscriptions publicFeedModel
                |> Sub.map PublicFeedMsg

        _ ->
            Sub.none
```

You check the current page with pattern matching. If it's PublicFeed, then you unwrap the inner model as publicFeedModel and pass it into PublicFeed.subscriptions. Similar to how you used Cmd.map and Html.map, you use Sub.map to wrap PublicFeed.Msg with PublicFeedMsg. If you have a different page, then you match it with _ and return Sub.none.

You also need to bring over the JavaScript port handling code to src/index.js. Update it like so:

single-page-applications/samples/index01.js
```
var app = Elm.Main.init({
  node: document.getElementById('root')
});

var socket = null;

app.ports.listen.subscribe(listen);

function listen(url) {
  if (!socket) {
    socket = new WebSocket(url);
```

```
    socket.onmessage = function(event) {
      app.ports.receive.send(event.data);
    };
  }
}
```

This code closely resembles the port-handling code from Chapter 5, Go Real-Time with WebSockets, on page 85, with a small change. You define the socket variable outside of the listen function and set it initially to null. Inside listen you only open a new WebSocket if you don't have an existing socket. You'll find this change useful later in the chapter when you need to close or reopen the WebSocket when changing routes.

Start the development server and visit http://localhost:3000 in your browser. The original Picshare application should load and fetch three photos. If you wait a few seconds, it should also receive new photos via WebSockets.

You've now built an awesome SPA with two real components. At this point you might have noticed a couple of issues, though. Wiring up components required some effort and led to duplicated code. You'll deal with the duplication in a later challenge. The application also provides no navigation links between the two pages. Let's fix that next.

## Navigate Between Pages

Modern SPAs depend on the pushState() method of the JavaScript history object. The pushState() method changes the current URL's pathname in the address bar without navigating to a new page. Tons of JavaScript frameworks and libraries use pushState() to update the pathname and notify your application so it can display the appropriate content based on the new pathname.

Elm is no different. The Browser.Navigation module uses native JavaScript code to wrap over history.pushState() with its pushUrl function. The pushUrl function accepts a Browser.Navigation.Key and String path and returns a Cmd. This Cmd instructs the Elm Architecture to call history.pushState() with the provided path. Let's use pushUrl to add navigation to the SPA.

Open up Routes.elm and add a helper function called routeToUrl:

single-page-applications/samples/Routes02.elm
```
routeToUrl : Route -> String
routeToUrl route =
    case route of
        Home ->
            "/"

        Account ->
            "/account"
```

The routeToUrl function accepts a Route and converts it into a string path via pattern matching.

Next, import Html and Html.Attributes:

```
import Html
import Html.Attributes
```

Then, add a href function:

```
href : Route -> Html.Attribute msg
href route =
    Html.Attributes.href (routeToUrl route)
```

The href function accepts a Route and returns Html.Attribute msg. It converts the route into a string with the routeToUrl helper and pipes the result into Html.Attributes.href. Routes.href will let you build links to your pages via Route constructors. This lets you avoid retyping the string paths throughout your codebase.

Expose href from Routes before moving on:

```
module Routes exposing (Route(..), href, match)
```

Before adding navigation links, you need to share the header from PublicFeed with Account. Remove the header from the view function in Feed.elm so you have this remaining:

```
single-page-applications/samples/Feed01.elm
div []
    [ div [ class "content-flow" ]
        [ viewContent model ]
    ]
```

Go back to Main.elm and create a viewHeader function:

```
single-page-applications/samples/Main03.elm
viewHeader : Html Msg
viewHeader =
    div [ class "header" ]
        [ div [ class "header-nav" ]
            [ a [ class "nav-brand", Routes.href Routes.Home ]
                [ text "Picshare" ]
            , a [ class "nav-account", Routes.href Routes.Account ]
                [ i [ class "fa fa-2x fa-gear" ] [] ]
            ]
        ]
```

You still create a div tag with a header class. Inside it, you add a div tag with a header-nav class. Inside the header-nav div, you build two anchor tags that link to the Home and Account routes via Routes.href. The account link displays a gear with an i tag and Font Awesome classes.

Inside the view function, add viewHeader to the list assigned to the Document record's body field:

```
, body = [ viewHeader, content ]
```

Save and view the application in your browser. You should see the following items displayed at the top.

If you click on the Picshare and gear links, nothing happens. When you click on the links, you generate Visit messages via the onUrlChange field supplied to Browser.application. Recall that you ignore Visit with the wildcard match in the update function. Fix that by handling Visit like so:

```
( Visit (Browser.Internal url), _ ) ->
    ( model, Navigation.pushUrl model.navigationKey (Url.toString url) )
```

You match the Visit message in the first position of the tuple and ignore the second tuple item. Remember that Visit wraps either an Internal or External UrlRequest. You only handle Internal, so you unwrap it to get the requested url. You ignore External with the catch-all wildcard match at the bottom of update. You ignore it because you won't use any external links in the application.

You return the existing model and generate a command with Browser.Navigation.pushUrl. You convert the url into a String with Url.toString and pass it and model.navigationKey into pushUrl. This will cause the Elm Architecture to call history.pushState with the correct route path.

To sum up what's happening, when you click on "Picshare", the application will trigger a Visit message with an Internal UrlRequest for /. When you click the gear icon, it will trigger a Visit message with an Internal UrlRequest for /account.

Then, Elm will call history.pushState with the path, the URL will change in the browser, and Elm will deliver the onUrlChange NewRoute message with the route to the update function.

Save the file and visit your application in the browser. Click on the links. Each page should load instantly and fetch the data it needs. You can check the network tab in your browser's devtools to verify that the browser doesn't send new page requests.

You may notice that the WebSocket feed stops working after you leave and revisit the home page. This is due to the changes you made in index.js. Let's fix this before wrapping up here.

## Clean Up the WebSocket

The application only needs the WebSocket open on the home page, so you need to enhance the WebSocket port module to close the socket when you leave the home page. Add a close port to WebSocket.elm and expose it:

single-page-applications/samples/WebSocket01.elm
```
port close : () -> Cmd msg
```

Because outgoing ports always require an argument, you just use the unit argument. Modify index.js to handle the close port:

single-page-applications/samples/index01.js
```
app.ports.close.subscribe(close);

function close() {
  if (socket) {
    socket.close();
    socket = null;
  }
}
```

You add a close function and pass it into the close port subscribe() method. Inside the close function, if the socket is set (non-null), you call the socket.close() method. This closes the connection to the server. You also set the socket to null so you can open the connection again later.

Back in Main.elm, you need to ensure that the application closes the WebSocket with the WebSocket.close port whenever the page changes. The NewRoute branch in update sounds like a great place to make that happen.

Import the WebSocket module:

single-page-applications/samples/Main03.elm
```
import WebSocket
```

Then, modify the NewRoute branch of update like so:

```
( NewRoute maybeRoute, _ ) ->
    let
        ( updatedModel, cmd ) =
            setNewPage maybeRoute model
    in
    ( updatedModel
    , Cmd.batch [ cmd, WebSocket.close () ]
    )
```

You call setNewPage like before, but instead pull out the updatedModel and cmd from the tuple. Next, you return the updatedModel as the first item of a new tuple, but call a Cmd.batch function as the second item of that tuple.

You can only give the Elm Architecture one Cmd at a time from the update function. Thus, you need a way to hand off the cmd from setNewPage and the WebSocket.close Cmd. Cmd.batch has your back. It takes a list of Cmds and combines them into one Cmd that dispatches the original list. In this case, you pass in a list with cmd and WebSocket.close. Note that you have to call WebSocket.close with the unit value. The new batched command will ensure that Elm handles both commands.

Save all the changes. Go back to your browser. Visit the home page, leave it, and visit it again. You should see the WebSocket feed reappear.

You have now constructed a bona fide Elm SPA with pushState and components. What a huge accomplishment! Verify your code matches index01.js, WebSocket01.elm, Main03.elm, Routes02.elm, and Feed01.elm in the code/single-page-applications/samples directory from this book's code downloads before proceeding.

## Handle Dynamic Routes

Up to this point, you've used static URL paths such as / and /account that fetch static resources. Many SPAs also access dynamic resources through parameterized paths. For example, a path of /photo/42 would fetch and display the photo with an ID of 42.

In this section, you will learn how to handle dynamic paths. You will add the ability to view an individual user's feed of photos. You will create a parameterized route for a user's feed. Then, you will make wrapper components that reuse the Feed component to display the public feed and user feeds.

You will use usernames to fetch user feeds, so start by displaying the username associated with a photo. Open Feed.elm in your editor. Add a String username field *below* the comments field in the Photo type alias:

single-page-applications/samples/Feed02.elm
```
, comments : List String
, username : String
```

You need to modify the photoDecoder too. Add a new required pipe below the comments required pipe:

```
|> required "comments" (list string)
|> required "username" string
```

Finally, display the username inside the viewDetailedPhoto function. Add an h3 tag with an anchor tag between the h2 tag and call to viewComments like so:

```
, h2 [ class "caption" ] [ text photo.caption ]
, h3 [ class "username" ]
    [ a [] [ text ("@" ++ photo.username) ] ]
, viewComments photo
```

You render the photo.username field with an @ in front to signify that it's a username. Save the file, start the server, and visit http://localhost:3000 in your browser. After the feed loads, you should see usernames with each photo similar to this screenshot.

*Surfing*

**@surfing_usa**

**Comment:** Cowabunga, dude!

## Create Wrapper Components

Currently, you display a public feed of photos in Feed.elm. Ideally, you could reuse this code to display a user's feed, but the Feed component uses a hard-coded public feed URL. You could copy the Feed component to make a new UserFeed component with a different URL, but that would lead to a lot of hard-to-maintain duplication.

Instead, let's parameterize the Feed component. It can accept the feed URL and WebSocket URL as arguments. Then, you can wrap Feed inside PublicFeed and UserFeed modules that fill in the URL arguments and reuse the Feed component.

Back inside Feed.elm, delete the baseUrl and wsUrl constants. Update the fetchFeed function to accept a URL argument:

```
fetchFeed : String -> Cmd Msg
fetchFeed url =
    Http.get
        { url = url
        , expect = Http.expectJson LoadFeed (list photoDecoder)
        }
```

You assign the url argument to the url field inside the record passed into Http.get. Next, change the init function's argument from () to a record with two fields, feedUrl and wsUrl, and use the fields like so:

```
init : { feedUrl : String, wsUrl : Maybe String } -> ( Model, Cmd Msg )
init { feedUrl, wsUrl } =
    ( initialModel wsUrl, fetchFeed feedUrl )
```

You have a String feedUrl field and a Maybe String wsUrl field. The eventual user feed page will not have a WebSocket feed. Instead, you will use Maybe for wsUrl to indicate if there is a feed to connect to. You'll see what I mean when you create the UserFeed module in a bit.

You use record destructuring on the argument to extract each field into its own local constant. This saves you from naming the argument and using record dot access to retrieve the field values. You pass feedUrl into fetchFeed. You also pass wsUrl into initialModel as if it were a function—and you'll convert it into a function in a moment.

Because you use wsUrl to connect to the WebSocket inside the update function, you will need to store it in the model until it's time to connect. Add a wsUrl field to the model type:

```
, wsUrl : Maybe String
```

Now change initialModel into a function that accepts wsUrl and assigns it to the model:

```
initialModel : Maybe String -> Model
initialModel wsUrl =
    { feed = Nothing
    , error = Nothing
    , streamQueue = []
    , wsUrl = wsUrl
    }
```

Above the update function, add a new function called listenForNewPhotos to connect to the WebSocket if the wsUrl is available:

```
listenForNewPhotos : Maybe String -> Cmd Msg
listenForNewPhotos maybeWsUrl =
    case maybeWsUrl of
        Just wsUrl ->
            WebSocket.listen wsUrl

        Nothing ->
            Cmd.none
```

You accept the argument as maybeWsUrl and use pattern matching on it. If it's Just, then you unwrap the URL as wsUrl and pass it along to WebSocket.listen. If it's Nothing, then you return Cmd.none.

Finally, modify the LoadFeed (Ok feed) branch of update to call listenForNewPhotos with model.wsUrl:

```
LoadFeed (Ok feed) ->
    ( { model | feed = Just feed }
    , listenForNewPhotos model.wsUrl
    )
```

Now that you have parameterized Feed, you can build wrapper components. Make a PublicFeed.elm file. Inside, import Feed and Html, exposing the Html type:

single-page-applications/samples/PublicFeed01.elm
```
import Feed
import Html exposing (Html)
```

Next, you will basically alias or wrap everything that Feed exposes. Follow these steps:

1.  Create type aliases to Feed's Model and Msg types. Yes, you can type alias other type aliases. In fact, you must alias them if you want to expose them from PublicFeed. A module can only expose what it defines.

    ```
    type alias Model =
        Feed.Model

    type alias Msg =
        Feed.Msg
    ```

2.  Add URL constants for the public feed and WebSocket stream.

    ```
    feedUrl : String
    feedUrl =
        "https://programming-elm.com/feed"

    wsUrl : String
    wsUrl =
        "wss://programming-elm.com/"
    ```

3.  Create an init tuple by calling Feed.init with a record that contains the feedUrl and wsUrl constants you just defined. Make sure you wrap wsUrl inside Just. This is how you will make the PublicFeed component fetch the public feed of photos but still reuse the Feed component to update and display the feed.

    ```
    init : ( Model, Cmd Msg )
    init =
        Feed.init
            { feedUrl = feedUrl
            , wsUrl = Just wsUrl
            }
    ```

4. Create view, update, and subscriptions functions that simply alias to the Feed's view, update, and subscriptions functions.

```
view : Model -> Html Msg
view =
    Feed.view

update : Msg -> Model -> ( Model, Cmd Msg )
update =
    Feed.update

subscriptions : Model -> Sub Msg
subscriptions =
    Feed.subscriptions
```

Because Elm treats functions as values, you can assign view, update, and subscriptions constants to existing functions instead of creating new functions.

5. Declare the PublicFeed module up top and expose Model, Msg, init, subscriptions, update, and view.

```
module PublicFeed exposing (Model, Msg, init, subscriptions, update, view)
```

You now have a PublicFeed component that uses Feed's functions to fetch, display, and update a public feed of photos. Create a similar UserFeed component. Copy PublicFeed.elm to make a UserFeed.elm file. Make these adjustments to UserFeed.elm:

1. Rename the module to UserFeed.

2. The UserFeed module won't display a WebSocket stream of photos, so remove the wsUrl and subscriptions constants. Also, make sure you don't expose a nonexistent subscriptions in the top module definition.

3. Change feedUrl to a function that accepts a username argument and returns the full URL for a user's feed. Follow this format: /user/<username>/feed.

```
single-page-applications/samples/UserFeed01.elm
feedUrl : String -> String
feedUrl username =
    "https://programming-elm.com/user/" ++ username ++ "/feed"
```

4. Modify init to accept the username argument and pass it into feedUrl before calling Feed.init. Also, set the wsUrl field passed into Feed.init to Nothing.

```
init : String -> ( Model, Cmd Msg )
init username =
    Feed.init
        { feedUrl = feedUrl username
        , wsUrl = Nothing
        }
```

At this point, verify your PublicFeed.elm and UserFeed.elm files match PublicFeed01.elm and UserFeed01.elm in the code/single-page-applications/samples directory from this book's code downloads. Let's set up a route for the user feed next.

 Recall you can run the server locally to fetch from the API endpoints and receive WebSocket events. Follow the instructions in Appendix 2, Run the Local Server, on page 267, and replace https://programming-elm.com with http://localhost:5000 in the feedUrl constants and wss://programming-elm.com with ws://localhost:5000 in the wsUrl constant.

## Create a Parameterized Route

You need a route that indicates which specific user feed to fetch. Open Routes.elm in your editor. Add a UserFeed constructor to the Route type:

single-page-applications/samples/Routes03.elm
```
| UserFeed String
```

The UserFeed route accepts a String argument which will be a username. Add a branch for UserFeed to routeToUrl so you can visit UserFeed URLs:

```
UserFeed username ->
    "/user/" ++ username ++ "/feed"
```

You unwrap the username to reconstruct the /user/<username>/feed path. Next, you should add a UserFeed URL parser to routes, but first you must expose something new from the Url.Parser module. Modify your Url.Parser import to look like this:

```
import Url.Parser as Parser exposing ((</>), Parser)
```

You expose a </> operator. Notice that you have to wrap it in an extra set of parentheses when importing. In addition to types, constants, and functions, some Elm packages sanctioned by the core team may define and expose custom operators. The </> custom operator lets you concatenate multiple path segments. Use it to add the UserFeed parser to routes like so:

```
routes =
    Parser.oneOf
        [ Parser.map Home Parser.top
        , Parser.map Account (Parser.s "account")
        , Parser.map
            UserFeed
            (Parser.s "user" </> Parser.string </> Parser.s "feed")
        ]
```

Inside the parentheses, you start with Parser.s and "user" for the first /user segment. Then, you concatenate it with the Parser.string parser via the </> operator. The operator mimics the / in URL paths.

Parser.string generates dynamic path parsers. It accepts whatever the next path segment is and captures it as an Elm String. Finally, you concatenate Parser.string with Parser.s and "feed".

Because this URL parser captures a dynamic String value from Parser.string, Parser.map expects the UserFeed constructor to accept a String argument, which it does. So, when your match function matches the path /user/photosgalore/feed, it will capture photosgalore and pass it into UserFeed. This lets you store the username for later use.

## Wrap Up with Wrappers

Now that you have a parameterized UserFeed route, let's wrap up by using it along with the Feed wrapper components in the Main module.

Change the Feed as PublicFeed import to just import the PublicFeed wrapper component. Also, import the UserFeed wrapper component:

single-page-applications/samples/Main04.elm
```
import PublicFeed
import UserFeed
```

Because you had previously renamed Feed to PublicFeed, all your existing code that references PublicFeed will still work. Instead, it will refer to the PublicFeed wrapper component now. You still need to handle the UserFeed wrapper component, however. Add a Page constructor called UserFeed that wraps a String and UserFeed.Model. You wrap a String as well so you can store the username for later access:

```
| UserFeed String UserFeed.Model
```

Next, add a UserFeedMsg wrapper to the Msg type:

```
| UserFeedMsg UserFeed.Msg
```

Then, add a UserFeed branch to viewContent that mimics the branches for PublicFeed and Account:

```
UserFeed username userFeedModel ->
    ( "User Feed for @" ++ username
    , UserFeed.view userFeedModel
        |> Html.map UserFeedMsg
    )
```

You also unwrap the username to build a dynamic title based on it.

Inside setNewPage, remove the () argument to PublicFeed.init in the Just Routes.Home branch:

```
( publicFeedModel, publicFeedCmd ) =
    PublicFeed.init
```

Then, add a branch for the UserFeed Route:

```
Just (Routes.UserFeed username) ->
    let
        ( userFeedModel, userFeedCmd ) =
            UserFeed.init username
    in
    ( { model | page = UserFeed username userFeedModel }
    , Cmd.map UserFeedMsg userFeedCmd
    )
```

This branch almost exactly mimics the other route branches except you unwrap the username from the UserFeed route. Then, you pass the username into UserFeed.init to obtain the initial userFeedModel and userFeedCmd. This ensures you only fetch and display the feed for a particular user. You also pass the username into the UserFeed Page constructor along with userFeedModel.

Finally, add a branch to the update function that resembles the other message-page tuple branches. Make sure you match on UserFeedMsg and the UserFeed Page. Also, make sure you unwrap the username and pass it back into the UserFeed Page when you reassign the model's page field:

```
( UserFeedMsg userFeedMsg, UserFeed username userFeedModel ) ->
    let
        ( updatedUserFeedModel, userFeedCmd ) =
            UserFeed.update userFeedMsg userFeedModel
    in
    ( { model | page = UserFeed username updatedUserFeedModel }
    , Cmd.map UserFeedMsg userFeedCmd
    )
```

Leave the subscriptions function alone. Recall that you don't use a WebSocket stream in UserFeed, and the current subscriptions function only hands off subscriptions from PublicFeed.

You've wired up the UserFeed wrapper component. Now you just need to navigate to a user's feed. Open Feed.elm in your editor.

Import Routes:

```
import Routes
```

Then, update the username anchor tag in viewDetailedPhoto to use Routes.href with the UserFeed Route:

```
[ a [ Routes.href (Routes.UserFeed photo.username) ]
    [ text ("@" ++ photo.username) ]
]
```

You call the Routes.UserFeed constructor with the current photo's username to ensure you visit the specific user's feed.

Ensure that you've saved all your open files and start the development server. Visit the application in your browser and click on a username such as elpapapollo. A new feed should load with only photos by elpapapollo. Click on the Picshare header link to go back to the public feed, and all public photos should load again.

Whew. You did it. You were able to reuse an existing component to make two separate feeds with a static and a parameterized route. You've built a fairly complex SPA with the power and safety of Elm. Great job!

If you encounter any issues running the application such as pages not changing with the URL, ensure that you're parsing the correct URLs and handling all your Route constructors inside the routes constant in Routes.elm. If pages do change, but they don't seem to fetch data or update, make sure you're handling all possible messages and pages inside the update function in Main.elm. Finally, you can always check that your files match the completed Account01.elm, Feed02.elm, Main04.elm, PublicFeed01.elm, Routes03.elm, UserFeed01.elm, WebSocket01.elm, and index01.js files in the code/single-page-applications/samples directory from this book's code downloads.

## What You Learned

And...that's a wrap. You achieved a lot in this chapter. You parsed static and dynamic URL paths with the Url.Parser module. Then, you used the Browser.application function along with the Elm Architecture to access the browser's current URL and convert it into a route and page. You built components and updated their state through the Elm Architecture. Finally, you used your components to display different pages depending on the current page state.

The duplication code smell still remains in setNewPage and update. Wiring up each component leads to extremely similar code. As a challenge, create a helper function that sets the model's page field with the appropriate Page constructor and page component model, and maps the command with the appropriate wrapper message.

Your helper function should accept a Page constructor, a Msg wrapper, the Main Model, and the model-command tuple produced by each component's init and update functions. This will let you reuse your helper function in both setNewPage and Main.update. Recall that the UserFeed Page constructor also accepts a String username argument, so you'll want to use some partial application when you call your helper function on it. If you need some help, you can check out the MainRefactored.elm file in the code/single-page-applications/samples directory from this book's code downloads. Look for the processPageUpdate function and its usage in setNewPage and update.

For another challenge, render a different message in Feed if the feed is empty. You'll likely want to use nested pattern matching with Just [] in viewFeed since it accepts Maybe Feed.

You are now able to build your own modular single-page applications with lots of pages, all in Elm. Let's build upon constructing complex applications in the next chapter by analyzing and improving performance in Elm applications.

# CHAPTER 11

# Write Fast Applications

In the previous chapter, you created a single-page application with the Browser, Browser.Navigation, and Url modules and components. You can now build and deploy your own Elm applications that vary in size and complexity. Although Elm touts a fast runtime and virtual DOM, your applications may encounter performance challenges. Don't worry. Elm *is* fast. Performance issues usually surface when code does more work than needed.

In this chapter, you will explore common examples where implementation details drastically impact performance. For example, traversing lists several times and eagerly evaluating expressions when unnecessary can slow down code. You will measure performance with elm-benchmark, diagnose the source of slower code, and improve performance with faster list algorithms and lazy design patterns. You will also use browser profiling tools to evaluate an application's performance. Then, you will use the Html.Lazy module to dramatically speed up parts of the application. When you complete this chapter, you will be able to measure the performance of your own applications and make them faster.

## Benchmark Code

Before we begin, I must caution you: You should only optimize code when performance becomes an issue. Focus on making your code correct. *After* you have a functioning application and if you suspect performance issues, *then* diagnose and improve performance. Early optimization can create complex, hard-to-maintain code. It also derails you from quickly implementing features and shipping a finished application.

Even after you've built an application, optimization can add hard-to-maintain complexity. The benchmarking tools that you'll explore in a moment can help you measure performance and decide if the performance improvement justifies the code complexity.

With that out of the way, let's investigate performance. In this section, you will discover performance issues when traversing lists. You will use the elm-benchmark package to measure a function's runtime and improve performance with a different implementation.

## Help Rescue Me

The Saladise company appreciated your help in Chapter 6, Build Larger Applications, on page 103 so much that they referred you to a nonprofit pet rescue organization called Rescue Me. Rescue Me wants to improve the performance of their codebase. You start investigating their modules for potential performance issues. You confront a function called dogNames.

```
fast/fast-code/DogNames01.elm
dogNames : List Animal -> List String
dogNames animals =
    animals
        |> List.filter (\{ kind } -> kind == Dog)
        |> List.map .name
```

It accepts a list of Animals, filters the list for Dogs, and returns the dogs' names. Here is the Animal type.

```
type Kind
    = Dog
    | Cat

type alias Animal =
    { name : String
    , kind : Kind
    }
```

The Animal type is a record with a String name and a kind of type Kind. The Kind type has two values, Dog and Cat.

Return back to dogNames. It pipes the animals list into List.filter with an anonymous function. The anonymous function destructures the kind field and checks if it's equal to Dog. Then, dogNames pipes the filtered list into List.map with .name. This isn't a syntax error.

When you type a dot and a field name without a preceding record, you create a *record access function*. A record access function accepts an extensible record with the given field name and returns its value. In this case, .name returns a record's name field.

```
.name { name = "Tucker" }
-- returns "Tucker"
```

Combined with List.map, record access functions such as .name let you extract a field value for multiple records.

You suspect that dogNames could use a performance boost. Functions can run slower if they traverse lists multiple times. In this case, dogNames traverses the list twice, once for List.filter and once for List.map. Granted, List.map likely traverses a smaller filtered list, but you could still improve performance by traversing less.

Fortunately, the built-in List.filterMap[1] function can filter and map lists in one traversal. Here is its type signature.

```
(a -> Maybe b) -> List a -> List b
```

It applies a function that returns a Maybe type to every value in the list. You can map a value and wrap the result in Just to keep it. Otherwise, you can return Nothing to drop the value. Let's implement a new dogNames with filterMap.

Create a new fast-code directory. Inside your directory, initialize an Elm project:

```
elm init
```

Create a DogNames.elm file in the src directory. Transfer the contents of code/fast/fast-code/DogNames.elm from this book's code downloads into your Dog-Names.elm file. Add a new dogNamesFilterMap function after dogNames:

```
fast/fast-code/DogNames02.elm
dogNamesFilterMap : List Animal -> List String
dogNamesFilterMap animals =
    animals
        |> List.filterMap
            (\{ name, kind } ->
                if kind == Dog then
                    Just name

                else
                    Nothing
            )
```

You pipe animals into List.filterMap with an anonymous function. Inside the anonymous function, you destructure every animal's name and kind fields. You check kind inside an if-else expression. If it is Dog, then you return the name field inside Just. Otherwise, you return Nothing. List.filterMap unwraps the Justs and removes the Nothings to yield a list of dog names.

---

1.  https://package.elm-lang.org/packages/elm/core/latest/List#filterMap

## Run Benchmarks

You wrote a new implementation but you should confirm that it's faster. Let's benchmark both implementations with the elm-benchmark[2] package. Inside your fast-code directory, install elm-benchmark:

```
elm install elm-explorations/benchmark
```

After the package installs, import it like so:

```
import Benchmark exposing (..)
import Benchmark.Runner exposing (BenchmarkProgram, program)
```

You expose everything from the Benchmark module and expose the BenchmarkProgram type and program function from the Benchmark.Runner module. Next, add an initial benchmarking suite after dogNamesFilterMap:

```
suite : Benchmark
suite =
    describe "dog names" []
```

You create a suite constant of type Benchmark, which comes from the Benchmark module. Then, you build a Benchmark instance with the describe function from the Benchmark module. The describe function takes a string description and a list of other Benchmark instances to group together. This syntax closely resembles test suites from Chapter 9, Test Elm Applications, on page 175.

Before you add benchmarks to the list, you'll need a sample list of animals. Place the sample list above the suite constant like so:

```
benchmarkAnimals : List Animal
benchmarkAnimals =
    [ Animal "Tucker" Dog
    , Animal "Sally" Dog
    , Animal "Sassy" Cat
    , Animal "Turbo" Dog
    , Animal "Chloe" Cat
    ]
```

You build a list of five animals: three dogs and two cats. Now, add some benchmarks to the empty list in suite:

```
describe "dog names"
    [ benchmark "filter and map" <|
        \_ -> dogNames benchmarkAnimals
    , benchmark "filterMap" <|
        \_ -> dogNamesFilterMap benchmarkAnimals
    ]
```

---

2. https://package.elm-lang.org/packages/elm-explorations/benchmark/latest/

The benchmark function mimics the test function from test suites. It accepts a string description and an anonymous function. Inside the anonymous function, you execute the code you want to measure. The elm-benchmark package uses the anonymous function to run the code multiple times over a certain time period to estimate the code's performance. It determines the number of runs based on calculations explained later on. In your suite, you create two benchmarks, one for dogNames and one for dogNamesFilterMap.

You run benchmarks in a browser, so you need an Elm program. Luckily, the program function from Benchmark.Runner wires up the Elm Architecture for you. Create a main constant with program like so:

```
main : BenchmarkProgram
main =
    program suite
```

You pass suite into program, which returns a BenchmarkProgram. The BenchmarkProgram type aliases to Elm's Program type to hide its internal Model and Msg types.

Instead of manually compiling DogNames.elm, let's use the convenient elm-live[3] package. The elm-live package runs a development server that automatically recompiles Elm files when they change and refreshes the browser. It resembles create-elm-app minus the ability to generate applications. Install elm-live with npm:

```
npm install -g elm-live
```

Then, start the development server:

```
elm-live src/DogNames.elm --open
```

The previous command should compile the file and open a new tab in your browser. You should see something like the following screenshot.

## Benchmarks Running

dog names
    filter and map                              Warming JIT

dog names
    filterMap                                   Warming JIT

The program displays each benchmark with a status message. The first status message is "Warming JIT". Modern browsers' JavaScript engines use a JIT (just-in-time) compiler. Typically, JavaScript engines interpret JavaScript code. When they notice a program running a particular piece of code multiple

---

3. https://github.com/wking-io/elm-live

times, they compile it to machine code to improve performance. Compilation costs time, so these engines won't compile until the benefits outweigh the costs. You could say it's just in time.

Because elm-benchmark runs your code several times, JIT compilation could skew the results. The JavaScript engine could interpret some runs and execute compiled code for other runs. The compiled runs would likely be faster. So, elm-benchmark runs your code multiple times before it takes measurements, to force JIT compilation.

Before collecting performance data, elm-benchmark also measures how often it can run your code over a small time period. Each benchmark should eventually display a "Finding sample size" status during this step.

Finally, elm-benchmark will start collecting samples. It collects multiples of the previous measurement to approximate the number of runs per second for your code. You should see the current progress of each benchmark as a blue bar.

## Benchmarks Running

Once elm-benchmark finishes, it should display each benchmark's results similar to this.

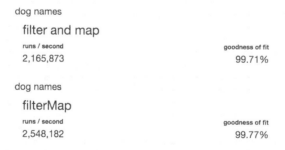

Each box displays a runs-per-second prediction and a goodness-of-fit measurement. The higher the runs per second, the better. Goodness of fit indicates elm-benchmark's confidence in its prediction. You want this number to be as close to 100% as possible or at least greater than 95%. If you get less than 95%, then close other computer programs that could interfere with your results.

According to my results, dogNamesFilterMap outperforms dogNames (2,376,242 is greater than 2,088,998). Your results will likely differ, especially based on your browser and computer. I used Chrome 70.0.3538.102 on a MacBook Pro to produce these results. I recommend using Chrome so you'll have results more consistent with mine. For example, Firefox's JavaScript engine can yield drastically different results.

These measurements indicate that dogNamesFilterMap is faster, but we really want to know *how much* faster it is. You can measure that with the Benchmark.compare function. Replace the two benchmarks like so:

```
fast/fast-code/DogNames03.elm
describe "dog names"
    [ Benchmark.compare "implementations"
        "filter and map"
        (\_ -> dogNames benchmarkAnimals)
        "filterMap"
        (\_ -> dogNamesFilterMap benchmarkAnimals)
    ]
```

Benchmark.compare takes a description and then individual descriptions and anonymous functions for each implementation. Notice that you call the qualified Benchmark.compare instead of compare by itself. Elm automatically exposes the built-in Basics.compare function, so the compiler wouldn't know which function you want without a module qualifier.

Save the file. The application should refresh and run a comparison benchmark. The eventual results should look like this.

dog names

implementations

| name | runs / second | % change | goodness of fit |
|---|---|---|---|
| filter and map | 2,165,977 | - | 99.81% |
| filterMap | 2,495,280 | +15.2% | 99.78% |

The results appear in one box along with a percent change in performance. In my results, dogNamesFilterMap was +15.2% faster. Again, your numbers will probably differ.

This is great. The results suggest that the new implementation performs better. But before you switch to the new implementation, you should consider how list size impacts performance. Before we dive into that, make sure your code matches code/fast/fast-code/DogNames03.elm from this book's code downloads.

# Traverse Large Lists

Whenever you fine-tune function performance, make sure you test different inputs, especially inputs you expect in production. One input's results may lead you to accept an implementation that performs worse on realistic inputs. In the case of dog names, you should ensure that dogNamesFilterMap performs well with larger animal lists.

In this section, you will benchmark the "dog names" code with various list sizes. You will learn about the list data structure, learn how to describe algorithm runtimes with *Big O notation*, discover recursion, and use list folding to write a faster dogNames implementation.

## What's in a List

I briefly compared lists to chains in Chapter 1, Get Started with Elm, on page 1. Each list element "links" to the next one. Lists are actually tree data structures (not Elm trees) with two types of nodes: *cons cell* and *nil*. Let's break down those unhelpful names.

Historically, cons is short for construct. It constructs a node that holds two values. In terms of lists, a cons cell holds a list item and a reference to the next cons cell or nil. Nil is an empty node. It holds no values and signals the end of a list. The list [ 1, 2 ] would look like the following figure.

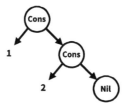

Functions such as List.map and List.filter follow each cons cell's child node reference to traverse a list tree. When they reach nil, they stop. Because List functions traverse a whole list, their performance depends on the list's size. The longer the list, the more time to traverse. So, you can express a function's performance in terms of input size. Programmers typically characterize a function's runtime with Big O notation.

Big O notation describes an upper bound on how a function's runtime grows with input size. For example, most List functions are O(n). The n means that the runtime grows linearly with input size. For example, if it takes 1 microsecond to visit one node, then it takes n microseconds to visit n nodes.

The dogNames and dogNamesFilterMap functions are both O(n). Recall that dogNames traverses the list twice, so you might think it is O(2n). In Big O notation, you remove constants that don't depend on input size, so you drop 2. You primarily use Big O notation to approximate a function's runtime growth rate. However, you'll use it in a bit to compare the performance between two functions.

## Increase List Size

Let's vet the superior performance of dogNamesFilterMap on larger lists. Update the benchmarkAnimals list like this:

```
fast/fast-code/DogNames04.elm
[ Animal "Tucker" Dog
, Animal "Sally" Dog
, Animal "Sassy" Cat
, Animal "Turbo" Dog
, Animal "Chloe" Cat
]
    |> List.repeat 2
    |> List.concat
```

You pipe the list into List.repeat. List.repeat creates a new list of a given item repeated a specific number of times. For example, you can repeat "Hello" three times in the REPL like this:

```
> List.repeat 3 "Hello"
["Hello","Hello","Hello"] : List String
```

For the benchmarkAnimals list, you repeat the entire list two times, which gives you a list of two lists. Look at this simpler REPL example to understand.

```
> List.repeat 2 ["Hi", "Hello"]
[["Hi","Hello"],["Hi","Hello"]] : List (List String)
```

The example repeats the list ["Hi", "Hello"] twice inside a new list. But, you want a list of animals, not a list of lists of animals. To fix this, you pipe the result into List.concat. List.concat flattens a list of lists into a list of items from the inner lists. Here's the previous REPL example with List.concat.

```
> List.repeat 2 ["Hi", "Hello"] |> List.concat
["Hi","Hello","Hi","Hello"] : List String
```

The example creates a list of four strings. With the benchmarkAnimals list, you generate a list of ten animals.

Make sure elm-live is still running. Save the changes and watch the new benchmark run in your browser. The results should change from the last benchmark. You should see dogNamesFilterMap's performance improvement decrease. In my results, it only had an 8% improvement compared to the previous 15.2% improvement.

This new implementation looks suspicious. Let's increase the list size more. Repeat the list three times to generate a list of 15 animals. Save and examine the results. Now dogNamesFilterMap should have little performance improvement over the old implementation. My results showed around a 2-4% improvement. Your results might be worse.

Repeat the list five times and save. Refresh your browser to run the benchmark a few times. The results should indicate no significant performance improvement. My runs showed the new implementation improving or hurting performance by around 1%. Try increasing the list size more. You will likely see the new implementation perform slightly worse in most instances. At best, the new implementation performs equally to the old implementation.

More than likely, the overhead of creating and unwrapping Just instances negatively impacts performance with larger lists. Elm represents Just instances with JavaScript objects. So, the JavaScript engine constructs a new object for every Just. The old implementation doesn't have to build these intermediate objects. Also, the JavaScript garbage collector might delete old Just objects while the new implementation is still traversing the list, which would slow down performance.

Rescue Me manages rescue animals from all over the United States, so you should expect a large list of animals. You need an implementation that traverses large lists once and avoids object creation overhead. Let's explore that next. Make sure your code matches code/fast/fast-code/DogNames05.elm from this book's code downloads before proceeding.

## Fold Your Laundry Lists

The List module has a handy List.foldl function that converts lists into other values. The foldl name is short for "fold left." Developers also refer to folding as reducing. Essentially, with foldl you fold, or reduce, a list to some other type of value. For example, you could implement your own sum function with foldl. Try this in the REPL:

```
> sum list = List.foldl (\item accum -> accum + item) 0 list
<function> : List number -> number
> sum [1, 2, 3]
6 : number
```

List.foldl accepts a *reducing* function, an initial value, and a list. The reducing function receives the current item in the list and the currently folded value.

Functional programmers typically call the folded value an *accumulated* value. The previous example notes this via the shortened accum argument name.

In the example, you add the current item to the accumulated value to eventually add all the numbers together. List.foldl makes the initial value the first accumulated value. In this case, that's 0. Whatever you return from the reducing function becomes the new accumulated value. List.foldl returns the final accumulated value when it reaches the end of the list.

You can use List.foldl to implement your own version of filterMap that traverses the list once. Add a new dogNamesFoldl function after dogNamesFilterMap like so:

```
fast/fast-code/DogNames06.elm
dogNamesFoldl : List Animal -> List String
dogNamesFoldl animals =
    animals
        |> List.foldl
            (\{ name, kind } accum ->
                if kind == Dog then
                    accum ++ [ name ]

                else
                    accum
            )
            []
```

You pipe animals into List.foldl with a reducing function; the empty list is the initial accumulated value. Inside the reducing function, you check the animal kind. If it's a Dog, you add the name to the end of the accumulated list with the ++ operator. Otherwise, you return the current accumulated list and drop the animal. When List.foldl finishes, it returns a list of only dog names.

Let's benchmark this new fold implementation against the first implementation. Replace the description and anonymous function for the filterMap implementation with this:

```
"foldl"
(\_ -> dogNamesFoldl benchmarkAnimals)
```

Also, make sure you repeat the benchmarkAnimals list five times (so, a total list of 20 animals). Save the file and look at the results. You should see a slight improvement. I saw an 11% improvement. This looks promising, but let's make sure. Repeat the list six times, giving you a list of 30 animals. The performance improvement should decrease or the foldl implementation should even perform worse.

Uh oh. Repeat the list 10 times for a big jump. You will then have a list of 50 animals. The fold implementation should definitely perform worse. My results indicated a performance decrease of 20%. Let's investigate further. Make sure your code matches code/fast/fast-code/DogNames06.elm from this book's code downloads.

## Prepend and Reverse

The previous results let us down. We're supposed to traverse the list once, and we don't have the overhead of Just objects. Instead, we have a subtle problem. The implementation actually traverses lists multiple times. Look at the list concatentation inside the reducing function.

```
accum ++ [ name ]
```

Concatentation must traverse the list on the left to replace its nil with the list on the right. So, thanks to concatenation, you will traverse the accumulated list for every item in the original list. The accumulated list will likely grow larger, which causes longer traversal times. You can approximate this implementation as O(n$^2$). The runtime grows *quadratically* instead of *linearly* with input size, so it eventually always performs worse than an O(n) implementation.

You can fix this with the cons :: operator. You've used it before to prepend items to lists. The :: operator creates a new cons cell where the left operand is the inner value and the right operand is the child node. Creating a cons cell takes constant time, or O(1) in Big O notation. So, you can traverse the input list without an extra traversal inside the reducing function. You'll return to an overall runtime of O(n).

Unfortunately, :: will build the dog name list in reverse because it prepends instead of appending. You can offset that with List.reverse, which—surprise—reverses a list. Copy dogNamesFoldl to a dogNamesFoldlReverse function and use :: and List.reverse like so:

```
fast/fast-code/DogNames07.elm
dogNamesFoldlReverse : List Animal -> List String
dogNamesFoldlReverse animals =
    animals
        |> List.foldl
            (\{ name, kind } accum ->
                if kind == Dog then
                    name :: accum

                else
                    accum
            )
            []
        |> List.reverse
```

Replace the dogNamesFoldl benchmark description and anonymous function:

```
"foldl with :: and reverse"
(\_ -> dogNamesFoldlReverse benchmarkAnimals)
```

Save the file and check the results. You should notice a huge improvement. My results showed around a 40% improvement. But, wait a minute. List.reverse adds a second list traversal. The old dogNames implementation traverses the list twice as well. These two implementations should perform similarly.

The performance difference comes from how Elm implements List.map and List.filter with a function called List.foldr. List.foldr acts like List.foldl, except it traverses the list backwards (from right to left).

Elm implements List.foldl and List.foldr with *recursion*. A recursive function is a function that calls itself to compute its result. For example, you could implement a recursive sum function like this.

```
sum : List number -> number
sum numbers =
    case numbers of
        [] ->
            0

        x :: xs ->
            x + sum xs
```

You pattern match over the list. Skip over the first branch for a moment. Just as you can add items to the start of the list with the :: operator, you can also retrieve the first item of a list with :: and pattern matching. That's what you do in the second branch of the case expression. You grab the first item in the list as x and the remaining items in the list as xs.

You add x to the result of recursively calling sum on the remaining list. Eventually, the recursive calls will hit the empty list. This is the first branch in the case expression. Any recursive function you write must have a stopping point called the *base case*. The base case for sum is the empty list, so you return 0. At this point, sum can start actually adding the numbers together. For example, if you called sum with [1, 2, 3], the recursive calls would execute like this.

```
sum [1, 2, 3]
1 + sum [2, 3]
1 + 2 + sum [3]
1 + 2 + 3 + sum []
1 + 2 + 3 + 0
1 + 2 + 3
1 + 5
6
```

This is a nice, elegant implementation but it suffers from one problem. Every recursive call adds a new *stack frame* to the *call stack*. JavaScript (and transitively Elm) tracks function calls with stack frames. A stack frame keeps a record of the function being called along with its arguments. The call stack stores stack frames in the order the functions were called. Each stack frame adds slight overhead because it consumes some memory. The larger the list input, the more stack frames to add to the call stack.

Because List.foldr is recursive, it adds stack frames to the call stack for every item in the list as well. However, the recursive List.foldl function, surprisingly, *doesn't* add stack frames for every recursive call. This is why the dogNamesFoldl-Reverse function performs better.

List.foldl doesn't create additional stack frames because it is a *tail recursive* function. A tail recursive function is a function where the last expression in the function is a recursive call or a value such as 0 or "hello world".

The earlier sum function is not tail recursive because the last expression in the second branch of the case expression is addition.

```
x + sum xs
```

You can't perform the addition until the recursive call returns a value. Thus, you necessarily have to add a stack frame. Contrast that with the following implementation of sum.

```
sum numbers =
    let
        sumHelp numbers_ accum =
            case numbers_ of
                [] ->
                    accum

                x :: xs ->
                    sumHelp xs (accum + x)
    in
    sumHelp numbers 0
```

You create a local helper function called sumHelp. It takes the list of numbers and an additional argument called accum, which is short for accumulated. You use the accum argument to keep track of the summed value. You again pattern match the list of numbers. Skip the first branch. For the second branch, you pull out the first number with :: pattern matching. Then, you immediately make a recursive call to sumHelp. Notice that you pass in the remaining numbers xs and the sum of accum and x.

You shift the addition into the accumulated value so that the last expression in the branch is the recursive call and not addition. Elm can detect when the last expression is a recursive call and perform *tail call optimization* (TCO). Instead of adding a new stack frame, Elm realizes that the result of sumHelp is the same as the result of the recursive call. It can replace the current stack frame with a new stack frame for the recursive call. In reality, Elm compiles the body of tail recursive functions into clever JavaScript while loops to avoid adding additional stack frames. When it hits the base case in the first branch, it returns the final accumulated value.

Removing the overhead of additional stack frames allows the List.foldl implementation of dogNames to perform better than the map and filter implementation that depends on List.foldr.

Let's verify that the new implementation performs well with even larger lists. Repeat the list 50 times to create a list of 250 animals. The performance improvement should stay around the same. Try even larger lists.

Make sure this implementation performs well on small lists too. Change the List.repeat to 1 for a list of five animals. The new implementation should still outperform the first implementation.

Awesome work. You wrote a new implementation that performs incredibly well and is still maintainable. More importantly, you better understand the list data structure and can more effectively traverse lists for better performance. However, you should always remember to focus on building functioning code first, before prematurely optimizing. Afterward, improve the performance if needed.

## Get Lazy

If you've ever wanted a reward for laziness, this section is for you. You will discover eager and lazy evaluation and how each impacts performance. You will use elm-benchmark and lazy design patterns to dramatically improve the performance of a function. Along the way, you will learn about thunks and the Dict type.

As you continue examining Rescue Me's codebase, you encounter a new feature to track dogs that know tricks. Rescue Me represents dogs with a record type and tricks with a custom type.

```
fast/fast-code/GetDog01.elm
type Trick
    = Sit
    | RollOver
    | Speak
    | Fetch
    | Spin

type alias Dog =
    { name : String
    , tricks : List Trick
    }
```

You find a getDog function that looks questionable.

```
getDog : Dict String Dog -> String -> List Trick -> ( Dog, Dict String Dog )
getDog dogs name tricks =
    let
        dog =
            Dict.get name dogs
                |> Maybe.withDefault (createDog name tricks)

        newDogs =
            Dict.insert name dog dogs
    in
    ( dog, newDogs )
```

The getDog function accepts a Dict of dogs and a dog name. It searches for the dog in the Dict by the name. If it doesn't find the dog, then it creates a new dog with the provided list of tricks. Dict[4] is a built-in type that resembles a dict from Python, hash from Ruby, Map from ES2015 JavaScript...you get the picture. It map keys to values. In this case, the dogs Dict maps String names to Dog instances.

The getDog function calls Dict.get with name and dogs to locate the dog. The dog may not exist, so it returns a Maybe Dog. Then, getDog pipes the Maybe into the Maybe.withDefault function. Maybe.withDefault accepts a default value and a Maybe. If the Maybe is Just, then withDefault unwraps it and returns the inner value. Otherwise, withDefault returns the provided default value. In this case, the default value is a new dog created from a createDog helper function.

Next, getDog inserts the previously found or created dog into the dogs Dict with Dict.insert. It assigns the new Dict instance to newDogs. Finally, it returns a tuple that holds the found or created dog and newDogs. Returning the updated Dict ensures that you find the dog next time.

---

4.    https://package.elm-lang.org/packages/elm/core/latest/Dict

Examine the createDog helper function next.

```
createDog : String -> List Trick -> Dog
createDog name tricks =
    Dog name (uniqueBy trickToString tricks)
```

The createDog function accepts a name and a list of tricks. It uses the Dog constructor to create a new Dog instance. Before passing in the tricks, it calls a uniqueBy helper function. Peek at the uniqueBy function above createDog.

```
uniqueBy : (a -> comparable) -> List a -> List a
uniqueBy toComparable list =
    List.foldr
        (\item ( existing, accum ) ->
            let
                comparableItem =
                    toComparable item
            in
            if Set.member comparableItem existing then
                ( existing, accum )

            else
                ( Set.insert comparableItem existing, item :: accum )
        )
        ( Set.empty, [] )
        list
        |> Tuple.second
```

The uniqueBy function uses an intermediate Set to remove duplicate entries from a list. Set operations are O(log(n)), and uniqueBy performs a Set operation for every item in the list via List.foldr. So, overall uniqueBy is O(nlog(n)).

The getDog function eagerly creates a new dog even if the dog already exists, so it always calls uniqueBy. That's a lot of unnecessary work that could hurt performance. It should only pay that cost when the dog doesn't exist. Let's fix that.

## Write a Lazy Thunk

Copy the code/fast/fast-code/GetDog.elm file from this book's code downloads into your fast-code directory and open it. This code houses the previously mentioned functions and types as well as an initial benchmarking suite. Let's implement a new getDog function and benchmark the two implementations.

You want to avoid creating the dog until necessary. Elm programmers refer to this as *lazy* evaluation. When I wait to do something later, I'm being lazy. The same applies to code. Why compute now what you can compute later. Create a version of withDefault that lazily evaluates the default value. After getDog, add this function:

```
withDefaultLazy : (() -> a) -> Maybe a -> a
withDefaultLazy thunk maybe =
    case maybe of
        Just value ->
            value

        Nothing ->
            thunk ()
```

You accept a Maybe as the second argument just like withDefault. For the first argument, you accept a function that takes a () argument and returns the default value. Functional programmers call this a *thunk*. A thunk is a function with no arguments that returns a value. You use thunks to delay computations. Elm functions require arguments, so you can mimic a thunk with the () argument.

You use pattern matching to unwrap and return the value inside Just. If the maybe argument is Nothing, then you call the thunk with () to return the default value.

Use withDefaultLazy to improve getDog. Copy getDog and paste it after withDefaultLazy. Name the copied function getDogLazy and replace Maybe.withDefault with withDefaultLazy:

```
|> withDefaultLazy (\() -> createDog name tricks)
```

You pass in a thunk that calls createDog. Now, if the dog exists, withDefaultLazy will unwrap and return the dog. Otherwise, it invokes the thunk, paying the cost of creating a new dog.

Compare the implementations of getDog inside the dogExists benchmark toward the bottom of the file. I've provided a sample list of tricks called benchmarkTricks and a sample Dict called benchmarkDogs. The Dict already contains the dog to locate.

```
dogExists : Benchmark
dogExists =
    describe "dog exists"
        [ Benchmark.compare "implementations"
            "eager creation"
            (\_ -> getDog benchmarkDogs "Tucker" benchmarkTricks)
            "lazy creation"
            (\_ -> getDogLazy benchmarkDogs "Tucker" benchmarkTricks)
        ]
```

Start the benchmark with elm-live:

```
elm-live src/GetDog.elm --open
```

You should see results similar to these.

getDog / dog exists

### implementations

| name | runs / second | % change | goodness of fit |
|------|---------------|----------|-----------------|
| eager creation | 699,960 | - | 99.56% |
| lazy creation | 10,981,472 | +1468.87% | 99.77% |

I audibly laughed at these numbers. The new implementation performed 1400.48% better. Being lazy pays off. You don't run the expensive uniqueBy function. Granted, these results only matter when the dog already exists. If the dog didn't exist, then you would pay the cost and have similar performance in both implementations.

## Delay More Work and Simplify

The new implementation performs amazingly, but you can improve it further. After you find or create the dog, you insert it into the Dict. But, you should only add the dog when you create it. Dict operations are O(log(n)), which is actually a good runtime but still unnecessary work if the dog already exists.

Move Dict.insert inside the call to withDefaultLazy. After getDogLazy, add a new function called getDogLazyInsertion:

```
fast/fast-code/GetDog02.elm
getDogLazyInsertion :
    Dict String Dog
    -> String
    -> List Trick
    -> ( Dog, Dict String Dog )
getDogLazyInsertion dogs name tricks =
    Dict.get name dogs
        |> Maybe.map (\dog -> ( dog, dogs ))
        |> withDefaultLazy
            (\() ->
                let
                    dog =
                        createDog name tricks
                in
                ( dog, Dict.insert name dog dogs )
            )
```

You check if the dog exists with Dict.get and pipe the result into Maybe.map. Recall that Maybe.map lets you transform inner Just values. In this case, you map the found dog to a tuple of it and the current Dict of dogs. Then, you pipe into withDefaultLazy. Inside the thunk, you create the dog, insert it into the Dict, and return a tuple of it and the new Dict. So, if the dog exists, you do no extra work because withDefaultLazy will unwrap the mapped found dog and original Dict from Maybe.map.

Update the benchmark to compare the previous withDefaultLazy implementation with this new one:

```
"lazy creation"
(\_ -> getDogLazy benchmarkDogs "Tucker" benchmarkTricks)
"lazy creation and insertion"
(\_ -> getDogLazyInsertion benchmarkDogs "Tucker" benchmarkTricks)
```

You should see a small improvement. My results showed around a 25% improvement. Lazily updating the Dict until necessary pays off. You could stop here, but let's evaluate the new implementation in terms of code complexity. You have to use a custom withDefaultLazy function and deal with mapping the found dog to a tuple. This code might initially confuse the Rescue Me's development team. You must decide if this optimization justifies the complexity cost.

In an ideal world, you could have performance benefits with no extra code complexity. And by golly you can here, too. Instead of writing custom helper functions and juggling thunks, simplify this code with a case expression. Add a getDogCaseExpression function after getDogLazyInsertion:

```
getDogCaseExpression :
    Dict String Dog
    -> String
    -> List Trick
    -> ( Dog, Dict String Dog )
getDogCaseExpression dogs name tricks =
    case Dict.get name dogs of
        Just dog ->
            ( dog, dogs )

        Nothing ->
            let
                dog =
                    createDog name tricks

                newDogs =
                    Dict.insert name dog dogs
            in
            ( dog, newDogs )
```

You use pattern matching to check if the dog exists or not. With Just, you unwrap the dog and return it with the current Dict in a tuple. Otherwise, you create the dog, insert it into the Dict, and return a tuple of it and the new Dict. Thankfully, case expressions only evaluate a branch when its pattern matches. So, each branch is lazy. Compare the last implementation with the case expression implementation.

```
"lazy creation and insertion"
(\_ -> getDogLazyInsertion benchmarkDogs "Tucker" benchmarkTricks)
"case expression"
(\_ -> getDogCaseExpression benchmarkDogs "Tucker" benchmarkTricks)
```

Astoundingly, the case expression outperforms the second withDefaultLazy implementation. My results showed around a 104% improvement. In the compiled JavaScript code, Elm implements pattern matching with fast if and switch statements. Also, the withDefaultLazy implementations suffer from the overhead of creating and calling anonymous functions. You produced a net win: faster *and* more readable code. Rescue Me praises your work so far. They now ask you to investigate performance issues in their main application.

# Build Lazy Applications

Fine-tuning function implementations can help application performance immensely. If your application works with large lists, you want to traverse lists efficiently and avoid heavy computations, when possible. However, implementation tweaks only go so far. You may still encounter performance issues in your view layer.

In this section, you will see those issues surface in Rescue Me's application. The application must display thousands of rescue animals at a time, which causes slowdown in a couple areas. Rescue Me admits that they should rethink their UI, but for now they need quick help to meet their initial release date next week. You will measure application performance with browser profiling tools. Then, you will use lazy design patterns with the Html.Lazy module to speed up the application.

## Get the Application

Try out the current application to witness the performance issues firsthand. Outside of your fast-code directory, create a new fast-application directory. Copy the contents of the code/fast/fast-application directory from this book's code downloads into your fast-application directory. Inside your fast-application directory, install dependencies with npm install.

Instead of a development server, you will run a production version of the application. The production version minifies and optimizes the compiled code. This prevents development-related code from interfering with performance measurements. Build a production application and serve it locally with these commands:

```
npm run build
npm run build:serve
```

Open http://localhost:5000 in your browser. You should see something similar to the following screenshot.

**Rescue Me**

Search Names:
Filter By Type:   All ⇕
Filter By Breed:   All                                   ⇕
Filter By Sex:   All ⇕

| Type | Name ▲ | Breed | Sex | |
|------|--------|-------|-----|------|
| Dog | Abby | Seppala Siberian Sleddog | Female | Edit |
| Cat | Abby | Japanese Bobtail | Female | Edit |
| Dog | Ace | Harrier | Male | Edit |
| Dog | Allie | Fila Brasileiro | Female | Edit |

The application will manage rescue animals across the United States. It currently loads a fake list of 300 animals. You can search, filter, sort, and edit the entries. Rescue Me says that the application slows down with a larger list of 4000 animals.

Open the Main.elm file in the src directory. Append a /large path to the url constant at the top of the file:

```
fast/fast-application/src/Main01.elm
url : String
url =
    "https://programming-elm.com/animals/large"
```

Run npm run build again and refresh your browser. The application should load the 4000-record list. The most noticeable slowdown occurs when a user edits an animal. Click an animal's edit button. The animal's information should display at the top right of the screen as in the following image.

**Selected Dog**

**Name:**
Abby

**Breed:**
Cierny Sery                                   ⇕

**Sex:**
Female ⇕

Save    Cancel

Change the animal's name. You should experience significant lag if you type quickly. Every state change causes Elm to rerun the view function. The application filters and sorts the list of animals inside the view layer, so it filters, sorts, and recreates the virtual DOM for each animal, every time Elm calls the view function.

The application shouldn't do all that work if nothing has changed about the list. The application stores the selected animal separate from the list. After you save the selected animal, the application updates the same animal in the list. At that point, you should sort and filter. Let's address this problem.

 You can run the server locally to fetch from the /animals and /animals/large API endpoints. Follow the instructions in Appendix 2, Run the Local Server, on page 267, and swap out https://programming-elm.com with http://localhost:5000 in the url constant.

## Use Lazy Html

You need to get lazy again to avoid doing unnecessary work. Luckily, you can handle this easily with the Html.Lazy module. Import it, and expose the lazy and lazy2 functions:

```
import Html.Lazy exposing (lazy, lazy2)
```

Visit the viewState function near the bottom of the file.

```
viewState : State -> Html StateMsg
viewState state =
    div [ class "main" ]
        [ viewAnimals state
        , viewSelectedAnimal state
        ]
```

The viewState function accepts a State type and returns Html StateMsg. It calls viewAnimals to display the list of animals and viewSelectedAnimal to display the selected animal. The State type alias contains application state, and the Model is a type alias to Maybe State.

```
type alias State =
    { animals : List Animal
    , selectedAnimal : Maybe Animal
    , sortFilter : SortFilter
    , dimensions : Dimensions
    }

type alias Model =
    Maybe State
```

The initial model is Nothing, so the main view function displays "Loading..." while the application fetches the list. Once the list loads, the update function builds the initial state and wraps it in Just. The update function also routes StateMsg values to a separate updateState function to keep the code modular.

```
update : Msg -> Model -> ( Model, Cmd Msg )
update msg model =
    case msg of
        ReceiveAnimals (Ok animals) ->
            ( Just (initialState animals), Cmd.none )

        StateMsg stateMsg ->
            ( Maybe.map (updateState stateMsg) model, Cmd.none )

        ReceiveAnimals (Err _) ->
            ( model, Cmd.none )
```

Return to the view layer. The viewAnimals function calls viewAnimalList to render the list of animals.

```
viewAnimals : State -> Html StateMsg
viewAnimals state =
    div [ class "animals" ]
        [ h2 [] [ text "Rescue Me" ]
        , viewAnimalFilters state
        , viewAnimalList state
        ]
```

The viewAnimalList function uses a sortAndFilterAnimals helper function to sort and filter the list.

```
viewAnimalList : State -> Html StateMsg
viewAnimalList { sortFilter, animals } =
    let
        sortedAndFilteredAnimals =
            sortAndFilterAnimals sortFilter animals
    in
    table [ class "animals" ]
        [ ... ]
```

The viewAnimalList function causes the lag when updating the selected animal's name because viewAnimals always calls it. You need to avoid calling viewAnimalList unnecessarily, but first, you should measure baseline performance. Then, you can make the change, measure again, and compare measurements to verify performance improved. Thankfully, modern browsers have great profiling tools.

I used Chrome's profiling tools for my measurements. I recommend using Chrome to follow along, but you're free to use another browser. However, your measurements may drastically differ. Refresh the application and click to edit an animal. Don't change anything yet. Copy another animal's name such as Allie to your clipboard.

Next, open the Performance tab in Chrome's devtools. You should see a record button along with other options.

Click on the record button. Paste the other animal's name into the name text box. Then, click the profiler's stop button.

You should see a result similar to the following screenshot.

The top timeline shows FPS (frames per second while rendering), CPU usage, and network traffic while you were profiling. Pay attention to the CPU usage. Notice the highlighted peaks when you changed the animal's name. Note: sometimes Chrome doesn't automatically highlight the peaks, which could skew the measurements you analyze. You can click and drag over the peaks you want to analyze specifically if Chrome fails to do it automatically. If you hover your cursor over peaks, Chrome will display a small preview of what it displayed underneath your cursor so you can determine which peaks to highlight.

The pie chart shows where the browser spent its time for the highlighted peaks. In my example, the browser took 94.8 milliseconds of scripting time, which is time in actual code. The application performed poorly. Ideally, scripting actions should take less than 16.67 milliseconds for an application to be perceived as fast. That number comes from dividing 1 by an ideal 60 frames per second. You can get away with slightly longer runtimes, but 94.8 milliseconds translates to around 10.5 frames per second. Clearly, sorting and filtering the list unnecessarily hurts performance.

You can use a function from Html.Lazy to lazily call viewAnimalList only when needed. Html.Lazy functions accept a function that returns Html and its arguments and creates a special Html node. Internally, Elm tracks these lazily called functions and their arguments. If the arguments remain unchanged during a re-render, Elm doesn't call the function. Elm checks arguments by reference. If the arguments change, then Elm calls the function to get new virtual DOM. If you're familiar with React, this mimics the shouldComponentUpdate method on class components.

Inside viewAnimals, you could call the lazy function from Html.Lazy on viewAnimals, but it wouldn't work as you would hope.

```
lazy viewAnimalList state
```

The state argument contains all state, so it would always change when you modify the selected animal. Since the argument changes, lazy would still call viewAnimalList all the time. Let's modify viewAnimalList's arguments to isolate it from selected animal changes.

Instead, use lazy2 and pass in the state.sortFilter and state.animals fields as arguments. The 2 in lazy2 means the function accepts two arguments. The sortFilter field holds information about how to sort and filter the list and the animals field is the list of animals.

```
lazy2 viewAnimalList state.sortFilter state.animals
```

Modify viewAnimalList to accept these arguments:

```
viewAnimalList : SortFilter -> List Animal -> Html StateMsg
viewAnimalList sortFilter animals =
```

Rebuild the application and refresh Chrome. Like before, copy a name to your clipboard. Use the same name for consistent measurements. Click edit on the animal you edited before. Before you start recording performance, clear the previous run with this button.

Then, start recording, paste in the new name, and stop recording. You should see a vast improvement. My scripting time decreased to around 20 milliseconds. Try quickly typing in the name text box. The lag should be almost unnoticeable. You can improve the runtime further, but you'll revisit that as an exercise later.

## Lazily Render Each Animal

Aside from sorting and filtering, generating virtual DOM for each animal when it doesn't change hurts performance. Look toward the bottom of viewAnimalList. It maps over the sortedAndFilteredAnimals with List.map and a viewAnimal function.

```
tbody [] (List.map viewAnimal sortedAndFilteredAnimals)
```

The application eagerly calls viewAnimal 4000 times with the current list. So, Elm has to compare at least 4000 virtual DOM nodes. The viewAnimal function has 12 nodes inside it, so that's really 48,000 nodes to compare. Let's measure the impact of these comparisons.

Clear the last performance profile and refresh your browser. Select an animal and change its breed. Start recording performance and click the selected animal's Save button. Stop recording. My scripting time lasted around 82 milliseconds. Make sure you highlight the appropriate peaks in the timeline.

You can effortlessly fix this with Html.Lazy. Update the List.map call to use the lazy function:

```
tbody [] (List.map (lazy viewAnimal) sortedAndFilteredAnimals)
```

Similar to lazy2, lazy takes a view function and arguments. In this case, lazy only accepts one argument for the view function. For this example, you partially apply lazy with the viewAnimal function. List.map provides the animal argument when it maps over the list.

Rebuild the application, clear the old results, and refresh your browser. Select the same animal and change to the same breed as before. Finally, start recording, click Save, and stop recording. My run spent around 27 milliseconds in scripting. That helped tremendously. It's not 16.67 milliseconds, but you can't avoid the cost of sorting and filtering the list.

Great. You've made noticeable improvements with relatively small changes. Html.Lazy lets you quickly speed up applications. But, just as I mentioned in previous sections, don't immediately reach for it until you need to address performance. Also, always measure changes with profiling tools to verify you're improving performance.

## One Last Challenge

Before we conclude, let's improve the Rescue Me application even more. In the search filters, the application computes the available breeds from the list of animals after every state change. The viewAnimals function calls viewAnimalFilters, which calls a breedsForSelectedKind helper function.

Inside breedsForSelectedKind and another helper function breedsForKind, the code calls three functions from the Animals module: dogBreeds, catBreeds, and breeds. Peek at those three functions. They traverse the list of animals to extract the appropriate breeds. You can improve performance by following these steps:

1.  Start by lazily calling viewAnimalFilters in viewAnimals. Adjust the arguments since viewAnimalFilters currently accepts all of the state. (Hint: you'll need three arguments, thus you'll need the lazy3 function.)

2.  The animal filters will need to re-render if you change one of the filter values or search for a name. But, you will still unnecessarily recompute the breeds. Refactor the application to cache a list of dog breeds, a list of cat breeds, and a list of all breeds in the Dimensions type alias at the top of the file. You should create and store these values inside the initialState function. Use the Animals module to create the lists.

    After those changes, update breedsForSelectedKind and breedsForKind to use the cached values. You can also reduce viewAnimalFilters' number of arguments to two, so switch to lazy2 to inside viewAnimals.

3.  The application has a bug in the animal filters. Select a dog breed, then select cats from the type dropdown. The breed dropdown should select "All" and only include cat breeds; the animal list below should only display cats. The breed dropdown options will change as expected but the list below will display nothing. The application doesn't actually change the selected breed.

    Dropdowns come from the Select module. The Select module has a type called Selection with two values, All and One. When filtering, the Select module uses All to allow all possible values and One to allow only a specific value.

    You need to update the selected breed when changing the animal type inside updateState. (Side note: to avoid conflicts with the type keyword, the code internally refers to an animal type as kind.) You should create a helper function to update the selected type and breed at the same time.

    Inside your helper function, if the currently selected breed is All, you can keep it. Otherwise, if it's One with a specific breed, then you need to check if the selected animal type can have that breed. Use the breedsForSelectedKind and List.member functions. If the breed is allowed, then keep it inside One. Otherwise, switch to All. You should also store a list of available breeds in Dimensions so you can more easily display them in the breeds dropdown when the animal type changes.

If you need some guidance, look at the code/fast/fast-application/src/MainFast.elm file for inspiration. After you make your tweaks, you should be able to get your previous measurements down under 16.67 milliseconds.

See if you can improve performance further. Look for other opportunities to use Html.Lazy. You could also investigate paginating the list to help with performance. In that case, you might want to add a button to the filters to only apply them on click. You will need to store the sorted and filtered list in the state. You can also look into using Elm's Array[5] type to simplify splitting the list of animals for pagination.

## What You Learned

Great job! Rescue Me thanks you for your hard work improving the performance of their application. They're ready to easily manage thousands of rescue animals.

You achieved a ton in this chapter. You learned about the importance of performance and when to investigate it. You used elm-benchmark to measure and improve the performance of functions. You learned more about lists, how to efficiently traverse them, and what recursion is. You got lazy to delay heavy computations and improve performance. Finally, you used Html.Lazy to obtain easy performance wins with little additional code. You also measured your changes with built-in browser profiling tools. You are ready to measure and improve the performance of your own applications with various techniques.

And...congratulations! You have reached the end of this book, but your Elm journey really just begins. You have gone from no Elm knowledge to building, deploying, testing, and tweaking your own Elm applications. Take what you've learned and create awesome applications. Good luck on your journey, and let me know what you build.

---

5.　https://package.elm-lang.org/packages/elm/core/latest/Array

# Install Elm

You need to add some dependencies to your computer in order to follow along in this book. This appendix will help you install everything you need to build your own Elm applications and set up a perfect Elm development environment.

## All Roads Lead to Node

And you thought you could escape JavaScript. All kidding aside, you will need a recent version of Node and npm. You will use them to install helpful tools and packages, develop locally, deploy applications, and test Elm code.

In case you're unfamiliar with it, Node is an implementation of JavaScript that runs directly on computers instead of browsers. Node uses npm as its official package manager for installing dependencies. You can also install dependencies for front-end applications with npm.

You'll need at least Node 12 to run some of the JavaScript code in this book. I recommend you install the latest LTS (long-term support) version of Node which includes npm. As of this writing, 12.16.1 is the current LTS version. You can install Node via the official website[1] or via a Node version manager such as nvm[2] or nodenv.[3]

## Install the Elm Compiler

The Elm compiler is built in Haskell.[4] You can download installation packages for macOS and Windows via the official Elm docs.[5] If you use a Linux distri-

---

1.    https://nodejs.org
2.    https://github.com/creationix/nvm
3.    https://github.com/nodenv/nodenv
4.    https://www.haskell.org
5.    https://guide.elm-lang.org/install.html

bution, or like to control installations through a package manager, you can install Elm globally via npm with this command:

```
npm install -g elm
```

The npm package provides the appropriate pre-built binary depending on your operating system.

Your Elm installation should include a few command-line tools:

- elm repl - try out Elm in an interactive shell
- elm init - bootstrap a new Elm project with elm.json and a src directory
- elm reactor - run a development server to build Elm applications
- elm make - compile Elm files
- elm install - install Elm packages
- elm publish - publish your own Elm package
- elm bump - change your package's version based on local changes
- elm diff - see changes between two versions of a published package

You will gain experience with most of these tools as you progress through this book.

## Install Development Tools

The Elm community has adopted an official style guide[6] for formatting Elm code. This book's code examples adhere to this style guide except where it might drastically increase page length or extend past margins. Instead of manually formatting code yourself, you can use the elm-format package to automatically format your code to community conventions. Install it with this npm command:

```
npm install -g elm-format
```

As of this writing, I used elm-format version 0.8.1 to format code samples in this book.

The elm-format repository[7] also provides links to integrate elm-format with your editor so you don't have to manually run it from the command line.

For more Elm integration inside your editor such as syntax highlighting and for other useful tools and resources, you can visit the awesome-elm repository.[8]

You're all set. Happy Elming!

---

6.   http://elm-lang.org/docs/style-guide
7.   https://github.com/avh4/elm-format
8.   https://github.com/isRuslan/awesome-elm

# Run the Local Server

Throughout this book, you build applications against API endpoints at programming-elm.com. If you lack Internet access while working through the book or have other reasons to work offline, you can run the same API endpoints locally. Follow these simple instructions to install and run the server.

## Install and Run the Server

The server code lives on GitHub,[1] a version control system for code. You will need a GitHub account and the Git command line tool installed on your machine to access the code. You can follow the download link on the Git website[2] to install Git if you don't have it.

Once you have a GitHub account and Git installed, run this command:

```
git clone https://github.com/jfairbank/programming-elm.com.git
```

The command should download the code into a new programming-elm.com directory. The server runs on the latest Node LTS (version 12.16.1 as of this writing). If you need Node, follow the instructions in Appendix 1, Install Elm, on page 265 to install it.

Inside the programming-elm.com directory, install dependencies with npm:

```
npm install
```

After you install the server dependencies, start the server with this command:

```
npm start
```

The server should listen on localhost:5000. You should see this message.

---

1.  https://github.com/
2.  https://git-scm.com/

```
Server listening at http://localhost:5000
```

Test that the server works by visiting http://localhost:5000/feed in your browser. You should see a JSON response similar to this (I have formatted and truncated the JSON result here).

```
[
  {
    "id": 1,
    "url": "https://programming-elm.surge.sh/1.jpg",
    "caption": "Surfing",
    "liked": false,
    "comments": [
      "Cowabunga, dude!"
    ],
    "username": "surfing_usa"
  },
  ...
]
```

You're all set. As you progress through the book, whenever a code sample refers to https://programming-elm.com, feel free to swap it out with http://localhost:5000 as long as your local server is running.

# Elm Package Versions

Inevitably, technical books will refer to outdated dependencies. If you find that the code samples in this book use an older version of an Elm package, refer to this appendix to ensure you install the correct older version.

## Install an Older Package Version

The elm install command only installs the latest version of a package. To install an older version of a package, you must change the desired version inside elm.json.

Let's say you installed elm/http with elm install. It installed version 2.0.0, but you wanted to use version 1.0.0. You can open your elm.json in your editor and change the version of elm/http located in the dependencies.direct field to 1.0.0 like so:

```
{
    "type": "application",
    "source-directories": [
        "src"
    ],
    "elm-version": "0.19.1",
    "dependencies": {
        "direct": {
            "elm/browser": "1.0.1",
            "elm/core": "1.0.2",
            "elm/html": "1.0.0",
            "elm/http": "1.0.0",
            "elm/json": "1.1.3"
        },
        "indirect": {
            "elm/time": "1.0.0",
            "elm/url": "1.0.0",
            "elm/virtual-dom": "1.0.2"
        }
    },
```

```
    "test-dependencies": {
        "direct": {},
        "indirect": {
            "elm/bytes": "1.0.8",
            "elm/file": "1.0.5"
        }
    }
}
```

Then, the next time you compile, Elm will download and use version 1.0.0 of elm/http instead.

If you find a mismatch between the code samples in this book for an installed package and the latest version of that package, modify your elm.json to use the versions below. (Or, you can attempt to adapt the code samples to the API of the newest version of a package if you prefer.)

| | |
|---|---|
| elm/http | 2.0.0 |
| elm/json | 1.1.2 |
| elm/url | 1.0.0 |
| elm-explorations/benchmark | 1.0.0 |
| NoRedInk/elm-json-decode-pipeline | 1.0.0 |

# Bibliography

[Lom15]    Andrew Lombardi. *WebSocket: Lightweight Client-Server Communications*. O'Reilly & Associates, Inc., Sebastopol, CA, 2015.

# Index

# Thank you!

How did you enjoy this book? Please let us know. Take a moment and email us at support@pragprog.com with your feedback. Tell us your story and you could win free ebooks. Please use the subject line "Book Feedback."

Ready for your next great Pragmatic Bookshelf book? Come on over to https://pragprog.com and use the coupon code BUYANOTHER2020 to save 30% on your next ebook.

Void where prohibited, restricted, or otherwise unwelcome. Do not use ebooks near water. If rash persists, see a doctor. Doesn't apply to *The Pragmatic Programmer* ebook because it's older than the Pragmatic Bookshelf itself. Side effects may include increased knowledge and skill, increased marketability, and deep satisfaction. Increase dosage regularly.

And thank you for your continued support,

Andy Hunt, Publisher

# Adopting Elixir

Adoption is more than programming. Elixir is an exciting new language, but to successfully get your application from start to finish, you're going to need to know more than just the language. You need the case studies and strategies in this book. Learn the best practices for the whole life of your application, from design and team-building, to managing stakeholders, to deployment and monitoring. Go beyond the syntax and the tools to learn the techniques you need to develop your Elixir application from concept to production.

Ben Marx, José Valim, Bruce Tate
(242 pages) ISBN: 9781680502527. $42.95
*https://pragprog.com/book/tvmelixir*

# Learn Functional Programming with Elixir

Elixir's straightforward syntax and this guided tour give you a clean, simple path to learn modern functional programming techniques. No previous functional programming experience required! This book walks you through the right concepts at the right pace, as you explore immutable values and explicit data transformation, functions, modules, recursive functions, pattern matching, high-order functions, polymorphism, and failure handling, all while avoiding side effects. Don't board the Elixir train with an imperative mindset! To get the most out of functional languages, you need to think functionally. This book will get you there.

Ulisses Almeida
(198 pages) ISBN: 9781680502459. $42.95
*https://pragprog.com/book/cdc-elixir*

# Seven More Languages in Seven Weeks

Great programmers aren't born—they're made. The industry is moving from object-oriented languages to functional languages, and you need to commit to radical improvement. New programming languages arm you with the tools and idioms you need to refine your craft. While other language primers take you through basic installation and "Hello, World," we aim higher. Each language in *Seven More Languages in Seven Weeks* will take you on a step-by-step journey through the most important paradigms of our time. You'll learn seven exciting languages: Lua, Factor, Elixir, Elm, Julia, MiniKanren, and Idris.

Bruce Tate, Fred Daoud, Jack Moffitt, Ian Dees
(318 pages) ISBN: 9781941222157. $38
*https://pragprog.com/book/7lang*

# Seven Languages in Seven Weeks

You should learn a programming language every year, as recommended by *The Pragmatic Programmer*. But if one per year is good, how about *Seven Languages in Seven Weeks*? In this book you'll get a hands-on tour of Clojure, Haskell, Io, Prolog, Scala, Erlang, and Ruby. Whether or not your favorite language is on that list, you'll broaden your perspective of programming by examining these languages side-by-side. You'll learn something new from each, and best of all, you'll learn how to learn a language quickly.

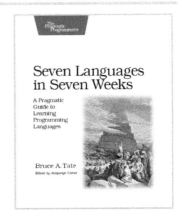

Bruce A. Tate
(330 pages) ISBN: 9781934356593. $34.95
*https://pragprog.com/book/btlang*

# Functional Programming Patterns in Scala and Clojure

Solve real-life programming problems with a fraction of the code that pure object-oriented programming requires. Use Scala and Clojure to solve in-depth problems and see how familiar object-oriented patterns can become more concise with functional programming and patterns. Your code will be more declarative, with fewer bugs and lower maintenance costs.

Michael Bevilacqua-Linn
(256 pages) ISBN: 9781937785475. $36
*https://pragprog.com/book/mbfpp*

# Functional Programming in Java

Get ready to program in a whole new way. *Functional Programming in Java* will help you quickly get on top of the new, essential Java 8 language features and the functional style that will change and improve your code. This short, targeted book will help you make the paradigm shift from the old imperative way to a less error-prone, more elegant, and concise coding style that's also a breeze to parallelize. You'll explore the syntax and semantics of lambda expressions, method and constructor references, and functional interfaces. You'll design and write applications better using the new standards in Java 8 and the JDK.

Venkat Subramaniam
(196 pages) ISBN: 9781937785468. $33
*https://pragprog.com/book/vsjava8*

## Programming Ecto

Languages may come and go, but the relational database endures. Learn how to use Ecto, the premier database library for Elixir, to connect your Elixir and Phoenix apps to databases. Get a firm handle on Ecto fundamentals with a module-by-module tour of the critical parts of Ecto. Then move on to more advanced topics and advice on best practices with a series of recipes that provide clear, step-by-step instructions on scenarios commonly encountered by app developers. Co-authored by the creator of Ecto, this title provides all the essentials you need to use Ecto effectively.

Darin Wilson and Eric Meadows-Jönsson
(242 pages) ISBN: 9781680502824. $45.95
*https://pragprog.com/book/wmecto*

## Property-Based Testing with PropEr, Erlang, and Elixir

Property-based testing helps you create better, more solid tests with little code. By using the PropEr framework in both Erlang and Elixir, this book teaches you how to automatically generate test cases, test stateful programs, and change how you design your software for more principled and reliable approaches. You will be able to better explore the problem space, validate the assumptions you make when coming up with program behavior, and expose unexpected weaknesses in your design. PropEr will even show you how to reproduce the bugs it found. With this book, you will be writing efficient property-based tests in no time.

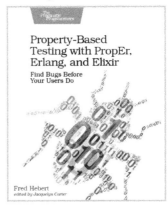

Fred Hebert
(374 pages) ISBN: 9781680506211. $45.95
*https://pragprog.com/book/fhproper*

# The Pragmatic Bookshelf

The Pragmatic Bookshelf features books written by professional developers for professional developers. The titles continue the well-known Pragmatic Programmer style and continue to garner awards and rave reviews. As development gets more and more difficult, the Pragmatic Programmers will be there with more titles and products to help you stay on top of your game.

# Visit Us Online

### This Book's Home Page
*https://pragprog.com/book/jfelm*
Source code from this book, errata, and other resources. Come give us feedback, too!

### Keep Up to Date
*https://pragprog.com*
Join our announcement mailing list (low volume) or follow us on twitter @pragprog for new titles, sales, coupons, hot tips, and more.

### New and Noteworthy
*https://pragprog.com/news*
Check out the latest pragmatic developments, new titles and other offerings.

# Save on the ebook

Save on the ebook versions of this title. Owning the paper version of this book entitles you to purchase the electronic versions at a terrific discount.

PDFs are great for carrying around on your laptop—they are hyperlinked, have color, and are fully searchable. Most titles are also available for the iPhone and iPod touch, Amazon Kindle, and other popular e-book readers.

Buy now at *https://pragprog.com/coupon*

# Contact Us

| | |
|---|---|
| Online Orders: | *https://pragprog.com/catalog* |
| Customer Service: | *support@pragprog.com* |
| International Rights: | *translations@pragprog.com* |
| Academic Use: | *academic@pragprog.com* |
| Write for Us: | *http://write-for-us.pragprog.com* |
| Or Call: | +1 800-699-7764 |

9 781680 502855